P9-ASF-500

Pragmatic Spirituality

Pragmatic Spirituality

The Christian Faith through an Africentric Lens

Gayraud S. Wilmore

NEW YORK UNIVERSITY PRESS

New York and London

NEW YORK UNIVERSITY PRESS
New York and London
www.nyupress.org

Library of Congress Cataloging-in-Publication Data
Wilmore, Gayraud S.
Pragmatic spirituality :
the Christian faith through an Africentric lens / Gayraud S. Wilmore.
p. cm.
Includes bibliographical references and index.
ISBN 0–8147–9395–9 (cloth : alk. paper) —
ISBN 0–8147–9396–7 (pbk. : alk. paper)
1. African Americans—Religion. I. Title.
BR563.N4W54 2004
230'.089'96073—dc22 2004003007

New York University Press books are printed on acid-free paper, and their binding materials are chosen for strength and durability.

Manufactured in the United States of America

c 10 9 8 7 6 5 4 3 2 1
p 10 9 8 7 6 5 4 3 2 1

For James Hutten Costen, Sr. 1931–2003

Pastor and preacher *extraordinaire*,
General Assembly moderator of the Presbyterian Church (USA), ecumenist, seminary president, benefactor of East African and African American higher education, a great family man, a faithful colleague, and devoted friend.

Contents

Acknowledgments

Most of my writings, in one way or another, have been influenced by the reflections and feelings of others—fellow laborers in the Lord's vineyard; women and men who have blessed me more than they will ever know. I include all those to whom I have been privileged to minister—in college and seminary classrooms, in churches, in congregational study groups, in academic meetings and conferences of every description—all over the world. I believe that every time we "gossip the gospel," even with skeptics and nonbelievers, some truth makes a home for itself in our soul—a firm residence in both our conscience and our subconscious that is ever present to correct and direct our beliefs and actions.

These particular essays, written over a period of forty or more years, owe much to my close collaboration with colleagues. There are too many to name—yet I dare not fail to acknowledge that, more than anyone else I can think of, James H. Cone and the late James H. Costen, in different ways and without always being aware of it, have resourced, replenished, and reinforced my intellectual storehouse for at least thirty-five of those forty or so years in which this work has been in progress. Though both were born later than I, their contributions to my development as a student of the religious history and faith of the African American people will never run out. I have not invariably agreed with either of them, but because of their sharp and creative intellect, friendship, and unselfish colleagueship over these years, my scholarship, writing, and teaching have flourished like the proverbial green bay tree.

I want to thank my former colleagues at the Interdenominational Theological Center in Atlanta, Randall Bailey and Jacquelyn Grant, for reading and commenting on portions of this book. I have received both objections and commendations from individual readers of most of these chapters since the 1960s. But I am especially grateful to Will Gravely, who made perceptive and extensive evaluations of the book proposal early on. Without their helpful suggestions my confidence in the likelihood of this project ever seeing the light of day would have flagged in the first months of putting it together.

To Larry Murphy, who teaches history at Garrett-Evangelical Seminary, and is the founder and curator of the video archives of the Society for the Study of Black Religion, I will be forever grateful for being the first to come up with the idea of my collecting and reworking some previously published essays that deserved to stay in print. He coaxed me out of the rocking chair of a shamefully carefree retirement to immerse myself once again in the tasks of scholarship—reading, thinking, writing, and producing what is very possibly my terminal volume that, I hope, will make a positive contribution to the academic study of religion and to what it means to be a Christian.

I would also like to thank the publishers of the original versions of many of these chapters, several of which have been substantially reworked for this book. Chapter 1, "What is African American Religious Studies," is reprinted by permission from *African American Religious Studies: An Interdisciplinary Anthology* (Duke University Press, 1989). All rights reserved. Chapter 2, "Reinterpretation in Black Church History," is reprinted by permission from *The Chicago Theological Seminary Register* (Winter, 1983). Chapter 3, "Black Religion: Strategies of Survival, Elevation, and Liberation," is reprinted by permission from *The Journal of the Interdenominational Theological Center,* vol. 21, no. 1 and 2 (Fall 1993/Spring 1994). Chapter 5, "'Doing the Truth': Some Criteria for Researching African American Religious History," is reprinted by permission from *African American Religion: Research Problems and Resources for the 1990s* (New York: Schomburg Center for Research in Black Culture, 1992). Chapter 7, "African Beginnings," is reprinted by permission from *Black Religion and Black Radicalism*, third revised edition (Maryknoll: Orbis Books, 1998). Chapter 8, "*The Black Messiah: Revising the Color Symbolism of Western Christology*," is reprinted by permission from *The Journal of the ITC*. Vol. 2 (Fall 1974, No. 1). Chapter 9, "Black Consciousness: Stumbling Block or Battering Ram," is revised and reprinted by permission from *Liberating the Future,* edited by Joerg Rieger, © 1999 Augsburg Fortress (www.fortresspress.org). Chapter 12, "Black Power, Black People, and Theological Renewal," is reprinted by permission from *Black Religion and Black Radicalism* (Maryknoll: Orbis Books, 1998). Chapter 13, "The Role of African America in the Rise of Third World Theology," is reprinted by permission from *African Theology En Route: Papers from the Pan African Conference of Third World Theologians, December 17–23, Accra, Ghana*, edited by Kofi Appiah-Kubi and Sergio Torres (Maryknoll: Orbis Books, 1979). Chapter 14, "What is the Relevance of Black Theology for Pastoral Ministry," is reprinted by permission from *The Pastor as Theologian*, edited by Earl E. Shelp and Ronald H. Sunderland (New York: The Pilgrim Press, 1988). Chapter 15, "Black Christians, Church Unity, and One Common Expression of Apostolic Faith," is reprinted by permission from *Black Witness to the Apostolic Faith*, edited by David T. Shannon and Gayraud S. Wilmore (Grand Rapids: W.B. Eerdmans Co., 1985) and from *Midstream/An Ecumenical Journal*. Chapter 17, "Struggling Against Racism with Realism and Hope," is reprinted by permission from *The Journal for Preachers*, vol. 23, no. 2 (Lent, 2000).

Before closing I must acknowledge my debt to Jennifer Hammer, my editor at New York University Press. I have done some serious editing of my own in past years and know what it takes to get an apparently successful manuscript to print. Jennifer Hammer labored over every page of my disorderly manuscript, critiqued, advised, and encouraged me far beyond what I would have done had our positions been reversed. If readers decide that this book succeeds in reassessing the meaning of spirituality in the service of God and humanity, Jennifer Hammer and her staff will have to stand up with me to receive whatever plaudits may come.

Finally, I want to thank one of my daughters-in-law, Carmen Falu Wilmore, for the clerical work she rendered when I was overloaded with other details; my grandson, Gayraud Aaron Wilmore, who knows about computers and kept mine working; and my wife of sixty years, Lee Ella Wilmore. "Through many dangers, toils, and snares," you have given me quiet support and wise counsel without which I would not have lived so long or accomplished as much as I have. God will judge the value of it all. Thanks be to our God and to all who made this book possible.

Introduction

The term *Africentric* is not likely to be familiar to the general reader of books on religion.[1] I imagine that readers, both white and black, may wonder what it means and, specifically, what the words "through an *Africentric* lens" signify. An African American reader may take this even further: "This brother evidently concedes from the outset that his understanding of the Christian faith is closely related to what is perceptible to his African-centered gaze—and somehow that makes me uneasy."

Let me begin by addressing that uneasiness.

Many good evangelical Christians I know would complain that a lens is not required for one to look upon the truth of God. They would say that, if a seeker comes to the Bible with a pure heart and unaided vision, the Spirit will open his or her eyes and provide the necessary understanding. My rejoinder is that most of us will already be wearing some kind of spectacles when we find ourselves gawking at spiritual mysteries that have astounded the most spiritually gifted and intellectually brilliant people in the world since the beginning of time. And, I believe, that is because of our infirmity and the nature of the truth we seek.

Indeed, we all need tinted glasses, so to speak, when we look upon the beauty of holiness in the unveiled countenance of the Almighty. The glory of the Lord is said to be like a "devouring fire" (Exodus 24:17) and it is doubtful that in this fallen world the naked, unaided inner eye can behold the ineffable glory of God and not be blinded instantly. That was the experience of the people when Moses ascended Mount Sinai to meet God. And a nineteenth-century American hymn writer averred that the awesomeness of the bleeding wounds of Jesus on the cross is such that even those as pure in heart as the angels turned away in fear and trembling:

No angel in the sky can fully bear that sight,
But downward bends his burning eye,
At mysteries so bright.[2]

I think, too, that we all need spectacles of some kind to refract the light of truth in the gospel in terms of the cultural context in which God finds us. We may make an existential decision over time to exchange the spectacles we habitually use for others that seem to fit us better. But spectacles there must be, in any case. Only so are we frail humans capable of appropriating the Word of life and gazing on the bright mysteries of faith in the darkness we have become accustomed to. As mature adults we choose our lens, unless we are content to continue to use those that our parents or Sunday School teachers chose for us. We select our spectacles in accordance with the imponderable realities and necessities of our personal search for meaning—such as the consciousness of who we are, who we belong to, and what our destiny is; the time, place, and circumstances of the summons some of us receive to follow Jesus, and the apprehension of the gifts and tasks which that following requires.

I believe that I must perceive the world and God's glory that shines through its darkness with the aid of my own chosen lens, and I think that you, my readers, must perceive those same indescribable wonders with the aid of yours. It seems that some of us, throughout our lives, continue to try on several sets of different lenses—like choosing sunglasses in an optician's shop. Most thinking people are engaged in an effort to see and understand the world and nature, their fellow human beings, and God, as best they can, whenever, wherever, and with whatever help a certain perspective may give that makes a real difference in their individual and collective lives.

In this book I use my Africenric lens for that purpose. I made that choice in the 1960s and have never regretted it. By "Africentric lens," I mean the lens that clarifies my perception of what, in this world, envelops and conditions me as an *African* American, as a descendant of a stolen and enslaved people of the continent of Africa, and also as a follower of Jesus Christ, who accosted me at the baptismal font of a black Presbyterian church in the ghetto of North Philadelphia many years ago and still pursues me through the ringing, vibrant, labyrinthine corridors of these closing years of my life.

A second question arises over the meaning of the term *pragmatic spirituality.* Recently, while dining with a new friend, I was asked: "But isn't that a contradiction in terms?" Why yes—in ordinary parlance—but in no sense more contradictory than the creedal affirmation: "Jesus Christ, God's only begotten Son, both God and man." "Pragmatic spirituality," as applied in this book, requires a careful explanation, which I will offer following a few preliminary remarks.

For more than half a century I have written, preached, and lectured about the faith of the Christian church from the perspective of many of my forebears. They were kidnapped men and women, boys and girls, on whom the religious customs and cultures of Europe were foisted, but who eventually molded and shaped the religious faith of their captors according to their own perceptions of its utility for maintaining selfhood and sanity under the conditions of dehumanizing bondage followed by a dubious emancipation.

That molding and shaping process, influenced by their dimming recollection of their ancestral religions, plus their own genius for combining and syncretizing diverse elements of belief, produced a peculiar set of lenses: A hybrid form of spirituality that was more than the solipsistic practices of holiness, the concentration on the presence of God and the feeling of personal fulfillment that sometimes comes with it. The spirituality of the African slave conjoined the sacred and the profane; the intuitive and charismatic apprehension of an invisible spirit world with the practical requirements of a visible physical world that, after more than six hundred years, continues to be oppressive and not infrequently brutal to people whose skin color is other than white.

Since the time I began graduate studies at Lincoln University, in Chester County, Pennsylvania, a student in its small, struggling Presbyterian theological seminary, I have understood my special vocation to be investigating and writing about the varied uses and abuses of religion and spirituality in the history of the African diaspora. "We have been believers!" sings Margaret Walker, in a moving poem that James H. Evans Jr. used as a preface to his book on African American systematic theology.[3]

We have been believers, indeed! Has any people in the United States believed more passionately, and acted out of those beliefs more aptly, than the descendants of those mournful but ingenious captives from Africa? Because of their beliefs, as a boy I yearned to be a believer, too, and I was baptized as a child and confirmed in the Christian faith while in high school, strangely enough, through readings in astronomy and metaphysics in the private library of the Benjamin Franklin Institute of Philadelphia. Let me explain how that happened.

I had been awarded a membership in the Benjamin Franklin Institute by winning first place in a citywide essay contest on Franklin and his contributions to the nation, sponsored by the elite Poor Richard Club of Philadelphia. In addition to receiving a handsome plaque and a five-year membership in the Franklin Institute, I was invited to ride, with my astonished father, at the head of a parade down the Benjamin Franklin Parkway to Logan Square, across from the main library whose roof garden I haunted almost every day. My winning that essay contest was as much of a shock to the illustrious gentlemen of the Poor Richard Club as it was to me, a poor black boy from the mean streets of North Philadelphia.

As a young member of the McDowell Presbyterian Church at Columbia Avenue and Twenty-first Street, and also an amateur metaphysician, I continued in college to investigate the beliefs of my people more closely by searching out the meaning of those beliefs, their truths and errors, their strengths and weaknesses. It has been an effort of a lifetime, and one that has brought both joy and sorrow, because what Margaret Walker in her poem calls "the secrets of the seeress and the magic of the charmers and the power of the devil's evil ones"[4] have not always been propitious. But for fifty years I have been plumbing the depths of those beliefs, and the many strange and frequently contradictory consequences that have flowed into our lives because of and in spite of them.

This book is a collection of essays, in my view, with the concurrence of a few former students and colleagues, that represents some of the best of those writings. Several were previously published in other books and journals; others were revised from formal lectures or unpublished manuscripts, and a few were written especially for this volume.

I call Africentric spirituality *pragmatic* because it is not particularly interested in mystical experiences, speculative theologizing, or idealizations of what it means to exist in the eternal presence of a Supreme Being who mainly deals with us in a nonmaterial, spiritual realm. To speak of the *pragmatic* character of this spirituality is to emphasize its interest in practical or human considerations and consequences—but not to the extent that all transcendence is summarily wiped out and religion thereby reduced to an especially moralistic kind of human engineering or an impersonalistic instrumentalism that seeks to calculate and program all human relationships. Quite the opposite! The pragmatic character of this spirituality is rooted in its human direction and goal, its propensity for loving service to others as an emulation of God's love of humankind that is manifested primarily in the biblical picture of Jesus' earthly ministry to "the least" of his sisters and brothers.

Without intending to be simplistic, "pragmatic spirituality" is street level–plain and profoundly sensible spirituality. Pragmatic spirituality focuses religion on the nitty-gritty problems and purposes of daily life. As such, it is very dynamic and adaptable. It is not static and brittle. Like water it conforms to the contours of its receptacle. Like the palm tree it bends in a hurricane. It could not be Africentric if it were not partly grounded in a transcendent and insubstantial world of sacred beliefs and traditions, in a certain style of divine worship and communion with an otherworldly Being or Beings who watch over and care for those who revere them. But this African and African American spirituality also projects itself onto the practical plane of life and grips the solid rock of empirical actuality. To be sure, it may luxuriate in flights of fantastic imagination and may have nothing against prayer and meditation, but it always comes spiraling back to earth to deal with the issues and problems of everyday life—that is, staying alive, "making do" with what is available, and also "doing more" to improve and enhance the possibilities of a this-worldly existence weighed and found wanting by comparison with another world to which we have not yet ascended. Let me be a little more specific.

Pragmatic spirituality is exemplified in the healing and liberating ministry of Jesus. It frees us to be human in a way that makes a palpable difference in other's lives. That is why Jesus, the Fixer, the Healer, the Liberating God, was at the center of black faith in the early African American churches and continues to be the same for most interpreters of black and womanist theologies today. Jacquelyn Grant, for example, speaks of black women as "the least" of all who suffer from racism, sexism, and classism in America and shows how black women in the past identified Jesus Christ preeminently with their salvation from suffering and ignominious servitude, and their liberation of self and others to humanity and self-determination.

> To affirm Jesus' solidarity with the "least of the people" is not an exercise in romanticized contentment with one's oppressed status in life. For as the Resurrection signified that there is more to life than the cross for Jesus Christ, for Black women it signified that their tri-dimensional oppressive existence is not the end, but it merely represents the context in

> which a particular people struggle to experience hope and liberation. Jesus Christ thus represents a three-fold significance: first he identifies with the "little people," Black women, where they are; secondly, he affirms the basic humanity of these "the least", and thirdly, he inspires active hope in the struggle for resurrected, liberated existence.[5]

What Grant says about Jesus and black women was also true for Jesus and black people in general, with women being most precisely the case in point. Black or Africentric Christian spirituality locates its source, example, and goal in Jesus, with all the problems for black women that the patriarchal interpretation of Jesus by black and white men entails. That needs to be discussed, but my main point here is that pragmatic spirituality "works" in the sense that Jesus worked. He did not sit around practicing "holiness" and the presence of God. He came down from the Mount of Transfiguration to heal and preach and unveil the Kingdom of God (Luke 9:28–62) with deeds of power. As the Negro Spiritual says, "No man works like him!" In the same sense, pragmatic spirituality *wants* to work like him—not to say that it expects always to succeed but that it aims for something that is creative and redemptive for all who suffer and struggle. It can be contemplative, but its overarching purpose and goal is to accomplish something for the good of humanity. It seeks to make real its vision of humankind as the New Being in Christ, its vision of the world as the consummate Realm of God's sovereign rule. Make no mistake about either its spirituality or its pragmatism. When it affirms and envisions a supernatural world, it does so in terms of the highest and noblest that the present world could produce if it would, but which it more frequently has withheld from the least of Christ's brothers and sisters.

When my ancestors sang, "I got shoes, you got shoes, all God's children got shoes," they were rejecting the idea of going without shoes on earth as a consequence of the selfishness of the plantation owner, and were voicing, at the same time, the expectation that in heaven they would enjoy putting on and taking off shoes to "shout all over God's heaven" whether white people liked it or not! Many of the spirituals were both otherworldly and pragmatic at the same time. Contrary to the stereotype about slave religion, black spirituality was not a crass and fatuous longing for "pie in the sky, when you die," but an empowering conviction that because God's will ought to be "on earth as it is in heaven," religion ought naturally to function as a goad in the struggle for an equal share of the material goods of this world and the freedom to exercise one's talents and potential as a human being in enjoying and utilizing and making them available to those most in need.

John S. Mbiti, perhaps Africa's leading theologian, forthrightly declares: "To live in the here and now is the most important concern of African religious activity and beliefs. . . . Man's acts of worship and turning to God are pragmatic and utilitarian rather than spiritual or mystical."[6]

John Lovell Jr., who I believe knows more about the spirituals than most theologians, preachers, and choir directors, devised a tabular comparison of the slave poet's vision of heaven and its rewards with his or her experiences of earth and what it lacked or had that needed to be shared more equitably. Lovell listed those earthly items or experiences that are glorified in the picture of heaven in the mind of the unknown bards who created the Negro spirituals. His table includes clothes, footgear, headgear, shoulder gear, living quarters, musical instruments, drinking water, food, types of punishment, transportation, meetings, family and friends, entrances and exits, and streets.

> If the reader thinks [the slave's] heav'm is a theological or otherworldly thing, the evidence ought to disabuse him. The heav'm of the Afro-American spiritual speaks more to the slave's appreciation and criticism of the things and values of his earthly life than it does to anything else. When he mentions a heavenly thing or value, he more than likely has an earthly thing or value in mind—like Homer who had two names for certain characters, one for earth and one for the heavens—and the reader should take pains to search his meanings. The spiritual poet was no visionary or speculator in the usual senses.[7]

In one of the chapters to follow I deal more fully with the nature and function of Black eschatology, to use a fancy academic word, but here I want to make patently clear its importance for my theory of pragmatic spirituality. That theory has been developing in my work since 1969 when I first read John S. Mbiti's assumption-shattering book on African religions and philosophy. Mbiti takes pains to assert that African ontology is unabashedly anthropocentric and pragmatic. He is careful in his generalizations about African religions because of significant differences between them. But what impressed me most was his firm assertion, for which considerable evidence has been amassed, that all loose talk about how otherworldly and spooky the religions of Africa are is wrong. If, as I believe, there are still distant echoes of this continent-wide religiosity in the spirituality of the African diaspora—particularly in the Western hemisphere—we should not be surprised that black people's faith has been so pervasively practical and "down to earth." Although the years pile up as time goes by, we are not so far spiritually from our foremothers and forefathers who were born across the sea. Mbiti speaks of their original belief systems as follows:

> The individual believes what others in his community believe: it is a corporate "faith." And this faith is utilitarian, not purely spiritual, it is practical and not mystical. The people respond to God in and because of particular circumstances, especially in times of need. Then they seek to obtain what He gives, be that material or spiritual; they do not search for Him as the final reward or satisfaction of the human soul or spirit. Augustine's description of man's soul being restless until it finds its rest in God, is something unknown in African traditional religious life.[8]

With this quotation from one of the most influential scholars representing the late-twentieth-century interest in African and African American religious studies, I return briefly to the topic I only touched on earlier, namely, why I chose to subsume my own lifetime of writing about religion under the banner "Africentrism."

Africentrism, as I apply the term in this book, involves doing intellectual work with Africans and African Americans—with their histories, their cultures, and their peoples—as one reflects on human affairs and what is transpiring in the world. Africentrism is the lens some people use to correct a distorted vision of reality that we inherited either by seduction or imposition. It involves centering the picture of the world that we have in our minds—namely, our worldview—so that our *actions,* our functional deportment, our modus vivendi will support the historic struggle of Africans and the African diaspora for freedom, justice, and equality in a world that has been colonized, dominated, and interpreted by white Europeans and Americans to the disadvantage and detriment of most people of color.

Professor Molefi Kete Asante, who prefers the word *Afrocentrism* to describe what I call *Africentrism,* for that reason and others, will not agree entirely with my definition. I believe, nonetheless, that Asante experienced remarkable moments of insight, which I might even call revelation, at Temple University in Philadelphia, where he heads the Department of African American Studies.

Asante has a tighter and somewhat narrower definition of Africentrism than I have. He puts the African continent at the center of the world, maybe at the center of the universe, and measures almost everything else in human history from that vantage point. This, of course, gives him a more triumphant and glorified characterization of "African-centeredness" than I have. At one place he writes:

> It [Afrocentrism] is about taking the globe and turning it over so that we see all the possibilities of a world where Africa, for example, is subject and not object. Such a posture is necessary and rewarding for Africans and Europeans. The inability to "see" from several angles is perhaps the one common fallacy in provincial scholarship.[9]

So far so good, but I have rather preferred the more rounded and modest explanation of Cain Hope Felder, a biblical scholar at the Divinity School of Howard University in Washington, D.C., who puts the matter this way:

> Afrocentricity is the idea that the land mass that the ancient Romans routinely called Africa and persons of African descent must be understood as having made significant contributions to world civilization as proactive subjects within history, rather than being regarded as merely passive objects of historical distortions. Afrocentrism means reestablishing Africa as a center of value and source of pride, without in any way demeaning other people and their historic contributions to human achievement.[10]

The "centrism" about which I speak in the title of this book is not so much geographical or even ideological as it is perspectival, spiritual, and open-ended. It is peculiarly suited to the way I look at the Christian faith, as well as the world of oppression and suffering to which that faith calls me to revolutionary action. Nevertheless, I believe that both Professors Asante and Felder recognize, as do I, that putting African and African American lenses into the spectacles with which people view the faith and the world will help those people, whose eyes (and souls) were otherwise out of focus, to see and respond to voluminous data and phenomena from "an alternative perspective" that is beneficial not only for black people but for everyone!

A theologian whose views I feel quite compatible with in this regard is Professor J. Deotis Roberts of Duke University Divinity School, whose book *Africentric Christianity: A Theological Appraisal for Ministry* is mandatory reading for anyone interested in using the lens of Asante's concept without making it a substitute for the Christian faith. That, I feel sure, is not Asante's intention, but Roberts's work ensures that we will not be so careless as to slip into that error unaware. His approach to the Africentric perspective is heuristic; it asks questions, explores new answers to old queries, and probes dogmatic positions with a willingness to reject them if they prove to be contrary to his faith commitments.

> As the term clearly implies, Africentrism is a way of viewing reality other than from a Eurocentric outlook. It entails a serious attempt to understand the manner in which Africans have viewed reality in their context of culture for thousands of years before they encountered the Western worldview. African Americans attempt to recover their classical roots through empathy, knowledge, and experience. Through new looking glasses, we peer into this Africentered world to observe what may be useful in our commitment to Christianity. What is useful? What must be rejected? What will enrich and empower our Christian way of life?[11]

The chapters in this book do not all conform to a strict definition of Africentrism that would be acceptable to the most radical leaders of the movement. Nonetheless, most of what readers will find here is the result of looking at the world I know as an African American Christian and being open to angles of vision that differ from Euro-American interpretations of history and ways of understanding the Christian faith. I believe that these chapters deserve the term *Africentric* because they are informed and inspired by my personal experience as a member of the African diaspora and of the Christian church, and because they look toward Africa and the diaspora, rather than toward the North Atlantic community, for authentication and authority.

Accordingly, I wish to register the following statement as my own heuristic definition of Africentrism, and I ask the reader to evaluate what follows in these pages in terms of conformity to this definition and to the gospel of Jesus Christ.

Africentrism is not defining everything in the world in terms of what Native Africans have done, thought, or believed; it is equally focused on the history and culture of African Americans. Nor is it a total rejection of the value of European, Euro-American, or any other civilization. It is not an anti-white version of black nationalism. Africentrism is rather a studied openness to the knowledge, wisdom, and spirituality of Africa and the African diaspora, and the willingness, on the strength of that acquirement, to always ask the question, "What does this datum of insight, knowledge, or experience have to do with the suppression of truth about black people and the oppression of the black world, and to what extent will it detract from or enhance liberation, justice, and democratic development for Africans, the diaspora, and all poor and oppressed people throughout the world?"

I am aware that most African Americans are abysmally ignorant about African culture and that many Americans, both white and black, are indifferent. They will wonder why I am at such pains to be identified with the struggling nations and ethnic groups of that long-subjugated land whose recent history is so tragic. It is precisely because of the historical astigmatism of the African American church and community that some of us are under a sacred obligation to open the eyes of the blind and unstop the ears of the deaf. Despite the tyranny, the genocide, and HIV-AIDS, we see a world aborning across the Atlantic that will come into its own one of these days and may yet call out to our unborn children, long after we have passed from the scene, to come and reclaim a heritage that we ourselves let slip from our hands.

The essays that follow do not make the case for Africentrism as strongly as I do here, but the reader will doubtlessly recognize the historic wells from which they draw water. They represent research and writing in a wide, interdisciplinary field, but their common focus on the history, culture, and religion of black people binds them together as reports of sightings that some of us have made of a yet inadequately explored terrain—through the lens of Christian Africentrism.

The "God of Ethiopia," as some of our great-grandparents were not afraid to call the God and Father of Jesus Christ, is the God of all oppressed peoples and holds out to both Africans and African Americans of the twenty-first century yet another opportunity to redeem not only the land that was alienated from its original possessors but to reinvigorate a spiritual inheritance that actually belongs to all God's children.

I hope that these chapters will speak not only to people intrigued by the ideology and theology of blackness in the new millennium but also to those who espy a multicultural future and want to contribute to it. If successful, these writings may show those sincerely desiring to participate in that great project how much they need to be chastened, instructed, and encouraged by the history of African American Christians and humanists over the last two centuries. The spirits of Daniel Coker, Edward Wilmot Blyden, Amanda Berry Smith, Henry McNeal Turner, Maria Fearing, Alexander Crummell, Marcus M. Garvey, Zora Neale Hurston, W. E. B. Du Bois, Charles Copher, and Cheikh Anta Diop—I love to call the roll of these hallowed names!—brood over the following pages. Long may they live in our thinking hearts and feeling minds!

PART I

Teaching African American Religious Studies

1

What Is African American Religious Studies?

African American religious studies refers to a field of research that suddenly burst upon graduate theological education in the late 1960s.[1] Serious inquiry and debate about the religious sentiments of black slaves and free persons in the Americas date from a much earlier period. However, it was not until the black studies movement, part of the artistic and intellectual efflorescence of the civil rights period, erupted on theological seminary campuses where there were critical masses of African American students that we began to hear talk of black church studies or African American religious studies programs.[2] Because various terms have been used to denote the academic study of the religions of African Americans and the requirements of an effective ministry with black congregations, differences of opinion remain about the precise nature of the field. In this chapter I advance a working definition of what I think the term *African American religious studies* should imply. But first a few preliminary remarks.

First, while it was inevitable that the earliest serious inquiries into the nature of black religions would occur in the context of scientific research by black scholars like W. E. B. Du Bois, Carter G. Woodson, Ruby F. Johnston, E. Franklin Frazier, and Benjamin E. Mays, it would have been strange had these inquiries remained at an academic level of sheer objective description and disinterestedness. The practical needs of the black church and community were too pressing on African American intellectuals. The extraordinary influence of the church could not but help make the training of pastors in the practical demands of ministry the dominating consideration for shaping courses of religious studies, at least in the black academy. African Americans could rarely afford the luxury of "scientific studies" of religion that were unconcerned about social matters and the preparation of a professional leadership class. After all, with the exception of the family, the church has always been the most important institution in the individual and collective lives of black people in this country.

Second, with the possible exception of the famous Myrdal studies,[3] the most serious investigations of African American religions before the 1960s were done over many years by students and professors at an obscure Methodist school for blacks in the South, Gammon Theological Seminary in Atlanta, and the Howard University School of Religion in Washington, D.C. These were the first fully accredited, predominantly African American graduate schools of religion. Most of their pre-1960s dissertations and monographs have either gone with the wind or are buried in neglected archives, having served the eminently practical purpose of "equipping the saints for ministry" in days long past.

Third, the comprehensive cultural and holistic character of African American religion itself militates against the epistemological split that often characterizes much of what is called Religious Studies in the prestigious white theological schools and university departments of religion. The best religious scholarship in the African American academy is, perforce, faith-based or "believing scholarship," accepting all the risks that such a position entails.

It scarcely could be otherwise. The centuries-old struggle for black humanity in a racist society never encouraged the development of a dispassionate, armchair study of religion for preparing the leadership of the embattled African American churches of America. Whatever titles may have been given to programs designed for the study of the religions of the African diaspora in the New World, most of them have had in common the ultimate purpose of faithful and pragmatic service to a disenfranchised and oppressed people.

The definition that follows will reflect this commonsense attitude toward research and teaching that comes out of the ethos of the historic African American community and its struggle for freedom and equality. African American religious studies, therefore, may be briefly described as an academic area that investigates the religions of people of African descent and their practice of ministry in the segregated and marginalized world in which they live. As we shall see in this chapter, the field takes on richer, interdisciplinary implications and practical uses that involve all levels of education among black believers, that regulate a certain cultural and religious interaction between blacks and others, and that facilitate the deployment of the African American church as an agency of social, political, and economic change. What follows below is a more comprehensive definition that I recommend for critical discussion, especially by church-affiliated scholars.

> African American religious studies refers to the investigation, analysis, and ordering of a wide variety of data related to the religions of persons of African descent, for the purpose of authenticating and enriching personal faith and preparing both clergy and laity for a ministry in the African American church and community. Such a ministry is understood to be competent and faithful leadership in worship, evangelism, and nurture, and to incorporate social, political, and economic action on behalf of God's mission of liberation and justice for all people.

The definition is, of course, open for experimentation and revision as we gain greater experience in research and teaching. It also presupposes provisional answers to several questions that need to be addressed. For example, what is an acceptable and useable definition of African American *religions?* And, incidentally, acceptable and useful by whose standards? What is the place of ethnicity and commitment to special interest groups in theological education? What are the appropriate pedagogical requirements of graduate theological education as opposed to Bible colleges or lay education? What is the relationship between African American religious studies in the seminary and the same area of study in the university or the university-related divinity school? What is the scope of African American religious studies? Should it include, for example, courses in black Judaism, Islam, neo-African religions, and the new urban sects and cults in the black community? Finally, how does African American religious studies intersect with black studies, African studies, and multicultural studies that focus on research which includes adherents of Euro-American, Hispanic, Asian, and Native American religions, and the religions of the Third World or, perhaps better put, the Two-Thirds World?

I do not intend to delve into all these perplexing questions, but I present them here as critical and urgent examples for the African American church and academy. My interest in this chapter is solely to unravel the definition of African American religious studies posed above so as to make a case for (1) an interdisciplinary theory that explains the nature and significance of the African American religious experience in North

America; (2) the exploration of some aspects of an experimental model for teaching and researching black religion from the perspective of both the theological and secular disciplines, crafted for use by African American scholars in those fields who want to help revitalize the African American church and community; and (3) a critique of American cultural, political, and economic conditions implicit in an approach that posits African American congregations as agents of change toward a more just society.

What the definition above intends to suggest, therefore, is a prolegomenon and context for understanding the unifying substance and underlying purpose of an Africentric approach to theological studies and pastoral ministry. Many African American scholars of religion widely agree that their vocation is about helping black people think more clearly and productively about God, about who they are as a people in a world that has been dominated primarily by racist white people; it is also about how black Christians can, with the help of their historic religious institutions, participate more meaningfully and effectively in God's mission of liberation from the power of racism, sexism, classism, and oppressions of every kind.

Let us begin, therefore, by turning to the definition itself to ascertain whether it indeed lends itself to these objectives and what problems we may encounter along the way

> *African American religious studies refers to the investigation, analysis, and ordering of a wide variety of data related to the religions of persons of African descent.*

The emphasis here is on the systematic examination and presentation of what we already know and what we still need to learn about the nature of religion and its relationship to other cultural phenomena in the African American subcommunity. Obviously one of the first tasks is to design a heuristic definition of black religion itself. I am using the singular noun here to indicate that our search is for a definition broad enough to include a variety of experiences that reflect the collective consciousness of a common "ultimate concern" among black religionists, while at the same time specific enough, and sufficiently committed to the Christian faith, to be able to utilize some of what we have received from the traditional disciplines of the American "theological encyclopedia."[4]

In the quest for such a definition I have utilized the approach of symbolic anthropologists such as Clifford Geertz, John Morgan, and Ann Marie Powers. Attempting to break away from an overly narrow functionalist explanation of religion, these writers have sought to penetrate its meaning as a system or mosaic of symbols by which people "communicate, perpetuate, and develop their knowledge about and attitudes toward life," continuously shaping reality as well as being shaped by it.[5] Geertz's paradigm for the study of religion as a cultural system describes how sacred symbols serve to synthesize a people's ethos with their operative worldview in such a way as to make for a subtle circularity—a reciprocal confirmation or coherence between how they live (i.e., their patterned behavior) and what they actually believe about the world they live in (i.e., their specific belief system or, one might say, their operative metaphysics). Religion, therefore, in Geertz's understanding is "a system of symbols which acts to establish powerful, pervasive, and long-lasting moods and motivations in men [*sic*] by formulating conceptions of a general order of existence and clothing these conceptions with such an aura of factuality that the moods and motivations seem uniquely realistic."[6]

Such a definition has the advantage of giving us a useful model for developing a more specific grasp of black religion as a *particular* symbol system, marginal to the mainstream of American culture but characteristically exhibiting an extraordinary relationship to the African American subculture as a whole. For it seems quite clear that religion has played a role in black America that is considerably more holistic and efficacious than its more segmented role in most white American communities. The focus of the symbolic anthropologists on the relationship between religion and culture has helped us to understand how black faith extracts meaning out of the depths and crises of oppression under a dominating culture, and pours it into the cultural molds of the African American ghetto. At the same time African American religion itself is being molded, for both good and ill, for accommodation and protest, and for compromise and resistance, by the social, economic, and political realities of African American existence.[7]

Such an understanding of black religion and culture cannot be validated without reference to a variety of academic disciplines from both the theological seminary and the university. The basic paradigm is anthropological, but history, sociology, psychology, political science, literature, and ethnomusicology are all relevant to what this opening sentence of our definition calls for. When we add biblical studies, church history, theology, ethics, and the "practical disciplines" of the theological curriculum (preaching, counseling, church administration, etc.) it becomes clear what wide-ranging vehicles are needed to traverse the broad landscape of the distinctive beliefs, experiences, and practices that fall within the boundaries of that familiar ethnic designation—"persons of African descent."

What it actually means to be a person of African descent is not altogether clear. Most of us generally perceive some notable differences as well as similarities between such persons and white people who were born in Great Britain, Germany, or who are of Swedish or Italian descent. But casual perception is not enough for our definition. Nor is the argument about the retentions of attenuated African elements in black culture and religion sufficiently conclusive. Thus the question of the relationship of Africa to African American religious studies remains problematic. But we cannot avoid some tentative hypotheses that open up creative possibilities for exploration and study.

To consider only one illustration: it would be helpful to discover the extent to which a three-year seminary curriculum should give a student the ability to trace the movement of Egyptian, Ethiopian, and Nubian Christianity from the East to the West, its decay, diffusion, and Islamization among several African Traditional Religions in the cultural areas from which the majority of slaves were brought to the Americas. Should African American religious studies include investigating the course of West African religion through Americanization in the United States under the pressure of slavery, ghettoization, and secularization? These are difficult academic problems, but they illustrate the magnitude and complexity of any search for a comprehensive, interdisciplinary theory of the origin, evolution, and present structure of the belief systems and ritual patterns of adherents of the historic African American faiths.

Difficulties notwithstanding, the task of collecting, sorting out, and analyzing all kinds of data related to religions that are embedded in the social-structural and personality systems of the average African American will require an unparalleled collaboration between subject matters as diverse as the archaeology of West and Central Africa and the hermeneutics of three centuries of African American music, rhetoric, dance, and literature. Out of the welter of evidence, both ancient and modern, we may be able to verify the multiform character of black belief and—more important to activist scholarship—catch a glimpse of the common thread of ethnic suffering and struggle by way of migrations, slavery, decolonization, detribalization, and gender conflict and injustice that binds together, for good or ill, black believers in Africa and the diaspora in a seamless garment of pragmatic spirituality. It should be mentioned that white and other ethnic group scholars, as well as black scholars, have been at work on these problems since the 1970s. All people who are committed to correcting years of neglect and distortion in the study of African American culture are more than welcome to join this worthy enterprise.

To conclude the discussion of the first clause in our definition of African American religious studies let us propose the forthright proposition that the field involves, at the very least, an analysis of data—from an interdisciplinary perspective—dealing with the systems of sacred symbols that people of African descent have passed down from generation to generation, and which have given essential meaning and direction to their lives in this western hemisphere for more than four hundred years.

. . . for the purpose of authenticating and enriching personal faith and preparing both clergy and laity for a ministry in the African American church and community.

Here we come upon a highly debatable question that will separate African American religious studies, in the white and black seminaries where I have taught, from religious studies in most predominantly white seminaries and universities. Our focus unabashedly seeks to authenticate and enrich personal faith. This is critical and will be a stumbling block for many colleagues who will consider it inexcusably subjective. We mean, nevertheless, to assist students who need assistance to move, in due time during a three-year program, from *academic conceptualization* to *experiential appropriation.* This requires taking the student's personal faith and life experiences, and the life and faith of the local congregation she or he may be serving during the seminary years, with utmost seriousness. The objective is to contribute to the development and enhancement of personal faith not only by the acquisition of abstract knowledge but by the appropriation of *meaningful faith* about life and vocation. This means not only the "reconversion" of some students but also concern about the process by which his or her faith is developed, tested, corrected, and verified by the gospel and the church. We want, in other words, to subject academic conceptualization to both the authority of Christ and to the priority of the religious and cultural experiences of the people. I believe that theological education will have failed, despite having expertly decoded the black experience, if there is no faith decision, no new and enriching sentiment embraced by the student. The seminary always fails to fulfill its mission, in my opinion, whenever what it teaches is left untouched by the faith and experiences of those it purports to educate, both students and the churches in which they minister.

The discussion thus far has suggested two dimensions or levels of African American religious studies. On the first level the question is, what do these academic disciplines teach about the origin, nature, development, and influence of religion in the culture of persons of African descent, particularly in the United States? The question on the second level is, what precisely does this knowledge have to do with the personal conviction (or lack thereof) that Jesus is Lord and that his salvific messiahship is consistently made manifest in the affirmations, yearnings, and striving of the church and community that certain persons are called to serve?

The latter question is inescapable for black Christian scholars who insist on the appropriation, authentication, and enhancement of faith as one of the objectives of African American religious studies. We are obliged to be what we are—black or Africentric Christians. We begin with the assumption that the gospel itself stands in judgment on all human knowledge and endeavor, including that which is Africentric, and that we must permit it to certify our academic enterprise. Second, we assume that there is an important work of translation and interpretation to be done in two directions—from the theological academy to the African American community, and from the African American community to the academy. It is important to note that inherent in both these assumptions is the recognition of the equal relevance of the black religious experience for the education of white people who are preparing for ministry. It is, in other words, important for everyone involved in this field that the religious experience of black people—to whatever extent possible—be translated into the language and thought forms of the academy. But of equal or greater import is that scholarly judgments and valuations be first communicated to ordinary black Christians in such a way that the folk recognize the essential integrity between what they believe and practice, by the authority of the Scripture and the Holy Spirit, and what their half-educated, ostensibly sophisticated but inexperienced student preachers espouse. This does not mean that what the folk already believe and celebrate should always be the final authority. Rather, it means that the burden is on graduate theological education and educators to make themselves understood and validated by black folk who already know God in both the sanctuary and the streets.

> "Aunt Jane" is still in the pew on Sunday morning. These days she may have a high school or even a college diploma, a late model car in the church parking lot, and other appurtenances of a black middle-class lifestyle, but she still has a no-nonsense attitude about her religion. She wants it straight, no chaser. She remembers what racism and oppression are like, and sees their more subtle and disguised manifestations crippling her children and grandchildren. She knows that Jesus, the Holy Ghost, and the struggle for survival are real, and she expects her seminary-trained preacher to "tell the story" in symbols and images that rise to the heights of passion and creative imagination without losing a grip on the practical requirements of daily life—on whatever black people have to do to remain human in this world and secure for the world to come.[8]

Certainly African American religious studies must be critical of both the black church and "Aunt Jane," one of its saints on the battlefield. But it must also have its academic feet on the ground on which these saints are carrying on the battle. Propositions and presuppositions need to be tested by the people's faith that has "brought them a mighty long way" and has enabled them somehow to survive. What we are describing in this chapter as African American religious studies cannot exist without a dynamic relationship between the students, the teacher, the congregation, and the community—with God at the center. The student, as scholar and professional-in-training, should be taught to understand the nature of generic religion and of black religion in particular. But what is desirable is a "second conversion experience"—away from a naive faith that was unduly influenced by white Protestant evangelicalism during and after slavery, to a new *persona,* grounded in a mature reappropriation of faith in the "God of our weary years . . . of our silent tears . . . who hast brought us thus far along the way"—the liberating God of Africa and of African America.

This God alone is the source of the power that holds the entire system of black faith and praxis together with creative energies flowing back and forth between the student, the professor, and the congregation—all within the context of a specific, dynamic, sociopolitical situation in the real world—in a given time and place.

Such a ministry is understood to be competent and faithful leadership in worship, evangelism, Christian nurture, and corporate social, political, and economic action on behalf of God's mission of liberation and justice for all people.

Here "leadership" has to do with both the professional clergy and the laity, women and men, each of whom need African American religious studies in their respective contexts. In other words, the heart of the definition we have been reviewing stresses the instruction and guidance of the black church in the liberating and justice-making experiences of worship, study, and action. I will not attempt to deal with all the areas of witness specified in the definition. It should be clear that everything points to the goal of "equipping the saints for ministry" (Eph. 4:12). More specifically, everything points to preparing and participating in a ministry of personal development and social transformation that combats the demonic forces of institutional racism, economic injustice, and political oppression.

This brings us to a brief but necessary historical excursus.

African American religious studies, as we are defining it, evolved from the black studies movement of the 1960s. James H. Evans compares the critique by the death-of-God theologians of the absence of a theoretical basis for American religious practices to the less celebrated critique by African American college students of abstract academic teaching in the white universities during the same period. Black students, led by Bob Moses, Stokely Carmichael, H. Rap Brown, and James Forman, pronounced their anathemas on any educational curriculum that had no practical consequences for the freedom, justice, and general welfare of the community.[9] One of the primary emphases of the black studies movement was education for liberation, that is, for selfless service (which is the meaning of *ministry*) in the African American community. Manning Marable, in a perceptive essay on the African American intellectual tradition, concludes that "Black Studies reveals the historical evolution and social reality of American capitalist society from the perspective of 'the bottom up.' It embraces the totality of the social sciences and the humanities, and seeks to restructure the method and content of American education from the vantage point of the oppressed."[10]

African American religious studies programs in American theological schools were similarly motivated. In the late 1960s and early 1970s African American seminarians startled white faculties and boards of trustees with the declaration that theological education, which presumed to prepare men and women for ministry among black people, had a moral obligation to see that the students received the requisite knowledge and skills for the radicalization of the African American church for social transformation. They followed the example of the militant undergraduates who were forcing the concept of black studies on America's secular colleges and universities, including, incidentally, the HBCUs—the Historic Black Colleges and Universities.

The definition with which we have been working ends on a familiar note that other African American intellectuals have sounded over more than two hundred years before the idea of black studies was conceived. But the need for the study of African American religion to motivate and instruct the laity for struggle has never been more urgent than it is today. With the waning influence of the traditional civil rights organizations, the rapid demise of the Historic Black Colleges and Universities, and the dwindling number of teachers in black public schools in some sections of the country, the church may be the last bastion of African American culture and consciousness. The black preacher, therefore, has no option but to become once again the teacher, role model, and mentor for young people who are looking for a more radical analysis and response to the black condition in America's cities. Such an analysis, and its implications of collective action, seem unlikely at the grass-roots level unless the future leadership of congregations, denominations, and various religious organizations will have been exposed to an African American religious studies emphasis based on some version of the interdisciplinary, faith-based, political-activist theory of Africentric education that we are exploring in this discussion.

The need is for a pragmatic application of the study of religion to the mission and ministry of the church that will engage a cadre of committed women and men who have been taught by faithful professionals who themselves have been well grounded in this field. Thus the teaching responsibility of African American preachers becomes one of the highest priorities for theological education in the twenty-first century. Such teaching should not be limited to what is conventionally called "Christian education." Only to the degree that the entire life of the congregation—its worship and other participatory activities, its study and nurture, and its community outreach—is permeated with questions and answers about the past and how to think theologically about the present and future will the church be able to experience the impact it once had on our communities and on the nation as a whole.

The objective of the last part of our definition is to see that the worship and the intellectual and communal lives of the congregation fall within the ambit of what we are calling African American religious studies. Our congregations need to have a consciousness of their spiritual and political vocation that is called to critique the connections between American capitalism, bourgeois democracy, poverty, sexism, misogyny, and racism in the United States and throughout the world. Only such people can be expected to mount an inspired and sustained non-violent attack on destructive globalization, exploitation, and age-old oppressions. African American religious studies is the first stage of such an attack, but it cannot be restricted to the theological seminaries. It must have a base in our colleges and universities, in local congregations, in block clubs and neighborhood associations, the family, and other generative groups and structures of the community. The important point is not to force everyone into some rigid mold of thinking and acting but to help future generations to synthesize conceptualizations of reality, personal faith, and day-to-day experiences in a manner that brings together theory and praxis, that makes academic study and religious education an experiment in both personal transformation and corporate mission.

In this way African American religious studies becomes something more than a compartment in which to conceal our intellectual deficiencies behind theologically flawed gospel songs and loud preaching: another sequence of irrelevant and ego-massaging exercises leading to a professional degree in divinity. It becomes, at one and the same time, the intellectually responsible preparation for and the actualization of an Africentric Christian ministry employing all the disciplines of the academy in culturally appropriate ways for the work of humanization and liberation in communities that need both in order to survive and flourish. Such a program of reflection and action will succeed in maintaining, between the black church and the academy, a shared responsibility in which congregations and denominations are continuously drawn into the process of graduate theological education, and the seminaries, for their part, are drawn into the ministry of personal rehabilitation and societal transformation.

2

Reinterpretation in Black Church History

The one hundredth anniversary of the Divinity School of the University of Chicago was the occasion for the publication of the celebrated "Essays in Divinity," edited by Jerald C. Brauer, history of Christianity professor and dean of the Divinity School. The fifth volume in that series appeared in 1968 and was entitled *Reinterpretation in American Church History.*[1] In the 1930s Chicago was the center of the discipline of American church history, and the students of William Warren Sweet, including Winthrop Hudson, Sidney E. Mead, Jerald C. Brauer, and Martin Marty, addressed themselves in the 1968 publication to "the general problem of changing assumptions at work" in the field of church history in the United States. It was a fortuitous decision. The common theme running through their essays was the idea that the churches of North America were in the throes of a period in which there would be a critical reinterpretation of their history in terms of research, writing, and teaching.

It is no accident that all this talk about reinterpretation took place at a time when the "black revolt," to use the rhetorical phraseology of the period, and its cultural spillover, was shaking the foundations of both religious and secular historical scholarship in the African American community. The cause of our apprehension was patent. Today we look back with amazement on the white scholar who, in 1963, advised John W. Blassingame that if he wanted a career in the profession of history teaching he would have to discontinue his study of the black past. There was even a report circulating in the black academic community during the 1950s about a graduate student at one of the Ivy League universities who, when he told his professor that the topic he wanted for his Ph.D. dissertation was "Nineteenth-Century Negro Thought," the professor lifted his spectacles and asked, querulously, "Did they have any?"[2]

Happily the essay by Robert T. Handy, "Negro Christianity and American Historiography," which appears in the 1968 volume of the University of Chicago Divinity School series and which seminarians taking my courses were required to read the first week of class, reminds those who are interested in reinterpreting church history that one of the most urgently needed areas of reinterpretation is the religious history of the African American people. It is perhaps illustrative of one of the welcomed results of widespread reinterpretations in the classic academic disciplines and the interest in interdisciplinary studies that I write as a professor trained in the field of social ethics rather than history, yet can take the liberty to suggest, with Professor Handy, that the reinterpretation of American church historiography was sorely needed and should enlarge its scope to include the black church. Because my writings, for many years, have ranged restlessly over the territory that lies within and between social ethics, theology, and church history, I am persuaded that one of the most significant developments during the past twenty or thirty years is the breakdown of the assumption that we who teach at the university and seminary levels should operate in airtight compartments, each compartment considered off-limits to strange and uncredentialed creatures from other compartments. That battle has not been entirely won, but airtight compartmentalization has, at least, been challenged.

The emergence of black studies in the 1960s is responsible, to no small measure, for the near collapse of this and other traditional presumptions and prejudices. African American religious studies, demanded by black seminarians in the face of the resistance of academic administrators, faculties, and denominations, has revealed once and for all that the foppish emperor of scientific objectivity and doctrinal purity in theological education is wearing no clothes and, to make matters worse, that he is a racist.

I want to begin this discussion by describing three unfortunate racist assumptions in some white seminaries and Bible colleges about church history. These assumptions are largely responsible for the retardation of African American religious studies in the English-speaking world and for the shocking ignorance about the religious experience of black people on the part of the majority of white scholars, church members, and their denominational Christian education staff persons.

The first assumption is that real, honest-to-goodness church history is the history of the mainstream white denominations and their European antecedents. It has simply been taken for granted that from the primitive Christian communities of the Mediterranean basin to the great ecclesiastical structures of the Vatican and the World Council of Churches, true and reliable information about the faith and its normative historical development have flowed through the national histories and cultures of the white people of Europe and North America. Indeed, only through the Protestant and Roman Catholic institutions of the North Atlantic community has an acceptable form of Christianity come down to the people of the United States and Canada, and, among Protestants, primarily through the white Episcopal, Presbyterian, Reformed, Lutheran, Baptist, Disciples of Christ, and Methodist churches. The majority of the immigrant churches of America's white ethnic minorities have been absorbed by those denominations. Others who have resisted total assimilation exist on the periphery as curiosities nostalgically preserving the language and culture of a non-European past and, as in the case of African and African American churches, represent an aberrant form of Christian faith and practice that can be subsumed under the mainstream tradition. They require no special attention, unless one has a penchant for the exotic. Reliable knowledge about these aberrations, it is assumed, can easily be picked up by traversing the main tradition. Real church history, in other words, is white church history.

The second assumption is that any serious religious beliefs among blacks must have begun with the Portuguese attempt to Christianize the coasts of Africa from the last quarter of the fifteenth century. Of course, scholars acknowledge that Islam had penetrated the coastal areas and parts of the forest belt of the Gulf of Guinea after the thirteenth or fourteenth century, but the purists believe that much of Islam was corrupted by African Traditional Religions by the time of the Atlantic slave trade. Thus, it is thought, the blacks who were brought to North America, after the traumatic experience of the Middle Passage, were bereft of everything except the absurd practices of magic, superstition, and the barbaric rituals of more elaborate African religious traditions that rapidly faded into oblivion. It is, we are told, sheer myth-making in the interest of recasting the past in the image of racial chauvinism to imagine that there are any connections, actual or potential, between early Christianity in Egypt, North Africa, Ethiopia, and Nubia, and any of the black indigenous religions or black Christianity in either West Africa or colonial America. Any doctoral study to challenge that normative thesis is politely discouraged.

We were taught that the African Traditional Religions were primitive forms of animism and ancestor worship impermeable to any authentic syntheses with or reinterpretations of Islam and Christianity. As for the transplanted Africans on American soil, whatever true religion they were able to profess after learning the English language had to be crude adaptations of the pure Christian faith given to them by whites. There is, therefore, no such thing as a black or Africentric religion in North America, unless one only refers to the color of the skin of most of the descendants of Africans who, for one reason or another, chose to worship in corporate entities from colonial times until now. Stamped on the souls of African American religionists, of whatever stripe, are the words "Made in America," and what they believed, practiced, and institutionalized in religious organizations has always been little more than a shadowy reflection of the historic faith of white Christians. What may be called black, Africentric, or African American church history (if one insists on those misleading designations) really begins *after* the Civil War, when three or four black denominations could be differentiated from their white parent bodies by the fact that thousands of former slaves poured into them out of the churches of their former masters to set up their own imitations of what they had previously known.

According to this view, it is euphemistic even to speak of black church history before 1865, for prior to the war the data are not only meager and frequently unverified, but there is even some question about the theological integrity and good polity of most of the independent black religious bodies that were extant, judged by the norms and standards of the mainline white denominations. African American church history, in other words, is a dubious enterprise when it purports to be a serious academic discipline.

The third assumption (as if we needed another one to make a case for reinterpretation!) has been that African American church history, if one concedes that such a discipline does exist, is practically and morally dysfunctional inasmuch as it tends to preserve and encourage the continuing disunity of the One, Holy, Catholic and Apostolic Church of Christ. Moreover, it has meaning only for black people. There is nothing particularly compelling about this history that white people need or are obliged to learn that is not already available in much better form in the standard histories of the Church Catholic, written by white European and North American historians. Ethnic church historiography, exponents of this view would say, obscures rather than illuminates the meaning and message of Christian ecumenism.

This third assumption is illustrated by the paucity of courses in black church history in European and American theological seminaries and Bible colleges, and the lack of interest these institutions have in encouraging white students to enroll in such courses or requiring white professors to obtain the competence needed to teach them. American Protestantism, it is assumed, is moving slowly but surely toward organic union between its major branches, at least in the United States. Why becloud the issue of the origin and direction of historical Christianity by making a separate study of the black church? Why make an effort to wrest from such a study some transcendent meaning irrelevant to others in the household of faith, for example, the Native Americans, Hispanic Americans, and Asian Americans?

Those who hold one or all of these views are apt to argue that the academic study of the history of black religion, and its institutional expressions in Africa and the diaspora, is gratuitous at best and dangerous at worst. African Americans made progress in race relations without attempts to reinterpret history when relations were much worse between the races than they are today. Is it not reasonable to believe that we can do without such revisionist history now?

Aside from the fact that in all three of these assumptions we are dealing with racism, pure and simple, academic and otherwise, they all contain some elements of truth—a characteristic of the most disingenuous public asseverations. The way these half-facts and half-truths are handled does violence to extremely complex problems in historical scholarship by creating, from the beginning, a climate of disbelief and suspicion. For nothing can be more sadly misleading than to mistake part of a truth for the whole. That was the unfortunate problem with Joseph R. Washington's otherwise pathfinding study, in 1964, of black religion. A kernel of truth based on one aspect of a multifaceted reality is not enough to dash headlong into a denunciation of a whole people. By criticizing black folk religion as theologically deprived of the qualities of authentic Christian faith that he believed was resident in white Euro-American congregations, Washington failed (in his first but not in his subsequent books) to realize that he was dealing with a deceptive half-truth.

Most black scholars want to engage a larger and more holistic truth about African American religion that most white scholars have had difficulty understanding or believing. It has been hard for the latter to see that what is at stake for African American scholarship in religion is not some claim of epistemological purity, or the pretentious assumption of absolute objectivity, but the survival and liberation of a people, without which the study of history for us would be a vain and meaningless exercise.

Of course, it will not be easy to arrive at one mind about what American historians and theologians ought to make of the religious history and experience of African Americans, but it is certain that white scholars must take seriously, if not appreciate, the ways we are reinterpreting the past and why our conclusions frequently differ from theirs. Otherwise we can have no true dialogue with them, and it will be impossible to have a common commitment to a truth that can edify the whole Church of Christ in this part of the world.

I want now to sketch briefly, and I fear inadequately, three areas of inquiry and reinterpretation that both black and a few non-black scholars have brought to the study of the African American church and the black religious experience over the past twenty or thirty years. I must deliberately omit some developments that a fuller treatment would require. But within the limitations of this chapter the following discussion must suffice to illustrate the point I have made about the falsification of African American church history and the attempts to correct it that some black and white scholars have been making against the arrogant presumptions noted above.

The first chapter of William J. Walls's monumental history of the African Methodist Episcopal Zion Church is entitled "African Civilization and Religion"; his second chapter is "African Origin in Christian Religion."[3] Thus a prominent historian of one of the most enlightened black churches in America, writing as late as 1974, begins his monumental work with a discussion of the early encounters that Egypt and Ethiopia had with Christianity and recalls that famous though all but forgotten prophecy of Psalm 68:31 that was a favorite text of so many black preachers of the past: "Princes shall come out of Egypt, and Ethiopia shall stretch forth her hand unto God."

One significant area of reinterpretation, therefore, is the priority of the contact of both Judaism and Christianity with African people, and the recognition of the African continent as the appropriate place to begin a comprehensive chronology of African American religion. This emphasis on Africa as the place to begin our study has to do with what Professor Charles H. Long has described as "the religious revalorization of the land, a place, where the natural and ordinary gestures of the black man were and could be authenticated."[4] It also has to do with one of the most widely discussed topics among African American intellectuals at the turn of the nineteenth century and one to which scholars in Africa, the Caribbean, and the United States returned during the 1960s and 1970s, namely, the African genesis of civilization, including the institution of religion. More specifically, the discussion focuses on the early influences that shaped the Judeo-Christian religions and on the possibility of finding the roots of African American spirituality in the religious genius of black Africa, not to exclude ancient Egypt and Ethiopia.

The earliest serious scholarship of this genre goes back to men like Alexander Crummell, Edward Wilmot Blyden, George W. Williams, W. E. B. Du Bois, Carter G. Woodson, and Willis N. Huggins. It is important also to look at the more recent writings of Cheikh Anta Diop, Yosef ben Jochannan, John Henrik Clarke, Ali A. Mazrui, John G. Jackson, J. C. De Graft-Johnson, Maulana Karenga, Chancellor Williams, Ulysses D. Jenkins, and Molefi Kete Asante,[5] to mention only a few of the most prominent expositors of this view. The work of these and other African and African American writers who are reinterpreting African history is of uneven quality, as may be expected with any revisionist historiography, but to the extent that they are able to be critical of their own and one another's work, striving for more reliable data from various sources and for greater methodological refinement, their contribution to our understanding of Africa's relevance to contemporary black religion and culture is assured. The craft of the historian, perhaps more than that of other disciplines, requires a certain daring, a certain irreverence for conventional wisdom, a willingness to break out of old molds and explore new inferences and insights.

I remember my own excitement some years ago when I stumbled onto a group of black graduate students and their professors in New York City who were reading E. A. Wallis Budge, the great British Egyptologist, for the first time and discovering new connections to West African religions that most white scholars in America had never suspected.[6] A black history professor at New York University introduced me to that strange but exceedingly erudite book *Anacalypsis* by Godfrey Higgins (1773–1833), which was first published in England in 1833. Higgins's controversial study of antiquity and his unorthodox interpretation of the contribution of black Africa to the ancient religions of Africa and Asia stimulated Harlem intellectuals during the 1960s. It sometimes takes such arcane and incredible thrusts into the belly of what most scholars take for granted to get the creative juices of other seekers flowing. Only so are our younger students able to surprise us with marvelously insightful new treatments of old problems long since laid to rest by their teachers.

That is what produced the reinterpretation of black church history represented by the opening chapters of Bishop Walls's history of the Zionites and, more recently, dissertations presented to the Society for the Study of Black Religion (SSBR), such as the paper on the twenty-fifth, or "Nubian," dynasty of Egypt and its relation to the history of the Old Testament, which Professor Robert Bennett, of the Episcopal Divinity School in Cambridge, Massachusetts, read to the 1980 annual meeting of SSBR in New York City.

The attitude of some white scholars to this kind of historiography has too frequently been, "Well, suppose black people did have some influence on Judaism and Christianity in ancient Africa, and even suppose West African Traditional Religions dimly reflect some of that influence—so what?"

It is part of the task of black church history, as related to African origins and influences, to produce an answer to that cynical "so what?"—not so much to mollify the incredulity of mainstream historians but to prevent that kind of attitude from discouraging younger scholars who can be too easily intimidated by the requirements for promotion and tenure in white schools. Most of all, it is necessary to unravel the myriad implications of the African connection in order to enrich the beliefs and to enlarge the vision of ordinary African American church members.

No one is suggesting that the black churches of America are more Oriental than Western, or that historic influences on the faith and order of black religious bodies run through Coptic Christianity and Constantinople rather than Roman Catholic Christianity and the Protestant Reformation. But what reinterpretation helps to bring out is that the image of African or "Ethiopian" origins has long been handed down by generations of Christians of the African diaspora, and there are data suggesting tenuous connections between East and West African religions before and after the Atlantic slave trade. One cannot dismiss lightly the findings of C. A. Diop and what he called the "cultural unity" of African descended peoples.

From the first nationalistic aspirations of the African Methodist churches of Allen and Varick to Garveyism and the Ethiopian World Federation[7] the evolution of black Christianity has been skewed in a way that was never true for the churches of the sixteenth-century Protestant Reformation and white Protestant evangelicalism in the United States. Future scholars need to take this into account when writing the history of Christianity in America![8]

A second area of reinterpretation involves research focusing on the nature and function of slave religion. Here important questions in church history correlate with similar questions arising from new research on such secular matters as the sociology and economics of slavery, comparative studies of slavery in its hemispheric dimensions, folklore studies, ethnomusicology, and cultural anthropology—particularly with regard to the relationship of moral values, worldviews, and lifestyles to the function of black conventicles in the institutional networks of the New World African American communities. Some of these topics gained increasing attention over the last few decades as a consequence of academic research and intellectual debates exploring pragmatic questions radiating from the Civil Rights movement and the quest for black power.

At first whites showed little interest in such questions, assuming that they had already been settled by the sociological studies of Robert E. Park and the influential work of his student, E. Franklin Frazier, on the Negro family and their churches. Today, however, an increasing number of white scholars are taking another look at the religion and culture of the slave community, its continuity with the African past, and the significant role of the African American churches in the long struggle for racial advancement.

E. Franklin Frazier, of course, was one of our most able and esteemed sociologists, and his work has been extremely helpful to all of us. But Frazier died at the height of what I have called "attitudinal-change integrationism" of the 1940s and 1950s (in contrast to the "direct-action integrationism" of a later period). What hampered the esteemed Howard University professor's scholarly interest in the recovery of an African inheritance was the fear of playing into the hands of white segregationists who were only too happy to say: "See, we told you their customs and values were different from ours. Nigras are unmeltable. They obviously don't belong in the American melting pot."

Frazier believed that a sociology which celebrated differences risked doing damage to the enactment of public policy for an integrated society and that the black church would be the last institution in the African American community to wither away after integration became a national goal. He was convinced that such a sociology stood obstinately in the way of progress toward the integration of the races.[9]

For the past forty years we have been living in a different climate of opinion. By the time Princeton Theological Seminary generously offered me an office in its library in which to spend a 1970 sabbatical year writing the first edition of *Black Religion and Black Radicalism,* the sheen had worn off the apple of one-way integration, and the black church, under Dr. Martin Luther King Jr., had shown surprising effectiveness in the struggle for civil rights, not to mention the involvement of the churches in the Black Power movement under the influence of the National Committee of Black Churchmen.

I think that Vincent Harding and John Blassingame, more than any other black scholars, pointed the way to a reinterpretation of black religious history by suggesting three hypotheses on which I and others went to work during the succeeding decade: first, that blacks had a usable African past and that the slaves were not empty tablets on which white preachers of the eighteenth century wrote whatever they pleased; second, that black religion was a source of constant resistance and insurrectionary ferment in the slave community; and, third, that black power was not new but had religious and theological implications which had never been absent from the black folk community.[10] Other scholars, mainly African Americans, made significant contributions before this period, and most of them related in one way or another to these three affirmations, which provided a lively context for the task of historical reinterpretation.[11]

My work, *Black Religion and Black Radicalism,* raised both old and new questions and stimulated additional research that made a modest contribution to this reinterpretation.[12] Many others also helped in the reassessment which takes us beyond the Frazier-Herskovits debate about the quality and quantity of the African inheritance one can find in the history of the black church.[13] And there were still others who made signal contributions during the past decades.[14]

The picture of the development of the black church that emerges from this remarkable outpouring of literature by both secular and religious scholars during the last half of the twentieth century confirms many of Frazier's positions but also differs from his basic conclusions at several points. Instead of a tabula rasa, devoid of African retentions, we see the slaves holding on to certain patterns of motor behavior, musical and linguistic conventions, ways of viewing reality and the supernatural, religious customs and concepts, and synthesizing these with compatible elements of the "partly taught, partly caught" religion of Christianity. Instead of a faith centered on the biblical injunction that slaves ought to be obedient to their masters, that "you can take all the world, but give *me* Jesus," that there will be "pie in the sky when you die," in other words, a religion of fear and obsequious submission to white preachers, we see a religion that was, more often than not, a compassionate but hard-nosed, appreciative but selective, appropriation of white Christianity by shrewd black exhorters. These unlicensed exhorters and jackleg preachers successfully disguised the real meaning of their messages but occasionally permitted them to suggest varied forms of covert resistance and sometimes open rebellion.

Instead of a church that retreated into passivity following the Civil War, we see a church building on the wily self-help philosophy of Booker T. Washington, but meanwhile absorbing nonetheless the angry protest philosophy of Du Bois. The result was the development in both the North and the South of a pragmatic and sometimes militant program of community service, social and educational reform, and political action for racial justice by what Carter G. Woodson called the "institutional churches" of the black urban community after the First World War.[15]

This revised picture is not scientifically categorical, nor does it intend to present the black church in America as the nearest thing to the Kingdom of God on earth, but it does help to correct the older stereotype of a dysfunctional black folk church that was ridiculed by the cultured despisers of organized religion, of which more than a few were artists and members of the Negro intelligentsia. The mass black church was erected on the remarkable religious sensibilities of the slave and, in spite of the outrages of corrupt leadership and other kinds of betrayals, it has been a bastion of black liberation during most of the 138 years of its turbulent existence since the Civil War. Black Christians knew that the conditions under which they lived and worshiped in slavery were wrong and that their churches were as much, if not more, true Christian churches as the white churches that tried to maintain a system of supervision and repression over them.

I take John W. Blassingame's astute appraisal to be implicit support for this point of view and close to being the last word on this second area of reinterpretation. The black church was a freedom church, if anything and throughout and beyond slavery it worked both overtly and covertly to subvert the slave owners' Christianity.

> The slave's religious principles were colored by his own longing for freedom and based on half-understood sermons in white churches or passages from the Old Testament describing the struggles of the Jews, beautiful pictures of a future life, enchantment and fear, and condemnation of sin. The heaviest emphasis in the slaves' religion was on change in their earthly situation and divine retribution for the cruelty of their masters.[16]

The third area of reinterpretation in black church history challenges the assumption that the religious experience of African Americans is only a little eddy gurgling in the marshlands alongside the great rushing stream of American Christianity. It is really nothing to get exercised about this late in the game. If the phenomenon of the black church has any meaning, or so the argument goes, such meaning is located, found, and studied mainly among a decreasing segment of 40 million African Americans who are increasingly attracted to Islam, comprise only a small minority of Euro-American Christians, and may have taken themselves a mite too seriously.

One could go back many years to build up a case to challenge this assumption, but the truth becomes clearest when the so-called invisible institution began to become visible in the nineteenth century. Some of the most impressive data to be considered lie closer to our own time. I refer to the behavior of the black church during the civil rights period of the 1960s and how not only the white churches of the North but even national social, political, and economic structures were disrupted and turned around by black religious institutions. Moreover, no social reform movement in American history has been more interracial and ecumenical than the movement led by the African American churches in the 1960s.

Even before the Civil War black Christians played a dominant role in countering, and finally bringing to a halt, the American Colonization Society, which included some of the most prestigious and powerful white churchmen in America. No sooner was the Society organized in 1817 than African American leaders gathered at Mother Bethel African Methodist Episcopal Church in Philadelphia to denounce it. Thereafter black churches and denominations of the North applied steady pressure against colonization and helped to prevent it from gaining more ground in civil society and in the Congress. White friends and supporters like William Lloyd Garrison, who were at first persuaded by the idea of repatriating free blacks in West Africa or the Caribbean, were dissuaded and turned around by their association with black abolitionist preachers. Indeed, the movement for the abolition of slavery had been the foremost issue for black church people from the last quarter of the eighteenth century. It is impossible to appraise the rising tide of the conflict between the North and the South without calculating the influence of the black denominations. The black churches of the mid-nineteenth century was no little gurgling eddy to the mainstream. Comparing their activity to the wavering commitment of the white denominations, the distinguished historian Benjamin Quarles writes:

> The Negro church had no such squeamishness about bearing witness against slavery. . . . Negro churches generally conveyed a sense of sincerity, a quality which led such abolitionists as William Goodell and Joshua Leavit to attend them frequently. But from the viewpoint of social reform, the distinguishing mark of the Negro church was its independence from white control. Its money came from Negroes. Hence it could speak out on such an issue as slavery without fear of losing members or offending someone in the South.[17]

Part of the new understanding of black church history, in particular, and American church history, in general, has to do with correcting the impression that the black church was so busy with ecclesiastical housekeeping, prayer meetings, revivals, and temperance meetings that it had no time for abolitionism, which therefore had to be left to Mr. Garrison, a few John Brown types, and the Quakers. That the churches of free blacks were always busy trying to survive is certainly true, but they were also on the firing line. It is seldom mentioned that of the eight blacks who helped to found the American and Foreign Anti-Slavery Society, which helped to propel the whole movement against slavery toward radicalism after 1840, all were preachers and among the most powerful African Americans in the nation.

With respect to the postwar period I have seen two research papers, as yet unpublished, that throw new light on the role of black churches in Reconstruction politics, particularly the way Northern black Methodists changed the religious face of the South by challenging both the Northern and Southern Methodist churches for the loyalty of the recently freed people. In my own writings I have endeavored to show how "missionary emigrationism" and the concern for the political and spiritual liberation of Africa led black churches in the late nineteenth and early twentieth centuries to sow seeds of discontent and black nationalism in colonial Africa.[18] An important reason for revisiting this period is to document this involvement with Third-World liberation, for example, the influence of black Christian leaders like Bishop James Theodore Holly, Marcus Garvey (whose work as a religious leader has been helpfully demonstrated by Professor Randall Burkett), and Bishop Alexander Walters on the movement of Pan-Africanism, not to mention the wave of admiration and encouragement that swept over colonized peoples everywhere in response to the activities of black Christians in Montgomery, Alabama, in 1955.

In the history of African American sects and cults there is an intriguing connection between doctrinal heterodoxy and social revolution, between religious alienation and political alienation. Two black Pentecostal historians, James S. Tinney and Leonard Lovett, have documented the priority of black Pentecostalism among the several factors that triggered what is now the fastest growing evangelical movement in the world. Both scholars show the hitherto ignored relevance of black Pentecostalism for social transformation among the wretched of the earth.[19] No serious history of Christianity in America can be written in the future without a full appreciation of the influence of William J. Seymour's Pentecostalism on white churches and how, after 1906, concentric waves spread out from his Azusa Street Revival to carry Martin Luther King Jr. to the Mason Temple Church of God in Christ in 1968 and to the garbage workers strike in Memphis, where most of the strikers were members of that Pentecostal denomination.

African American church history since the Supreme Court decision of 1954 will also have to include in the future more accurate reporting of what the great black Baptist and Methodist denominations were doing during that period. It is correct to extol the work of the NAACP, the National Urban League, and other civil rights and labor organizations. It is right to credit the personal courage and charisma of Dr. King for much of what was achieved in terms of racial desegregation. But neither the civil rights organizations nor Dr. King could have been successful without the massive support of the black churches, expressed primarily by the thousands of unheralded, and not very well educated, laymen and laywomen in their respective congregations across the nation. They listened to their ministers and bishops and went out to carry the movement on their shoulders. They struck, boycotted, and raised money for bail bonds and other costs of the war against segregation. They sang and prayed, marched, prepared meals, distributed flyers, worked for white folks all day long, and rallied in their churches half the night to win the fundamental changes we enjoy today. That dramatic story remains to be told.

The standard line has been that the black denominations were barely involved in the movement. That allegation is the consequence of measuring the quality of Christian social action by the yardstick of the mainline white denominations that frequently received a disproportionate amount of attention, thanks to their well-financed public relations offices. The huge National Baptist Convention, Inc., had serious differences with Dr. King, as we all know, but it is incorrect to claim that it was uninvolved in social and political action for the same ultimate goals as the Southern Christian Leadership Conference. The Urge Congress movement of NBC, Inc. produced an intensive lobbying effort in Washington, D.C., that had much to do with the enactment in 1957 of the first civil right legislation since 1875. Later, when the existence of the National Association for the Advancement of Colored People (NAACP) was threatened by the Mississippi litigation in 1976, the Convention earmarked $500,000 in cash and loans as an emergency backup and set up another source of $500,000 should the NAACP require it.[20]

For its part black Methodism was in the forefront of the movement led by King. Already in 1948 the AMEs had risen to support one of their beleaguered pastors, the Reverend J. A. DeLaine of Clarendon County, South Carolina, who initiated one of the four school cases involved in the U.S. Supreme Court decision of May 17, 1954, that struck down school segregation. His church and home were burned down by irate whites, and DeLaine had to shoot his way out of South Carolina with the help of Bishop D. Ward Nichols, who organized a modern version of the Underground Railroad to bring the pastor safely to Trenton, New Jersey. Rosa Parks, the intrepid seamstress who lit the fire in Montgomery, was a member of St. Marks AME Church of that city—a church that was one of the sponsors of the boycott. Daisy Gaston Bates of Little Rock, Arkansas, who withstood the machinations of Governor Orval Faubus in the school desegregation crisis at Little Rock's Central High School in 1957–58, was an AME laywoman, and six of the nine courageous children who faced the mob at the school were members of AME congregations in Little

Rock.[21] In Charlotte, North Carolina, a black Presbyterian minister, Darius L. Swann, and his daughter were at the vortex of the struggle with Mecklenburg County, North Carolina, over school desegregation and brought about a landmark federal suit, with the backing of black Presbyterian congregations throughout the state, that became one of the successful cases in the long campaign to desegregate the public schools of North Carolina. All across the nation black churches were the seedbed of the movement to bring an end to legal segregation.

Not all black Christians agreed with King's strategies. That was evident in the rise of black power and the crisis over the Black Manifesto. But recent research has put to rest the assumption too many of us shared at the time that the mainline African American denominations were not doing their part. It was, of course, independent black church organizations and clergy groups like the Southern Christian Leadership Conference, the National Conference of Black Churchmen, the Baptist Ministers' Conferences, and the interdenominational urban caucuses, like the Philadelphia and Boston Councils of Black Clergy, that provided the primary organizational base. But those radical independent and interdenominational groups could not have done so without the kind of black denominational support represented, for example, by the vote on August 1, 1969, of the AME Zion Connectional Council, a body at the highest level of that church's Discipline, to affirm the Black Manifesto and the concept of reparations.[22]

The events of African American church history from 1954 to the mid-1970s are inseparable from what was happening in the African American community across the nation. The old adage "As goes the black community goes the black church" was never more true than after the Supreme Court decision of 1954 that abolished legal segregation. Developments within both the denominations and the secular community powerfully impacted the white church both for good and for ill—depending on how one regards what transpired in the predominantly white denominations and their local congregations. In any case, no accurate record of American religion in the twentieth century can be written without taking into full account the social witness of black churches against "America's original sin" and how that witness resonated throughout America's religious establishment and the nation as a whole.

During those memorable years I deemed it my sacred responsibility and privilege to be engaged in trying to reinterpret the history and experience of African American Christians as an indispensable part of the struggle. The racist assumptions of previous generations that the only real church history is the history of the mainline white denominations; that all black religion and church history worthy of the name began in a white incubator; and that the African American church story, such as it is, has significant lessons exclusively for African American Christians—being challenged by today's younger scholars who will explore and uncover data that some of us were too busy in the streets and courts of law to ferret out of the libraries and archives. This information will show that African American Christians have made an inestimable contribution to interracial and ecumenical developments in the United States.

American church history as a discipline has not always been an exciting enterprise, and certain large portions of it have been predictable, given that, from the beginning, the telling of the story in English devolved on armchair white historians who were elite beneficiaries of the slave-owning British colonies of North America. But God, once again, has moved in surprising ways among those at the bottom of the bucket. What God made of that ragtag, illiterate band of black believers, who dared to call themselves a proper church when most of them were still in chains, is one of the most inspiring stories of our era.

For those who are concerned about setting the record straight, whether black, white, red, or yellow, reinterpreting the standard version of Christianity in the Western hemisphere is a heavy and sometimes thankless responsibility. Nevertheless, we have the God-given task of revealing the truth and positive significance of America's ethnic and religious pluralism and, in the particular case of African Americans, of helping all Americans of whatever color, within and outside the churches, to lay claim to this great black Christian heritage that indeed belongs to us all.

3

Black Religion

Strategies of Survival, Elevation, and Liberation

In a classic essay on black religion W. E. B. Du Bois wrote: "Three things characterize this religion of the slave—the Preacher, the Music, and the Frenzy."[1] Although this classic description captures the dynamic of the Africans' earliest appropriation of evangelical Protestantism on both sides of the Atlantic, contemporary historical studies reveal a more complex and comprehensive pattern of religious development. From a perspective that includes not only what Du Bois called "an adaptation and mingling of heathen rites . . . roughly designated as Voodooism,"[2] but also the institutionalization of incipient slave worship in African American churches of the nineteenth and twentieth centuries, three dominant themes or motifs stand out as foundational from the Jamestown Landing to the present. They may be designated as survival, elevation, and liberation.

In teaching black church history I have been tempted to encompass the entire history of black religion in America by arranging these motifs in chronological order. In that case, paradigms of survival (the sheer effort to use religion to stay alive, to keep body and soul together) would characterize the earliest period of clandestine slave worship in the seventeenth and eighteenth centuries. A second period, from the ascendancy of the black middle-class churches during the 1850s and the "civilizing" efforts of white missionaries during Reconstruction through the first quarter of the twentieth century, would emphasize efforts of African American Christians to make religion a ladder for educational, moral, and cultural elevation. Finally, a third and partly overlapping period, ranging from the decade preceding the Civil War to the end of the twentieth century, would contain the paradigms of liberation—direct action on the part of churches and religious groups to free the slaves to combat racial segregation and discrimination after emancipation, and to make unprecedented efforts in our time to garner black political, economic, and social power.

On careful scrutiny, however, this neat chronological order, so useful in the classroom, breaks down. One sees these themes entwining and intermingling in various configurations at several points. Nevertheless, as this chapter will show, the chronological sequence, if not pressed too strongly, is useful. Yet, in the final analysis, it is more accurate to understand the strategies of survival, elevation, and liberation as major emphases that emerged simultaneously, depending on conditions in any given context, throughout the entire course of African American religious history.[3]

The African Heritage

It seems incontrovertible that the religious traditions brought from West Africa gave early comfort and consolation to the slaves as they were slowly acculturated to the new religion of Christianity in North America. The first Africans who were transported in the seventeenth and eighteenth centuries brought religious beliefs and modes of worship that prevented them from being totally dehumanized by chattel slavery. In their homeland they had shared, within many tribal groups, certain ancient ways of life—rituals, wise sayings, and ethical teachings—that had been handed down through the generations. Ancient beliefs, folklore, attitudes, and religious customs provided a holistic view of reality that made no radical separation between religion and daily life. There was no consciousness in the everyday affairs that one was being "religious" at one moment and "nonreligious" or secular at another. There was no difference between the life of the mind and the life of the spirit.

This is not to claim, however, and this is important, that the slaves and those they left behind in Africa did not perceive the difference between sacrificing a chicken to a familial god and hoeing a garden. Nor are we saying that Africans did not esteem some men and women more than others because of the special training and knowledge they possessed that could make the secrets of nature and God accessible. Precisely so. But there was no absolute disjunction between the sacred and the secular. What we must understand is that the African perspective looked upon the work of the intellect and that of the human spirit as a harmonious whole, as ultimately being about the same thing. Presuppositions and experiences of the unity of body and spirit, of what today we might call the profane and the holy, was the common privilege and obligation of everyone—not the guarded sinecure of intellectuals called philosophers and religionists called priests or preachers.

Modern people may find it almost impossible to appreciate fully the way of life out of which the slaves came. We have to change our habitual thinking entirely about the qualitative difference between reflection and action, between the commonplace or ordinary affairs of daily existence and what we vaguely put into a separate box and call the "spiritual life." Only thus can we begin to conceptualize the comprehensive, unitary character of the African consciousness. To be sure, some scholars contend that the past was almost completely obliterated in the slave brought to North America. But let us argue, for the moment that, for those who did remember anything about their former life (and it is unreasonable to suppose that everything was immediately forgotten as soon as they disembarked on the quays of Jamestown or Charleston), there was indeed no separation between religion and life, between the sacred and the profane. Experience was truth, and truth experience. The single entity—what we might call the "life-truth"—embraced the totality of existence. Reality was, at one and the same time, immanent and transcendent, material and spiritual, mundane and numinous.

One should not assume here that we are dealing with some simplistic and naive stage of becoming human. The folklore of Africa, comprising thousands of myths, folktales, and proverbs—and still being transmitted from one generation to another—is as subtle and complex in its probity as the choicest dialectical ruminations one can find in Plato's *Republic* or Machiavelli's *Prince*. As one scholar writes concerning the excellence of the proverbs of the Yoruba people of Nigeria:

> Surely these proverbs are indications of no ordinary perception of moral truths, and are sufficient to warrant the inference that in closeness of observation, in depth of thought, and shrewd intelligence, the Yoruba is not an ordinary man.[4]

Nor were Africans so unsophisticated in their ideas about God that the religions some slaves preserved in secret can be dismissed as grossly inadequate compared to the rarified theological cogitations of the missionaries. Not only had some slaves been introduced to Islam and probably to the Nile Valley religions and shards of Nubian Christianity in West Africa before the coming of the white man, but their traditional religions were not inferior in insight and coherence to those great systems of faith that came out of Europe and Asia. The Nigerian novelist Chinua Achebe catches the keen wit and pragmatism of the traditional religionist, Akunna, in a confrontation with Mr. Brown, an English missionary who came to Akunna's village.

> "You say that there is one supreme God who made heaven and earth," said Akunna on one of Mr. Brown's visits. "We also believe in Him and call Him Chukwu. He made all the world and the other gods." "There are no other gods," said Mr. Brown. "Chukwu is the only God and all others are false. You carve a piece of wood—like that one" (he pointed at the rafters from which Akunna's carved Ikenga hung), and you call it a god. But it is still a piece of wood."
>
> "Yes," said Akunna. "It is indeed a piece of wood. The tree from which it came was made by Chukwu, as indeed all minor gods were. But He made them for His messengers so that we could approach Him through them.
>
> "It is like yourself. You are the head of your church."
>
> "No," protested Mr. Brown. "The head of my church is God Himself." "I know," said Akunna, "but there must be a head in this world among men. Somebody like yourself must be the head here."[5]

Achebe's deftly drawn picture of Ibo life shows the inseparable connection between the soil in which the ancestors are buried, the community, and God. He calls into question all the facile assumptions of the West about the childishness of African religion and philosophy. Without it our ancestors, the African arrivals to the New World, would have been hollow men and women. With it they were able to survive with their bodies and souls intact for the long and rugged ascent into a perilous and uncertain future.

The Christianization of the Slaves

Any analysis of black religion in America must begin with two critical issues: the attitude of white Christians toward the conversion and emancipation of the slaves, and the nature of the earliest and largely unobserved slave religion. The first recorded baptism of an African in the American colonies occurred in Virginia in 1624, but there was no systematic evangelization until the eighteenth century. Even then, the colonists were in no hurry to introduce their slaves to the religion they themselves professed. The rationalization the English gave for the enslavement of both Africans and Indians was that the two groups were both different in appearance to themselves and that they were heathens. When it became evident that blacks were becoming believers despite widespread neglect by the official church bodies, Virginia was the first of the colonies to make short shrift of any attempt to make conversion an excuse for emancipation by declaring, in 1667, that "the conferring of baptisme doth not alter the condition of the person as to his bondage or freedom."

It was difficult enough to induce a healthy state of religion among the white population. Attempts by the Society for the Propagation of the Gospel in Foreign Parts, an outpost of the bishops of London, to encourage planters to provide religious instruction for their slaves, were largely unsuccessful, but almost from the beginning some blacks attended public worship with their masters and requested baptism. By the time of the American Revolution a few had become Roman Catholics, Anglicans, Presbyterians, Baptists, and Methodists. In South Carolina one missionary, Reverend Samuel Thomas of Goose Creek, reported, as early as 1705, that he had given religious instruction to as many as one thousand slaves, many of whom he claimed could read the Bible and had memorized the Creed.

Taking the gospel to blacks helped to ease the conscience of both the colonial Puritan and the Anglican establishments about slavery, but it did not solve the problem completely. All the American churches wrestled with the issue and, with the possible exception of the Quakers, finally compromised their ethical standards. Bitter contention raged between Northern and Southern churchmen, and, as early as 1837, there were splits among the Lutherans and Presbyterians. In 1844 the Methodist Church divided, North and South, over slavery, followed by the Baptists in 1845. The antislavery American Missionary Association virtually split the Congregational Church in 1846. The Presbyterians finally set up northern and southern branches in 1861, and a fissure that would have split the Episcopal Church was adroitly aborted in 1862 when the northern Episcopalians, desiring not to be separated from their southern brethren, refused to recognize that any controversy even existed. Both the Episcopal and Roman Catholic churches, with some difficulty, managed to hold on to a semblance of structural unity throughout the Civil War.

The Evolution of Black Christianity

During the anguish in the white churches over slavery, the special nature of the new African American Christianity asserted itself. We do not know when the first slaves stole away from the surveillance of the masters to worship in their own way. Two conjectures seem reasonable: First, it had to have occurred early in the seventeenth century, for Africans would not have neglected practicing their ancestral religions as best as they could; further, the whites cared little about what the slaves did, as long as they were peaceful, and so did little to induce them to adopt their masters' faith. Second, it is likely that the worship the first slaves to the colonies engaged in was replete with transplanted survivals or elements carried over from Africa.

Today most scholars accept the position of W. E. B. Du Bois and Melville Herskovits that fragments of African religions survived the Middle Passage and the "breaking in" process in North America to reappear under disguise in the early religious meetings of the so-called Invisible Institution—the proto-church of the slaves. One contemporary secular scholar writes:

> In the United States, many African religious rites were fused into one—voodoo. From the whole panoply of African deities, the slaves chose the snake god of the Whydah, Fon, and Ewe. Symbolic of the umbilical cord and the rainbow, the snake embodies the dynamic, changing quality of life. In Africa it was sometimes the god of fertility and the determiner of good and ill fortune. Only by worshiping god could one invoke his protective spirit.[6]

There is scant evidence that voodoo or some discrete form of reinterpreted African religion synthesized as effectively with Protestantism in the English colonies as it did with Roman Catholicism in the Caribbean and in Latin America. Nevertheless, reports of missionaries and the slave narratives show that the African conjurer and medicine man, the manipulation of charms and talismans, and the use of drums and dancing were present in the slave quarters as survival strategies, even after conversion to

Christianity. Selective elements of African religions were not easily exterminated. A Presbyterian missionary, the Reverend Charles C. Jones, described what he encountered among the slaves in Georgia as late as 1842:

> True religion they are inclined to place in profession, in forms and ordinances, and in excited states of feeling. And true conversion in dreams, visions, trances, voices—all bearing a perfect or striking resemblance to some form or type which has been handed down for generations, or which has been originated in the wild fancy of some religious teacher among them.[7]

Mr. Jones warned his fellow missionaries that the blacks displayed sophisticated perversions of the gospel accountable only to the influence of African survivals. So impressed was he with their covert resistance to white Christianity that he compared their objections to "the ripe scholarship and profound intelligence of critics and philosophers." Jones would have objected to the allegation of some fellow missionaries that African religions were "childlike."

The First Black Church

Although there was a black congregation on the plantation of William Byrd III, near Mecklenburg, Virginia, as early as 1758,[8] the first black-led churches were formed along the Savannah River in Georgia and South Carolina in the 1770s, and in Tidewater, Virginia, at about the same time. Immediately following the Revolutionary War black imitations of white Baptist and Methodist churches appeared in Philadelphia, Baltimore, and New York City. But in the Sea Islands off the coast of South Carolina and Georgia, in Louisiana, and on scattered plantations across the Upper South, a distinctive brand of black folk religion flourished and infused with the adopted white evangelicalism of the Baptists and Methodists along with selective retentions of African spirituality. A new and implacable African American Christianity was being created, much less puritanical and supramundane than its white counterpart.

The three best-known slave revolts were led by fervently religious men—Gabriel Prosser in 1800, Denmark Vesey in 1822, and Nat Turner in 1831. Studies of the music of the early black church show that hidden rebelliousness and a desire for emancipation were often expressed in song. The independent black churches—particularly the African Methodist Episcopal (AME) Church and the African Methodist Episcopal Zion (AMEZ) Church—were known to be "freedom churches" because their latent, if not manifest, reason for existing conspired with their determination to promote liberation from slavery and the elevation of their people to a higher plane of life through education and self-help.

David George, who served as the de facto pastor of an independent black congregation at Silver Bluff, South Carolina, before 1775; George Liele and Andrew Bryan of the First Colored Baptist Church in Savannah; Josiah Bishop of Portsmouth, Virginia: and other preachers—between 1760 and 1795—were all former slaves who ministered in territories hostile to black religion under the sponsorship and with the encouragement of a few radical white Baptist preachers. Some slave preachers, like the full-blooded African called "Uncle Jack"; "Black Harry" Hosier, who served the Methodist bishop Francis Asbury; and the many illiterate exhorters who are mentioned but unnamed in missionary reports and other sources—these preachers are legendary. Many of their sermons dealt with the deliverance of Israel from Egyptian captivity, the stories of heroism and faithfulness in the Old Testament, and the identification of Jesus of Nazareth with the poor and the downtrodden. Mainly untutored, but rarely ignorant, they told "many-a-truth in a joke," as the saying goes, slyly philosophizing about how "God don't like ugly" and "everybody talking 'bout heaven ain't goin' there." They obliquely reassured their congregations of the ultimate vindication of their suffering. Moreover, many animal tales, adages, and proverbs that make up the corpus of African American folklore were repeated from the pulpit as homemade homiletical devices, as one preacher said, to "explain the unexplainable, define the indefinable, and unscrew the inscrutable."

The theological motif of these early preachers was survival, by virtue of their belief in the supernatural power available to believers to keep them alive under a brutal system of enslavement. They were preoccupied with maintaining their people's sanity, keeping them on their feet, assisting them to retain some semblance of humanity and self-esteem in the face of massive dehumanization. Blassingame writes:

> One of the primary reasons the slaves were able to survive the cruelty they faced was that their behavior was not totally dependent on their masters. . . . In religion, a slave exercised his own independence of conscience. Convinced that God watched over him, the slave bore his

earthly afflictions in order to earn a heavenly reward. Often he disobeyed his earthly master's rules to keep his Heavenly Master's commandments. . . . Religious faith gave an ultimate purpose to his life; a sense of communal fellowship and personal worth, and reduced suffering from fear and anxiety.[9]

Development of the Northern Churches

A somewhat different tradition developed among black churches in the North. Many of their pastors also emerged from slavery and humble rural backgrounds, but in the freer atmosphere of the North and West the theological content of their religion took a different turn. It tended toward the ethical revivalism that inundated white Protestant denominations following the Second Great Awakening (1790–1815). Northern black Christianity was more urbane, more freely spoken, and more appealing to those blacks who were beginning to enjoy a relative measure of prosperity and greater educational and cultural opportunities.

The former slaves, Richard Allen and Absalom Jones, protested racial segregation by walking out of St. George's Methodist Church in Philadelphia. As early as 1787, they founded a quasi-religious community organization called the Free African Society that was replicated in several other places during the same period. In Baltimore, New York, Providence, and Boston, these associations—dedicated to the moral, educational, and religious uplift of Africans—became the scaffolding of the black churches of the North. Immediately following voluntary or forced separation from white churches, African Americans demonstrated an overwhelming zeal for social, economic, and political advancement by making their new churches the center of such activities. They were aided by white friends like the Quaker Anthony Benezet and Benjamin Rush of Philadelphia in organizing and funding their benevolent societies, but their local congregations were the main engines driving all "secular" enterprises concerned with improving their worldly situation. The primary impulse behind these Northern developments was a desire not so much for survival—that had already been secured to a large degree for those no longer in bondage—but for autonomy, racial solidarity, self-help, and individual and group elevation. Thus Peter Spencer formed a new denomination, the Union Church of African Members, in Wilmington, Delaware, in 1813;[10] Richard Allen became the first bishop of the African

Methodist Episcopal Church, founded in Philadelphia in 1816; and James Varick became the first bishop of the African Methodist Episcopal Zion Church, founded in New York in 1821. These men, together with Absalom Jones, rector of St. Thomas Episcopal Church of Africans in Philadelphia; John Gloucester, pastor of the First African Presbyterian Church of the same city; Peter Williams Jr., the first ordained black priest of the Episcopal Church in New York; and Thomas Paul, the founder of the first black Baptist Church, also in New York City, were all strong, progressive leaders who, in the first two decades of the nineteenth century, promoted education and social betterment as a religious obligation. They encouraged northern lay people to undertake racial-advancement programs and activities at a time when public meetings of blacks were forbidden in the South and even preaching was prohibited except under white supervision.

We can speak of these northern church leaders, therefore, as elevationists in the sense that their concerns went beyond mere survival. Although a physician and journalist, Martin R. Delany, of Pittsburgh, is a good example of the elevationist orientation before the Civil War. For Delany, education, self-reliance, a desire for equality, and racial progress were steps on the ladder of black elevation from degradation and "the means by which God intended man to succeed."

> If, as before stated, a knowledge of all the various business enterprises, trades, professions, and sciences, is necessary for the elevation of the white, a knowledge of them also is necessary for the elevation of the colored man. . . . What we desire to learn now is, how to effect a remedy; this we have endeavored to point out. Our elevation must be the result of self-efforts, and work of our own hands. No other human power can accomplish it.[11]

The concept of "elevation" appears, by the wide use of that very word, to be well established in African American literature throughout the nineteenth century. Black men and women, clergy and lay, envisioned a broad horizon of racial uplift and advancement through religion.[12] They were the people who dominated the free black communities of the North and the major cities of the South, when they could get away with it, to lead such causes as seeking opportunities for higher education for their children, the boycotting of goods produced by slave labor, resistance to efforts of the American Colonization Society to return them to Africa, and the promotion of moral reform, lyceums, and benevolent societies. As the clergy became more involved in and distracted by ecclesiastical responsibilities, the secular organizations that they had helped to spawn gradually became separated from the churches, although still under the parental influence of the larger congregations.

Such was the case with the American Moral Reform Society and the National Negro Convention Movement. The latter first met in a church in 1839 and held seven consecutive annual convocations on elevationist issues. Liberal whites attended many of these meetings, as they provided a rare opportunity to prevent the withering away of their fellowship with blacks as the latter became more independent (and also the chance to exercise subtle control when possible). That interracial connection and sometimes subordinate relationship between whites and African American Christians was made more difficult by the rapid development of separate black churches.

The regional and national conventions devoted to abolition and moral reform also represented what I call the "liberation tradition." It was the more pointed and aggressive emphasis of members of the black middle class, who considered legal or political equality with whites by means of the vote equally as necessary for upward mobility as elevation in manners and morals. The concern for complete liberation from white supervision, influence, and indirect management was soon extricated from the ecclesiastical control of black preachers and their congregations. Its real impulse was to come from church-related but intellectually independent laymen and women—like Paul Cuffee (the Massachusetts sea captain), Maria Stewart, Booker T. Washington, W. E. B. Du Bois, Ida Wells-Barnett, and Mary McCloud Bethune. In the antebellum period the themes of liberation and racial uplift were joined under the sponsorship of relatively wealthy laymen like James Forten, Robert Purvis, William Whipper, and William C. Nell. One of the most influential among them was the journalist David Walker, whose incendiary *Appeal to the Colored Citizens of the World,* in 1829,[13] inspired former slaves Frederick Douglass and William Wells Brown, and "free-born" propagandists Martin R. Delany, William H. Day, and H. Ford Douglass. But it was the women of individual black congregations, in both the North and the South, who broke away from the preachers and patriarchal church controls by the beginning of the twentieth century to become the fierce liberationists to whom the present-day black womanist movement turns for inspiration.

A Comparative Assessment of Motifs

There is an intricate and dialectical relationship between the survival, elevation, and liberation traditions in the African American church and community. All three were seminal in the churches of the nineteenth century and continued into the next century in various configurations and degrees of tension, depending on the situation that existed in different parts of the country. In the ghetto of central Los Angeles, between 1906 and the First World War, the survival-oriented followers of William J. Seymour and other charismatic evangelists produced an unprecedented display of African religious retentions that had lain dormant for a hundred years in the interstices of African American rural society. Thus black Pentecostalism was born in a city in the far West that had already been nurtured in the "invisible institution" of the South but had almost been extinguished by the elite Negro churches and white missionaries who came to the South with the Union Army. Holiness and Pentecostalism together claimed 34 percent of the black churches in New York City in the mid-1920s. In twelve other northern cities in 1930, 37 percent of the churches were neighborhood storefront missions that fostered a volatile combination of survival and liberationist hermeneutics. During and after the First World War this distinctive strain of lower-class religion, scorned and repudiated by the elevation-oriented churches of the growing middle classes, was radicalized. In the white-hot, purifying fires of its Africentric forge this originally survivalist stream of African American religion metamorphosed into various religio-political sects and cults, including black versions of Judaism and Islam.

Between the First and Second World Wars it was necessary to realign the survival, elevation, and liberation themes so as to create the kind of balance and harmony between them that would be conducive to racial advancement. It was the experience of African American leadership during the era of abolitionism and missionary emigrationism that when one of these themes or tendencies is either neglected or exaggerated above the other two, the result is that commitment to the biblical God and to a militant church, on the one hand, and to African American political, economic, and cultural life, on the other, fall apart. The center collapses, and chaos reigns. That happened during the Radical Reconstruction and again during the Great Depression of the 1930s. On both occasions the consequence was a kind of racial schizophrenia that left the masses in moral confusion and the middle classes in a spiritual malaise that rendered them powerless to give the kind of leadership necessary for realignment and a new beginning as soon as relative calm and prosperity returned.

Beginning in 1955 the genius of Martin Luther King Jr. brought the three motifs or traditions together again in a prophetic combination that wedded the deep spirituality and will to survive of the alienated and impoverished masses with the sophisticated pragmatism and determination to achieve equality and complete liberation that characterized the parvenu urbanites and the "New Negro" intelligentsia of the Harlem Renaissance. King embraced all three of these tendencies and created a multidimensional movement, inseparable from the African American church but not subservient to it. As a young Baptist preacher he set in motion social, political, economic, religious, and cultural forces that have not yet run their full course. Martin Luther King Jr. stands, therefore, at the pinnacle of African American religious and political developments in the twentieth century.

King, however, was not alone in pointing the way to a new future, for the Black Muslim minister Malcolm X forced a decisive break between a moderate reformism that to him seemed to compromise the liberation ideal and a form of protest that was truly revolutionary, one that ultimately radicalized King. But in King was the confluence of all the complex and variegated trends, traditions, and orientations that are summed up in our three motifs of survival, elevation, and liberation. Other leaders were to emerge out of the sacred ground on which he stood, yet beyond him lay unexplored heights that could not have been seen without standing on his shoulders.

The publication in 1969 of James H. Cone's thunderous challenge to Euro-American theological scholarship, *Black Theology and Black Power,*[14] made room for a bold alternative strategy for African American churches and introduced an intrusive new tenant in the halls of academe. This method of theologizing had not been altogether absent during the years before King but had sulked in the shadows outside the mainstream black churches and the ivy-covered walls of the Historic Black Colleges and Universities. Cone's first book gave a name to this neglected and ignored stream of African American religious thought that probably came into existence when the first slave tossed and turned all night on his straw mat, wondering why he should be expected to believe in a God who ordained all black people to perpetual bondage. The name Cone gave to what he saw pulsating just beneath the surface of King's more conciliatory Negro Social Gospel was "black liberation theology," the theological first cousin to the black power ideology popularized by Stokely Carmichael and Charles V. Hamilton.[15]

Before the end of the 1960s the liberation theme had once again regained ascendancy in the black church community and had proliferated beyond it to other venues. Liberation theology took root among oppressed campesinos and barrio dwellers in Latin America, among black Christians in South Africa, white feminists and black womanists in the United States, and even among the dark-skinned peoples of Australia and the islands of the South Pacific. Black liberation theology rapidly became a major topic among theologians on both sides of the Atlantic and in the circles of the World Council of Churches and the American hierarchy of the Roman Catholic Church. But the discussion was not limited to theological seminaries and church councils. A small but belligerent movement for black religious power and social transformation broke out under the aegis of a new coalition of African American church executives, pastors, and academics that called itself the National Committee of Black Churchmen (NCBC)—a northern version of King's Southern Christian Leadership Conference (SCLC) but considerably more interested in theology and solidarity with other ethnic groups in this country and with oppressed people in Africa, Asia, South America, and the Caribbean.

The watchword in important segments of the African American religious community was *liberation*—which is to say freedom from racism, poverty, powerlessness, and every form of white Euro-American domination. *Liberation* became a theological code word for the indigenous religious genius of the oppressed masses who had been passed over by upwardly mobile elites. On their part, African American theologians and ethicists, freed from being intimidated by, and feeling they owe deference to, ecclesiastical authority within both the white and black churches, began to teach and write a revolutionary Christianity that began with the historical Jesus whom they called the Black Messiah. Jesus was revered as the Oppressed Man of God who challenged the hypocrisy of his own Jewish religion. Black liberation theologians saw that hypocrisy recapitulated in the white Christianity of the North Atlantic community and in the defects and corruptions of Negro religion. They also found the unjust political and cultural domination of the Roman Empire at its height recapitulated in the worldwide political, economic, and cultural hegemony of the American capitalist system at the end of the twentieth century.

Facing the Present Crisis

Throughout their history African American churches have struggled to maintain a precarious balance between racial advancement on the secular front and winning souls on the Christian evangelism front. This has enabled African American churches to achieve three goals: first, to help individuals survive by enabling them, by amazing grace, to subsist in the face of the atrocities of white racism; second, to help the race free itself from legal slavery, economic exploitation, and the curse of second-class citizenship; and, third, to elevate the masses, particularly young people, to a level of moral and spiritual integrity through the kind of education in church and school that ennobled the individual and collective life of black people.

Today both individual and collective life remains in a kind of perpetual crisis. The desire for material goods, for experiencing pleasure, and for making money seems to have overridden the values of the civil rights era, which had opened up new opportunities for the black middle class while, unfortunately, leaving behind large segments of the race that continue to live in urban ghettos and rural slums. Seduced by the new politics of "keeping quiet and looking the other way," a by-product of conservatism; by a mindless emotionalism as a form of religious entertainment to drown out anxiety; and an outworn ecclesiasticism that stultifies and divides, the African American churches have lost the balance between what have been the basic characteristics of black religion for more than three hundred years. The disequilibrium affecting the historic motifs examined in this chapter has meant the loss of the churches' external mission to fumigate a white racist society, and the loss of the necessary cultural authority to prevent the trivialization of its internal mission to itself. Consequently the holistic character of black religion was fractured after King and Malcolm, and both the church and the culture, previously inseparable, became bereft of that essential connection and vulnerable to the malaise that brings on indolence, on the one hand, and corruption, on the other. Thus, today, both the church and the culture are, in the first instance, in the throes of a crisis of faith, and, in the second instance, in the grip of a crisis of meaning.

These internal crises cannot be resolved, however, by the "classes and the masses" repudiating religion or by grown men pretending that a transient youth culture, which glorifies volatility, disregard for serious commitments, and referring to black women as whores and bitches, is authentic African American culture.[16] To undermine black religion by accusing it of being perennially caught up in irrelevant mystification and to trivialize our black culture by denying its historic linkage to the church is only to deepen the crisis, not to eliminate it. Authentic black faith has nothing to do with the theatrical posturing of preachers who ape televangelists, who are essentially entertainers in four-thousand-dollar business suits, any more than Hip Hop and New Jack City have most to do with the rich vein of folk wisdom, African retentions, and African American intellectual traditions—from David Walker to Toni Morrison. Perhaps the time has come to reassert the great triad of traditions we have been examining, namely, survival, elevation, and liberation; to insert values that are truly Africentric; to rescue the inheritance of Martin and Malcolm from moral and spiritual annihilation by children who never knew them, children who, shamefully, have never been taught the truth about their forebears or why they themselves have fallen into this sorry plight.

This, I believe, is one of the purposes of black liberation theology. If the church returns to basics and once again taps into that ennobling and enlightening religion that brought blacks through the civil rights period and helped us to amass a modicum of countervailing power in American society, perhaps the crisis that continues into the twenty-first century will be surmounted and black folks can enter the future with integrity and hope. Martin Luther King Jr. anticipated this possibility. Indeed, it was a part of his dream that he left out of the Lincoln Memorial speech, probably in the interest of multiculturalism. King consistently advocated an embracing of enduring values that emerge from our past, an intelligent and liberal lifestyle based on a profoundly spiritual reorientation of black life, and a rejuvenation of the Africentric spirit that saw us through slavery and Jim Crow. This is what he meant when, at the end of his last book, he wrote:

> This is our challenge. If we will dare to meet it honestly, historians in future years will have to say that there lived a great people—a Black people—who bore their burdens of oppression in the heat of many days and who, through tenacity and creative commitment, injected a new meaning into the veins of American life.[17]

4

Womanist Thought as a Recovery of Liberation Theology

Serious theological reflection on the part of African American women who were conscious of egregious gender discrimination in the black church and community arose at a critical point in the development of black liberation theology. The theology that had been produced primarily by African American men in the late 1960s had become stagnant by the end of the 1970s, and today there is, among male thinkers, no predictable rejuvenation in sight. Moreover, the patriarchal assumptions in the work of black male theologians, with few exceptions, made it necessary for African American women to form an alternative school of theological reflection.

By the end of the 1960s the two leading exponents of the mainstream of black theology, James H. Cone of the Union Theological Seminary in New York and James Deotis Roberts of the Divinity School of Howard University in Washington, D.C., had published their most definitive works;[1] the responses of their male colleagues in the churches and theological academy were, in my opinion, minimal and somewhat disappointing. The rejoinders of their male peers added little to the debate about whether black theology was to be grounded in the concept of *liberation* for the poor and oppressed (including especially black women) or, more broadly, in the *reconciliation* of all persons to God and one another through the saving/liberating work of Christ. What came to be known as womanist theology was a radical juxtaposition of the major building blocks of black liberation theology. The consequence has been a vigorous emphasis on the existential concerns of black women about patriarchy and sexism from a somewhat different angle of attack than that of white feminists,[2] together with an insistence that the black church and the academy adopt a new agenda for dealing with the separate issue of black women's liberation. The question of reconciliation was not ignored; indeed, it was considered as urgent as liberation from all forms of oppression. Womanist theology seemed to promise a refreshing intellectual challenge from a new, more holistic approach to liberation. But what would it be?

The publication of *Black Theology: A Documentary History, 1966–1979,* which I edited with James H. Cone, gave notice that a revolution of black women against male-dominated theology was in the making, for we included in that anthology several articles by African American women.[3] Most notable among them was Theressa Hoover's previously published but generally neglected essay, "Black Women and the Churches: Triple Jeopardy," and a new essay by Jacquelyn Grant, then a doctoral student at the Union Theological Seminary in New York, her now celebrated tour de force, "Black Theology and the Black Woman." In dividing up the editing on this collection, it fell to me to prepare Grant's essay for the publisher. I remember using a heavy hand with what I confess first impressed me as a graduate student's work in progress rather than the mature introduction of a rebellious new way of thinking about the Christian faith that would rattle the hatches of the male-centered, male-dominated field of black God-talk.

Cone was more sensitive to these new developments and to the approaching collision than I. His subsequent writings testify to his much keener awareness of what was going on among black women to which black men were obliged to attend. That may have been because I was teaching women at the Master of Divinity level while he was preparing the first crop of black women doctoral candidates in systematic theology. But that is no excuse for my myopia.

In any case, taken as a whole, the section given to black women's religious thought in the first *Documentary History* was more fiercely articulate and more noteworthy than either James Cone or I had anticipated. Only a short time later, when black women seminarians at Union and around the country began to react with suppressed anger to the patriarchal and sexist attitudes and practices of their male student colleagues and professors, did it become evident to us both that the *Documentary History* had opened a Pandora's box. From that point on, it would be intellectually dishonest for theological scholarship and American Christians generally, black or white, to ignore or take lightly the determined resistance of black women to second-class citizenship in the church and in the theological academy.

Now, almost a quarter of a century later, it should be no surprise to anyone who has kept up with the development of black and womanist theologies that the contributions of African American women have surpassed those of men in the dialogue about the roots, character, and urgency of justice orientations in African American Christian thought about God, salvation, ethnicity, church history, the Bible, pastoral care and counseling, liturgical practice, Christian education, and social action in the African diaspora and on the continent itself. Indeed, it is only a slight exaggeration to say that black womanist thinkers have taken over the whole gamut of themes that had energized liberation theology from the 1960s on.

Since 1985 the writings of black women Christian theologians and ethicists have not only equaled in number the publications of their male colleagues but may have exceeded the latter in quality. Among the men who have been writing black theology in recent years, there are few whose contributions, in terms of originality, prominence in contemporary discussions taking place in the academy, and courage in demanding change on the part of the black church, compare to those of Delores Williams, Jacquelyn Grant, Evelyn Brooks, Diana L. Hayes, Ella Mitchell, Toinette Eugene, Cheryl J. Sanders, A. Elaine Crawford, Katie Cannon, Cheryl Kirk-Duggan, Kelly Brown Douglas, Marcia Y. Riggs, Karen Baker-Fletcher, Renita J. Weems, Cheryl T. Gilkes, Melva Costen, Emilie M. Townes, Mozella G. Mitchell, Jualynne Dodson, Vashti McKenzie, Rosetta Ross, M. Shawn Copeland, Jamie Phelps, Clarice J. Martin, Iva Carruthers, and Yvonne Delk—to name only those who come immediately to mind.[4] Several other sisters who write from the perspective of black church women could be mentioned. Also noteworthy is that the women seem ahead of the men in terms of the number of non-Christian writers (or writers and scholars not professionally related to the church) whose work in disciplines outside the theological curriculum are utilizing and buttressing what those of us in the church are saying and doing today. I may be wrong, but it seems to me that black male theologians and ethicists do not have as many secular writers and scholars whose research and analytical skills are being put to use or cited on behalf of black theology as is presently the case with womanist history, theology, and ethics.[5]

These observations are not meant to draw invidious distinctions. Nor am I saying that all this womanist literature comes to us with an even quality or that these sisters generally agree among themselves about what ought to be the norms and major themes of their Christian theology. But my purpose in calling the long, though incomplete, roll above is simply to direct attention to the remarkable efflorescence of writings on theology, history, ethics, the Bible, and black women in church and society that have, in the last two decades of the twentieth century, introduced the names and published the reflections of women we never knew or adequately recognized in 1979, indeed to call attention to women whose works have now taken their place beside the older works of African American male scholars whose books and articles are rapidly going out of print, notwithstanding that they first blazed a path for the academic study of African American religion. Although we men introduced a distinctively African American understanding of the meaning, mandates, and goals of authentic Christianity for oppressed people, the womanists have caught up, and in some instances, have forged ahead. In 1990 the late C. Eric Lincoln and Lawrence H. Mamiya wrote in their authoritative overview of the black religious situation:

> Womanist theology is only one form of the theological debate addressed by African American feminist theologians and preaching women. However, it is an important intellectual trend that is likely to continue to grow along with the dramatic increase of black women students now entering seminaries and divinity schools. How these trends will affect the membership of black churches in the future is still unknown since the movement is still in its infancy. And whether and to what extent black women preachers and theologians will be able to find significant response among the black women laity must also await the evaluation that only time can provide.[6]

The queries implicit in Lincoln and Mamiya's prediction have not yet been answered in terms of how these trends will influence the black churches and particularly black lay women. But there are sufficient indications that a new leadership group is growing among some African and African American church women, as well as a new recognition of black women scholars, to suggest that something of note is happening that will shape the way Christian theology is conducted in the black world.

It should also not escape notice that there are more black Catholic women in the world than any other group of black Christian women and that a womanist theology is stirring among them in powerful ways. Black Catholic theologian, Diana L. Hayes believes that the reinterpretation by black Catholic women of the role and presence of Mary will become their most significant contribution to black liberation theology in general and to black Christian women in particular.

> They relate to her by sharing in her experiences as women who are also oppressed but who continue to bear the burden of faith and to pass on that faith to generations to come. At a time when women were supposed to be silent and invisible, when women were considered of little importance, Mary accepted a singular call from God to stand out as "blessed among all women" as a young, pregnant, unwed woman who would have many difficult questions to answer within her community, but who had the courage to say a "yes" to God that shattered all of time. She is a role model, not for passivity, but for strong, righteous, "womanish" women who spend their lives giving birth to the future.
>
> It is African American Catholic women who have been the bearers and the preservers of their culture, of their heritage, of their faith, both Black and Catholic, and who have passed these treasures on to the next generations.[7]

The question I address in this chapter is whether womanist biblical scholars, historians, theologians, and ethicists, who are making the case against black male patriarchy and the indifference to women's liberation in early black theology, will be able to maintain their present advantage and what will be required for their analyses and recommendations to achieve the ends they envision. What emphases in womanist thought point to a recovery of liberationist religious thought so that the black people of Africa and the entire diaspora will be spiritually and materially enriched, and thereby helped to create a movement for justice and liberation that will be inclusive of all people?

The objection may be raised that no less can be demanded of the more narrow black Christian theology with which some African and African American men have identified. Why should we press such an exacting responsibility on black women? My answer is that womanist theology has evinced such vitality and creativity over the past twenty or more years that some of us men are willing to concede that the way forward more likely may be found in the new womanist platforms as described by such theological strategists as Karen Baker-Fletcher, Kelly Brown Douglas, Mercy Amba Oduyoye, and A. Elaine Brown Crawford.[8] Moreover, with women comprising an estimated 78 percent of the African and African American church membership, it seems reasonable to suppose, inasmuch as black women are moving rapidly into the church leadership, entering theological seminaries, and earning terminal degrees in increasingly large numbers, that womanist theology has a greater chance for acceptance in the African American religious community of the future than the now admittedly gender-biased theologies written by men. Mature womanist scholars like Jacquelyn Grant and Delores Williams may reject my assigning them an unequal burden of leadership, but younger women entering the academy are voicing the hope that present-day womanists will be called to seize an initiative that will bridge the chasm between women and men and redeem the race. Prof. A. Elaine Brown Crawford, coordinator of the Womanist Scholars Program at the Interdenominational Theological Center in Atlanta, writes:

> Traversing the chasm between oppression and transformation is a bridge—womanist hope. Womanist hope is an active hope in the struggle for resurrected transformed existence. It is the embodied hope of African American women that moves the personal, social, and political cogs in the wheels of the transformative process. Embodied hope is a lived witness that discerns God's presence in the experience of African American women. Womanist hope is the bridge constructed with theological belief and social justice that binds and strengthens the community.[9]

One of the differences between the kind of theology that black Christian womanists have developed over the past few years and black theology of the late twentieth century is the womanist theologians' point of departure from "a triple jeopardy" grievance package and their commitment to a broad and all-encompassing goal of social justice, a goal that goes beyond the usual focus on the male theologians' white racism and the search of many African American men for prestige, power, and material rewards on the level white men enjoy. That, at least, has been the argument of some black Christian womanists, and, unhappily, a certain measure of their allegations about black male Christian academics and activists are credible.

The womanists have also insisted that sexism is only one aspect of their passion for women's justice and liberation. Race, class, and environmentalism have given their struggle wider province than that of either white feminists or black men. Today black womanists further contend that their struggle has to do with the liberation not only of women of color in the First World but of women, men, and children in the Two-Thirds World who did not benefit from the limited successes of the civil rights movement in the United States or the fight for true democracy in South Africa and other newly independent states on the continent.

Together black men and white women have provided a convenient quarry for the most aggressive black womanists. It is well known, for example, that the legislative and regulatory mandates of affirmative action programs have led, not exclusively but primarily, to the liberation, equality, and wealth of millions of white American women and of a lesser number of middle-class black men. It is possible, of course, to contend that the white American woman was in the best position, educationally, socially, and politically, to take advantage of affirmative action, and perhaps, for that very reason, white feminists could join with black men in setting their sights on white men as the common enemy. A broader and more inclusive goal would have been to address and lift women and men who were the most victimized—the millions of non-white people worldwide who were never meant to share in the American dream and were deliberately left behind by the triumph of white male-dominated globalism fueled by rampant American capitalism.

Few womanist theologians have dealt forthrightly with the issue of lesbians and transgendered persons. Kelly Brown Douglas is a Christian womanist who does go beyond the gender, race, and class analyses to take seriously Alice Walker's definition of a womanist as "a woman who loves other women sexually and/or non-sexually."[10] Thus, in reconstructing a theologically salient image of the Black Christ, she is not afraid to suggest that Christ must not only be seen in the face of a black female but most vividly in the face of a poor and socially rejected black lesbian.

> My christological perspective is not limited to a tridimensional analysis. Instead, it stresses the need for a multidimensional and bifocal analysis that confronts all that oppresses the Black community as it impinges upon the community or is harbored within. This means that Christ is a sustainer, liberator, and prophet in the face of such evil as racism, sexism, classism, and heterosexism.[11]

Of course, black theology has not entirely ignored the homophobic character of worldwide oppression. In my introduction to part 1, entitled

"Black Theology and Pastoral Ministry," in volume 2 of *Black Theology: A Documentary History, 1980–1992,* I refer to the essay by an avowed gay-identified, bisexual black theologian, Elias Farajaje-Jones, as exploring for the first time, in a collection of essays on black Christian theology, "how homophobia remains behind a wall of silence . . . in the Black Church" and I welcome him to the black theological roundtable.[12] One has to concede, nevertheless, that the younger black male theologians have not taken up the topic of homophobia as readily as some womanists have, and this is one of the reasons why black male liberation theology remained stagnant in the 1990s while womanist thought advanced—however gingerly in this case—toward a more developed concept of wholeness that has excluded no area of contemporary African American life and culture.

It is difficult to find an area of application that was not covered to some degree by the early writings of Cone and Roberts, but the literature of the men who came after those two pioneers exhibited variety but not great creativity in forging new uses, new doctrines, new interpretive tasks that had not been previously investigated in the Cone-Roberts corpus. The books and essays written by younger men from the 1970s to the end of the century focused on racism, black biblical hermeneutics, the theology and ethics of King, the roots of black theology in slave religion, pastoral care, the preaching ministry, the freedom struggle in South Africa, folk ways, politics, and the disgraceful neglect of young African American males in or on the way to prison. On the whole, womanist theology seems equally multidimensional, but, in terms of larger theological and ideological building blocks, they have been willing to grapple with the *isms* that men neglected in the early stages of the National Committee of Black Churchmen, the black caucuses of the predominantly white churches, and the Society for the Study of Black Religion. NCBC, for example, paid little attention to cultural analysis and the sources of the data that women have had no problem using. The Christian womanists seem to have been more determined to escape the gravitational pull of Christian sources and to accelerate into orbits that are not controlled by the institutional black church.

Jacquelyn Grant makes the point that black women's theology has not only resisted American "bourgeoisification" but also African American "churchification" and, as a result, has opened up critical and constructive tasks which "take seriously only the useable aspects of the past."[13] If this is a programmatic challenge to her younger sisters it suggests a future for black Christian womanist thought that will produce a new Christology under multidimensional rubrics which will include racism, sexism, classism, and sexual preference, with an emphasis on "the least" of God's children. Grant is not afraid to follow her "holistic mission" beyond the boundaries of the historic Christianity that African American and African male theologians continue to exegete along lines that do not threaten their position in the black churches and in academia.

I doubt that womanist theology can accomplish this constructive program outlined by Grant and others without restoring and reinvigorating the collaborative relationship it once had with black liberation theology, when Pauli Murray, Theressa Hoover, Jacquelyn Grant, and others began to conceive of a partnership, but one they practically abandoned, as the new womanist thought sought independence in order to flourish. Perhaps it was for this reason that, in the 1990s, the work of black male theologians began to falter.

One might assume that some partnership is still being practiced whenever black women and black men get together to address common problems at the Society for the Study of Black Religion or at the regional and national meetings of the American Academy of Religion. That, however, has not been the case. There have been few planned and regular opportunities for programmatic collaboration. More frequently each group of scholars has gone its own way, leaving intriguing questions unanswered and vaguely overlapping areas of common interest still awaiting serious cooperative effort.[14]

It seems certain that more African and African American women will become pastors of black congregations on both sides of the Atlantic and even become pastors of an increasing number of non-black congregations worldwide. It also seems likely that in the near future the number of black women seeking a terminal degree in religious studies will exceed the number of black men earning a Ph.D. It is probable, too, that these women will have increasingly greater influence in determining the shape and direction of theological and ethical reflection in black communities at home and abroad.

It is reasonable to speculate further that both traditional Pentecostal and Spiritual or prophet-led church emphases will try to dominate the kind of theology that will emanate from black womanist thought and praxis in the twenty-first century. These are the dominant emphases today in the black churches of Africa, Europe, North America, and the

Caribbean where women's leadership is becoming stronger every year. Women have always been prominent in charismatic movements, and there is little on the horizon that promises to change that picture any time soon. We might hope for more enlightened leadership from our sisters. There are important exceptions, but Holiness, Pentecostal, and Spiritual churches have not been particularly interested in the kind of social transformation that has been a priority of liberation theology. The urgent question is whether womanist thinking, with its present accent on liberation from sexism, racism, classism, militarism, and homophobia, will be able to divert the historic tendency of these powerful churches from biblical fundamentalism and pneumatological sensationalism to wide-ranging political and social justice concerns.

Moreover, although womanists have been conspicuous in their broader concern for the whole spectrum of black reality, the weapons they have chosen to engage issues of justice have primarily been literary; that is, they have mainly used the writings of other black women as a major source for their theologizing, rather than choosing a praxiological approach that brings them into more direct contact with poor black women. They have not been in the streets with poor women and, on the strength of direct action, solidified their relationship with the oppressed so that they might develop their theology from the resistance of their less privileged sisters against crippling abuses and injustices at the grass roots.

Here is where I believe that closer collaboration is necessary between what we formerly regarded as black liberation theology conducted by men and black womanist theology if the full panoply of neo-African and African American religious thought and action—the pragmatic spirituality and Africentric orientation of black peoples—are to be available to Christian churches and other religious institutions throughout the world. After all, this is where black liberation theology began. It was in the 1960s when black liberation theology was deeply influenced by pastors in Brooklyn, Philadelphia, Rochester, New York, Detroit, Chicago, Watts, and the San Francisco Bay area, pastors who were in the streets with the people, working alongside community organizations that were challenging the white power structures and supporting such groups as the Interreligious Foundation for Community Organization, the Revolutionary Action Workers, the Pan-African Skills Project, the Patrice Lumumba Coalition, and the World Council of Churches' Programme to Combat Racism, groups that were all involved as well with the liberation movements in Southern Africa. It is this kind of alliance with people who are still fighting injustices on the ground that is missing today among black Christian womanists as well as among the younger black male theologians.

Of course, we can all be accused of armchair theologizing. It is a familiar malady of academics, but it can be ameliorated among black scholars in religion if they close ranks around local congregations and social activist groups in the African and African American communities. This confederation, however, is not likely to happen until black male theologians and church leaders become less enamored with academic and ecclesiastical issues and more involved with a "public theology" that is not afraid to deal with the nitty gritty realities of a pastoral and political ministry, preferring to get their hands dirty with local issues than to be recognized as spokespersons and national power brokers on prime-time TV.

This does not mean that the normal function of theology as the work of the church needs to be neglected. Both women and men must also examine the undue time and effort given to the struggle against white racism as the primary, almost exclusive objective of its polemics, and become more energetic about Christian education in the denominations and local churches so as to better inform and help shape beliefs and behavior from "the bottom up." Black theology must reinvigorate the work it began on the formulation, refinement, and catechesis of Christian doctrine and moral behavior. We urgently need to develop lay theologians who will help to contribute to the understanding and commitment of church-related brothers and sisters whose neighborhoods and community institutions are suffering from racism and oppression in the many new guises that they assume today.

This will require some radical reshuffling of priorities by the men in order to see that the doors are opened today for greater participation by women in theological education, in the national denominational and ecumenical leadership ranks, and in the development of programs in Christian education, missiology, and social action for local congregations. For its part, womanist theology must disavow its latent and overt separatist tendencies and propose short-term and long-term worship, study, and action agendas that not only address the thorny problems that continue to embitter the dialogue with black men but also draw them into collaboration on neglected issues of holistic liberation at all levels of the African and African American churches and communities.

Womanist theology is not a branch of black theology, nor is it a substitute for black theology. Womanist theology *is* black theology. It is black theology with a special laboratory for testing its liberative efforts in the company of females and with a special message for black girls and women, gay and straight, rich and poor, in Africa and in the diaspora, helping them to work themselves out of an inferiority complex and into equality and collaboration with their brothers, fathers, and sons. Womanists seem peculiarly suited to giving leadership in Christian action that will lead to a new ecumenical and interfaith dialogue. It almost goes without saying that African and African American churches and communities are a part of a changing world order that cannot help but be instructed and enriched by a theological revolution that brings the Christian faith into a dynamic synergy with African Traditional Religions, progressive Islam, and other non-Christian faiths and ideologies, and that will benefit all peoples by virtue of its religious humanism and justice-making involvement in a world beloved by its Creator.

Katie G. Cannon, one of the earliest of the black women ethicists, represents those women scholars who find in black theology and ethics the possibility of collaboration for a bipolar theology of liberation. She recognized that neither Howard Thurman nor Martin Luther King Jr. wrote expressly about women's liberation, but she believes that both were liberation theologians of the highest order who emphasized God's love as the basis of moral agency and of the beloved community of men and women. Cannon links their emphasis on justice and love with the extraordinary perception and wisdom of Zora Neale Hurston, the womanist thinker and writer without peer, thereby demonstrating the possibility of the kind of dialogue and collaboration that womanist scholars, writers, and leaders can offer to a recessive, male-dominated theology.

> The centrality of moral agency is a response to divine love, wherein grace initiates experience of God's love which in turn commissions each person to a ministry of love. Thurman advocated a love-ethic which impacts social situations by affirming the inter-relatedness and inter-dependence between each individual. The fullest meaning of love can be known only when human beings, in tune with the infinite, shape a loving reality (community). Thurman's love-ethic calls Black women forth to test and confront all barriers to common unity.[15]

Cannon finds a similar possibility in King's interpretation of "the beloved community" but with a greater concern for a pragmatism that leads to nonviolent direct action and has a special relevance to Hurston's refusal to tolerate dehumanization by either legal or illegal norms and customs. Cannon concludes her analysis with an insightful comment that helps to clarify what I have tried to describe as the role of womanist thought in the recovery of a valid Africentric liberation theology that knows no basic disjunction between the liberative task of black women and black men:

> Neither Howard Thurman nor Martin Luther King, Jr. reflect directly on the Black woman's experience, but emergent in their theologies is the strong affirmation of the dignity of all Black people grounded in God, precisely the starting point of Hurston's vision. This theme resonates with Zora Neale Hurston's deepest conviction and what she mirrored as a portrayer of Black life. Hurston insisted that Black women seek the realization of their dignity as persons. This dignity is a birthright, a non-negotiable need. . . . Hurston's suspicion of the Black religious tradition is valid. Black male theologians continue to ignore the victimization of gender discrimination. However . . . I signal three basic theological themes in the ethics of Thurman and King that can sustain the politics of justice, which Black women need. What Hurston was denied, Black women of today must have. Black women intellectuals must transform the tradition so as to enable Black women, who celebrate Black life, to make a reaffirmation of their spiritual roots.[16]

We have come too far, together, to separate on the cusp of the New World that is aborning, a world that will refuse to be divided up into camps of nationalities, skin colors, males and females, sexual orientations, sexes, and even rigid, uncompromising religions, but one that will, unfortunately, find it exceedingly difficult to escape the harvest of evil that those divisions have sown in the fields of human endeavor for at least two thousand years. There is still much work to be done by churches, mosques, educational institutions, and democratic societies. Christianity and Islam, by themselves, will not be able to wipe away the hates and injustices of the past twenty centuries. Each has too many blemishes itself. And together they have been notoriously complicitous in those very hates and injustices.

But a renewed Christian ecumenism and humanism, exemplified by African and African American women and men—who are certainly among those who have suffered most from "man's inhumanity to man" since the Middle Ages of European history—should be able to fashion new possibilities of collaboration and community, across the ancient lines of demarcation between the genders, that point to a new world of justice and love. A more complete renovation of womanist theology and black theology, crafted primarily by patriarchs like me and by the macho men who were the vast majority of my students during the second half of the twentieth century, might be, in the Christian churches and the theological academies of the twenty-first century, one place to begin.

5

"Doing the Truth"

Some Criteria for Researching and Teaching African American Religious History

I first began seriously to research and teach African American religious history late, as late as the summer of 1974, when I became a fledgling member of the church history faculty at Colgate Rochester, Bexley Hall, Crozer Theological Seminary, a consortium of historic schools of theology in Rochester, New York, hereafter referred to as CRDS. Working in African American religious history was a relatively new challenge for me, because my brief teaching career at the Presbyterian Seminary in Pittsburgh, Pennsylvania, and at the School of Theology at Boston University had not been in the field of history but in that of social ethics and, given the times and the seasons, with a strong emphasis on moral and ethical issues incident to the Civil Rights movement that was in high gear during the 1960s.

One of the initial lessons I learned in the movement between 1963 and 1972 was that one could not understand the struggle for desegregation and racial justice without first understanding the religious history of African Americans and the responses white Christians made to the persistent demands of black people. For nine years, sandwiched between sojourns in ethics at Pittsburgh and Boston, I had been trying to put into action what I had put into words in *The Secular Relevance of the Church*, my first attempt to be a scholar in religion.[1] The book was written during my doctoral studies at Drew University and Temple University, which had to be aborted after, in a fit of excitement, I quit the classroom, at Pittsburgh, to become executive director of the new Commission on Religion and Race of the United Presbyterian Church.

That was during the tumultuous summer of 1963. I had decided to take a job that was supposed to help Presbyterians catch up with Dr. Martin Luther King Jr. The unlikely and surprising directive of the United Presbyterian General Assembly to the newly formed Commission in San Antonio in the spring of 1963, was to insert the struggle against racial segregation and discrimination into the top of the agenda of the denomination, an upper-middle-class, wealthy, and predominately white Protestant church.

It did not take long for me to discover that a knowledge of religious history on both sides of the color line was indispensable to anyone occupying that unprecedented national staff position in race relations to which I had been appointed in 1963. For almost ten years I and my staff battled as best we could to fulfill the promise that this powerful white church had made to the black people of America. When I left New York in 1972 for the King chair that Preston Williams had occupied at Boston University and came to another King chair at CRDS in 1974, I was fired up, particularly in Rochester, to immerse myself in African American religious studies, particularly in history.

During the years 1974 to 1983, when I resigned from CRDS to become professor of black church studies and dean of the Master of Divinity program at New York Theological Seminary in Manhattan, I metamorphosed from a battle-tested social ethicist to a self-made church historian. This may have bothered some of my scholarly white colleagues, but it never bothered me or my students. They knew that I had mastered my stuff in the field and was ready to take it into the classroom. I have always been convinced that the kind of activist scholarship that was incumbent on African American teachers of men and women preparing for the Christian ministry required an in-depth knowledge of both the ethical norms and behavior of black Christians, the history of African American religious institutions, and the determination to put one's body where one's mouth was—that is, in the thick of the struggle. Indeed, the rapid development of African American religious studies, as a separate academic field, made it abundantly clear by the 1980s that research and teaching in graduate theological schools had to be unashamedly activist and self-consciously interdisciplinary if students were to appreciate the context of ministry in the embattled inner city of the metropolis, and be inspired and equipped to lead people, white and black, in the struggle for truth, justice, and liberation. "Doing the truth," as a teacher and role model for future ministers in the 1960s, meant being involved yourself and helping your students to be involved in the implementation of justice and liberation strategies from many different perspectives and in the variety of ways of doing research, teaching the truth that transforms people, and radicalizing the church in America.

Since 1974 I have advocated a generalist approach to theological education made to order for the local congregation in situations of crisis, and I have insisted on the interdisciplinary and nontraditional nature of our work in African American Religious Studies. My agenda for researching and teaching achievable objectives and predictable problems in this field is obviously only a partial listing—a modest beginning—and is based on criteria that are, by no means, value-free. I believe that while the Bible and theology are the king and queen of the normative theological curriculum, the religious history of Christian action is the prime minister and mover in the African American academy. But it is important to note that the central role it plays must be augmented by the contributions of several secular and religious disciplines, and that any proactive ministry in the world, within or outside the churches, must discern where God is at work, bringing to naught the things that exist and bringing into existence the things that do not exist.[2]

Since I am more concerned about finding the best way to make steady progress toward the goal of full humanity and liberation for African Americans than I am about a sightseer's impression of what lies out there in the delightful gardens of academe, I shall begin this chapter by recommending three criteria that I have used in my own career to help me decide what I should make an effort to *look for,* as opposed to what might *just happen to come into view* as I explore this problematic terrain of African American religious studies.

Black scholars in the field have understood, at least since the days of Carter G. Woodson, Anna Arnold Hedgman, Mordecai Wyatt Johnson, Benjamin Mays, and Howard Thurman, to mention only a few of the Venerable Ones, that the black scholar must know everything that his or her white colleagues know, and then something extra that most of those colleagues will know little about and about which they probably couldn't care less. Some of us who came on the scene late tended to be less impressed or intimidated by what white scholars thought worthwhile or worthless than did our predecessors, but even in this later period we, too, recognized the importance of knowing something about what interested our white counterparts, and most of us opted to share some—not all—of those interests, and to offer other interests that seemed to have particular importance in the African American community. The main point here, however, is that what the white academy values deserves to be only one criterion for our work, and then not necessarily the most important one. There are other equally consequential criteria for researching, teaching, and resolving problems in religion whose solution should prove to be a great boon to our teaching and to all African Americans. I would argue that these other criteria are important for white scholars and teachers, too.

The criteria I have been using to decide on and lift up some unresolved problems that students of African American religion might usefully explore are these: First, does the particular study or inquiry in question contribute anything to our knowledge of the truth? As a people who have so frequently been victimized by lies—scholarly, pseudo-scientific, and otherwise—we want to be as sure as we can that we are "speaking the truth," to borrow the title of one of James H. Cone's books. But we ought also to be sure that speaking the truth depends on first *seeking* the truth, then *knowing* the truth, and finally, and indispensably, *doing* the truth. These three requirements are inseparable and point to the seriousness with which we approach the work of scholarship in African American studies. As the saying goes, "If you can't walk the walk, don't talk the talk." That matter of *doing* brings me naturally to a second criterion.

Does research on the question being considered for investigation contribute to theory—and not just any theory but a broad and illuminating theory about African American life and culture that connects different aspects of our problematic and leads to knowledgeable and informed action on behalf of the black community? To put the matter somewhat more elaborately, does the contemplated research project make possible and feasible a more comprehensive and holistic hypothesis for understanding and appreciating African American life and culture in their national and international contexts? And this not merely for academic purposes but in order to direct us back into the community as teachers/learners, activist scholars, and agents of renewal, social justice, and liberation?

Third, I ask myself, does this study or area of research have significant social, economic, political, and spiritual implications? In other words, when considered against the background of social, economic, political, and religious realities, does the area of research provide the African American church—and, by extension, the religious communities of other marginalized and oppressed people—with data and experience that contribute to survival, self-determination, and spiritual as well as political liberation, rather than to further underdevelopment, dependency, and bondage? Put differently, does this study and research help me and my students to *do* the truth?

How does one do the truth? That is not an easy question to answer, but for me, as a black Christian activist teacher/learner who is open to truth from other faiths and other ideologies as well, the answer is a "work in progress" that is identified, carried out, tested, and evaluated by these three critically necessary criteria. Ultimately, "doing the truth" forces me back to my personal faith in Jesus as Lord and Liberator and to God's mission to unbind the whole creation from its bondage to decay and to reconcile all peoples to God's self.

This final consideration is not a mega-criterion incumbent on all of us who are involved in research, writing, and teaching, but it is inescapable for me, and I mention it here mainly to indicate that, for some of us who are Christians, *doing* the truth is fundamentally an attribute of discipleship, of being a follower of the one who said of himself: "I am the way, and the truth, and the life." The rest of that text says that those who come to the truth and to God, the author of truth, must come through Christ. This is not the place to argue about that imperious claim. Let it suffice for the moment simply to say that I believe that we can proclaim Jesus Christ as the truth without insisting that only "born-again" Christians can come to God. Having made that personal confession, I turn now to the specific question of African American religious history.

I am using the term here to include the history of the black religious experience from the continent of Africa to the Caribbean to Central and South America and to North America, but also the history of black religious institutions: the denominations, local congregations, church-related self-help and benevolent associations, schools, colleges, and universities, sectarian groups, cults, and ecumenical agencies. Since the subject of religion has been raised I want to make it clear that most Christian scholars have short-changed Islam and Judaism. No study of African American religion can henceforth be complete without attention to both these "religions of the Book" that have always drawn black people to plumb the depths of their sacred revelations.

There are still enormous gaps in our understanding of these groups that belong to our past as well as our present. As long as the gaps remain we will continue to be uncertain about what worked or failed to work at other periods, and therefore what consequences we ought to anticipate from our present choices and actions. It is commonplace to say that religion has played a primary and powerful role among all African people, but there is a dearth of synthetic histories (such as, for example, Roger Bastide's *African Civilizations in the New World* or George Eaton Simpson's *Black Religions of the New World*) written by black authors that explain precisely how religion functioned at the most critical moments of our history.[3] Why were religion and religious institutions so influential in this history? How have those resources of the spirit nourished us in the past? And how can they provide us with the transcendent and humanistic powers we need for the purposes of humanization and liberation today? We know a great deal about African American religion in bits and pieces, but who can help us to articulate an integrated, holistic picture of what black people have believed and practiced under the rubric of religion? What do we really understand about this new institutionalized Islam that today is as indigenous as Christianity in many key black urban communities? Who will help us to understand and deal with this contemporary black church of the metropolized middle class in a way that will help this church to do the truth as well as preach it to the rapidly deculturated, trivialized, and normless black society of the twenty-first century?

Most of the denominational histories we are using are out of print and contain misstatements of fact and, to say the least, some glaring omissions. Even the classic work of Carter G. Woodson, *The History of the Negro Church,* is woefully inadequate, although we have no choice but to assign it over and over again in our course work because in more than sixty-five years nothing has been published to replace it.[4] The source book *The Black Church in the African American Experience,* by C. Eric Lincoln and Lawrence H. Mamiya comes closest to doubling as a general survey of denominational history and a sociological analysis of organized African American Christianity today, but it does not pretend to be comprehensive and many small but significant details that one might find in encyclopedia articles on individual black churches could not be included in this otherwise excellent synopsis.[5] We are equally grateful for the work of Albert Raboteau, James M. Washington, Leroy Fitts, Lewis Baldwin, Othal Lakey, David Daniels, and Ann H. and Anthony B. Pinn for published histories over the last ten or twelve years, but there are reams of source material in libraries and dusty archives (not to mention old trunks in somebody's attic or basement) that we have not even begun to tap. Many more researchers, perhaps an army of graduate students, like the Works Progress Administration Writers' Project of the 1930s, must be enlisted and put to work before we will be able to say that significant progress has been made in the reconstruction of African American church history.

While we welcome the excellent studies by white scholars, such as Eugene Genovese, David Wills, Richard Newman, Randall Burkett, and Mary Sawyer, that have been available over the last few years, African American scholars should not lose control of the field by default. Some self-deluded people may take this as a racist statement, but honest students of history on both sides of the color line will agree that most histories that are written by representatives of the group in power are generally considered more authoritative than those by others, though they are likely to ignore or leave out important information that submerged or marginalized groups might have included if they had an opportunity to speak for and about themselves. The attitude some of us express, for example, "Let the white people who can get the good grants do the digging; I'm too busy with my lecture circuit and preaching engagements," has spelled nothing less than the death of black religious historiography written from the perspective of those who should know precisely what it feels like to be black in a dominating white world. A few white scholars may accept the criteria I have posited in this chapter, and we welcome them with open arms. But I fear that most will not, mainly because of what they mistakenly regard as our ethnic chauvinism. At the same time, however, some of them are prepared to do research and write books about African American religious history for professional advancement and other purposes quite unrelated to the survival of the African American community and the mission of the black church.

Let us now look briefly at specific areas that offer fertile ground for future research in religious history.

First, we need more studies of the religious experience of the slave community between 1619 and 1750. We could use more studies like St. Clair Drake's classic text, *The Redemption of Africa and Black Religion*, and James W. St. G. Walker's *Black Loyalists: The Search for a Promised Land in Nova Scotia and Sierra Leone, 1783–1870*, on the fugitive slave preachers who established the first black independent churches in Canada, the Caribbean, Bermuda and the Bahamas, South America, and West Africa.[6] We need to know much more about the churches they left behind and the Pan-African connection in religion they forged and that is carried on today by jet-hopping black preachers and evangelists who traverse the skies between North America, unknown venues in the West Indies, England, the European continent, and Africa. I and a few colleagues, when traveling abroad, have been astonished to accidentally encounter such persons, generally without a degree and unheralded, in strategic parts of Africa and the diaspora, standing in the customs lines or at airport hotels. Like so many unknown black women preachers, they invariably belong to an almost invisible group of self-made ministers and local church missionaries who continue to exist in the shadows of the inner city and whose sympathies for and connections with Africa are unknown to most of us who work for established churches and prestigious educational institutions.

There are lacunae in our church history that have either been dismissed or are filled with largely unsupportable inferences. For example consider the following:

1. What was the role of African American church leaders in predominantly white denominations in the antebellum period, and what effect did they have on those churches in subsequent years?
2. What should we know about the Baptists who came out of Lynchburg College and Seminary in Lynchburg, Virginia, who are reported to have inspired revolutionary missions to Africa at the turn of the nineteenth century?
3. What was the role of mysticism and occultism in the careers of black women preachers and missionaries in the nineteenth century?
4. Is it really true that the black church was "hopelessly accommodationist" between 1900 and the Montgomery bus boycott, and who were the local preachers and church members who laid the foundation for the Civil Rights movement prior to Martin Luther King Jr.?
5. How did the so-called New Negroes of the Harlem Renaissance (such as Zora Neale Hurston and Ruby F. Johnston) try to reinterpret black folk religion, and what can be learned from the period between the two world wars about the church and the "cultured despisers" of black religion today?
6. Why have church union efforts failed so miserably among the historic black denominations that had no difficulty in participating in the Consultation on Church Union and the National Council of Churches?
7. Why has a large segment of African Americans opted for Roman Catholicism and Islam, and why has another considerable segment

shown a preference for the episcopal system of church government despite the well-known tyrannies which that polity has exercised over some African American constituencies?

8. What important lessons can we learn from new biographical studies of persons such as William J. Seymour, Ida Wells-Barnett, George Alexander McGuire, Nannie Helen Burroughs, Bishop Ida Robinson, and Father Divine?
9. What evidence is available to show that black women are the backbone of the African American church as reputed, and to what degree has their predominance in the pews moved the churches in the direction of political conservatism rather than liberalism?
10. What conclusions can we draw from the failures or the short-lived careers of black ecumenical agencies, such as the Fraternal Council of Churches, the Southern Christian Leadership Conference, the National Conference of Black Christians, and the national black caucuses of the predominantly white denominations, that can help us to plan and implement more effectively a comprehensive urban strategy for the African American church in the twenty-first century?

Such are the tantalizing questions we need to pose to the enormously rich deposits of black religious history remaining to be mined by intrepid researchers. Some of these deposits are being rapidly depleted by obsolescence and disuse, for we are notoriously poor keepers of records. Unless we move swiftly, much of the data required for answering these and other urgent questions that continue to perplex us will sink into oblivion forever. This unhappy state of affairs suggests one concluding observation about requirements in the field of African American history—the great need to accelerate the collection and transcription of oral and videotaped history.

Many of older people in the field have grossly underestimated what we, as historians, can do with the humble tape recorder. The history of many ordinary preachers, church members, choir directors, Sunday School superintendents, and leaders of neighborhood organizations and community groups that were organized in the churches during the Great Migrations from the south and rural areas can only be reconstructed by means of the tape recorder. But only a few years remain before even that possibility will cease to exist.

We cannot afford to be cocky and excessively self-confident about the direction and quality of our work in the future. There is covert resistance in the profession to the very kind of interdisciplinary research and generalist approach to which I alluded at the beginning of this chapter. One of the greatest threats to the advancement of African American religious studies is our own failure to understand the ideological and political advantage and power of elitist scholarship in a society where black academics can be a conspicuous target in hostile territory. All of us can testify, if not for ourselves then at least for friends and colleagues who, because of prejudice, broken promises, professional jealousy, or resentment over old affirmative action politics, were betrayed by people whom they trusted and chatted with amicably at faculty meetings but who either helped to drive them out into the cold or made them languish on the borders of academic skid row.

There exists the belief among some African American scholars that it is imprudent and unprofessional to appear to be too political or ideological, or too identified with the underclass. We fear being labeled as unreconstructed black nationalists. We have the naive notion that only if we are scientifically objective or disinterested or wear the mask about which Paul Lawrence Dunbar wrote[7] can we be sure that the serious and responsible work we do, or want to do, will invariably be authenticated on its own merits, as is usually true of many of our white colleagues. This, unfortunately, is a sad illusion.

We have to organize, to demonstrate unanimity of purpose and solidarity, to "do the truth" come hell or highwater. We particularly have to be sensitive to the problems encountered by black women in as many black as white colleges and universities. Joan M. Martin, who has studied the problems of work for African American women from the white mistress's kitchen to the plush executive positions in Washington, D.C., New York, Atlanta, and Los Angeles, writes:

> All along this journey, African American women have faced personal, cultural, and institutional discrimination as enslaved women and as the descendants of enslaved women. As a testimony to the human spirit, they have maintained a critical sense of the meaning of work and its value to their communities and to Christian faith in the context of our society.[8]

Too many of our colleagues look askance at African American religious studies because they regard work in this field as basically oriented to black nationalism and as not only spurious but also irrelevant to anyone who is not of African descent. One has only to be around predominantly white institutions a few years to discover that there are white scholars who want desperately to believe that there is neither an advantage nor a disadvantage in being white or black when it comes to scholarship in a law-abiding and democratic society. That is an ideological gloss over reality that we must expose and repudiate every chance we get.

The black scholar must constantly be aware, as Cornel West has reminded us, that "race matters." She or he must be cognizant of the advantages and disadvantages, the rewards and penalties, for being black in America, without becoming mired in either self-pity or self-adulation. We must realize that in this society it is next to impossible to discern reality from unreality, or truth from falsehood, without taking into strict account the factor of non-white ethnicity, class, and gender in the search for and the utilization of knowledge. That is why it is so important not to be satisfied simply with knowing the cognitive difference between truth and untruth. One has to *do* what is truth in order to really know what it is and be able to teach it to others. The matter is put squarely for the Christian scholar in I John 1:6–7: "If we say that we have fellowship with him [that is, with the Truth] while we are walking in darkness, we lie and do not do what is true; but if we walk in the light as he himself is in the light, we have fellowship with one another, and the blood of Jesus his Son cleanses us from all sin."

Those brave and brilliant men and women who preceded us in the nineteenth and early twentieth centuries, many of whom did not have half the education and privileges we enjoy, who were barely out of slavery and yet as learned as we are, and could express themselves with even greater eloquence—those first African American scholars and scholars in the making—knew that the black race had been disparaged, maligned, and virtually shut out of the annals of Western civilization. Most of them were followers of Jesus Christ. But whether they were Christians or not, they decided long ago that whether white people believed them or not, whether the white press published them or not, whether they were appointed to prestigious white faculties or not, they would speak the truth, and do the truth, by working against all odds for the liberation and elevation of the people. We who are their descendants can do no more. We dare not do less.

PART II

The Quest for an Africentric Cultural Identity

6

What Is African American Christianity?

Let us first attend to the terminology.[1] When words such as *African American, Euro-American, white,* and *black* are used to modify nouns such as *religion* or *Christianity,* many people are quickly turned off. Most of us prefer to believe that because we live in the modern or postmodern world where everyone wants to be recognized first as a human being, created in the image of God, there is no reason to classify one another in ways that draw attention to our differences. Why is it necessary, some will ask, to throw up artificial barriers between us by insisting on a black or African American Christianity instead of just plain Christianity, or black or white Roman Catholics, Baptists, or Presbyterians instead of just plain Roman Catholics, Baptists, or Presbyterians? It is sad enough to have to admit our denominational differences, why add an additional embarrassment with racial and ethnic divisions among Christians? Using such terms in the 1960s might have made sense because we Americans were in the midst of an unprecedented cultural revolution, but why should anyone, at the beginning of the third millennium of the Christian era, take seriously the present chapter, which asks the question, "What is African American Christianity?"

Some readers may have an even more basic objection. "What," they may ask, "does the Bible have to say about a black Christianity or a white Christianity? Show me those terms in my family Bible, Professor! Then maybe we'll have something to discuss. Otherwise, just talk to me about Christianity, pure and simple, and leave out all the racial and ethnic stuff."

Of course, such a sincere request is not unreasonable; it just happens to be pointless if we are really interested in examining the state of the Christian faith in the world we live in and read about every day in the newspapers. If ever there was anything about Christianity that was "pure and simple," it disappeared sometime before the end of the first century A.D. The way Christianity has come down to us today makes it a very mixed bag of racial and ethnic and national, or cultural and religious, habits, traditions, and understandings that may or may not—depending on how they are transmitted to whom and by whom—help someone to know who Jesus Christ is and what he wants his present-day disciples to believe and to do.

Nor is it possible to run to the Bible every time we try to escape this problem. We cannot even hear or tell a simple biblical story about the birth of Jesus, his first sermon in his hometown of Nazareth, or the parable he told about the man who was robbed on the Jericho road, without consciously and unconsciously filtering it through the sieve of our different human languages, the time and place of our rearing, our age and gender cohort, our racial, ethnic, and cultural locations in the biosphere, our educational level, our vocational or occupational choices and experiences, our psychosomatic condition, our economic and social status, our political convictions, and so forth.

The Bible does not address us as if we were purely disembodied spirits floating around in some celestial vacuum but, rather, in the only way human beings can hear God's voice and recognize it as truth for themselves. The Bible speaks to us in a way that takes into account all the dirt and grime of our personal and social existence, who we really are in the bathroom as well as in the sanctuary, our given time and place in history. If we insist, therefore, that the Scriptures must be the exclusive judge of how the term *Christianity* should or should not be modified, we should at least be aware that the word *Christian* appears only three times in the Bible (Acts 11:26 and 26:28; and I Peter 4:16) and the word *Christianity* does not appear at all! We use both these terms to describe the special religion that formed itself, albeit by the power of the Holy Spirit, around the personality and ministry of Jesus of Nazareth long after both he and those who knew him in the flesh had passed from this earthly scene.

So where does that leave us?

We are left with the difficulty that when we use the term *Christianity* we are speaking, whether intentionally or not, as if we were primarily concerned with history, with systems of belief, practices, and social structures that have grown up around the memory and teachings of the man called Jesus. You can accept it or not, but you cannot use the word *Christianity* if you mean the religion about Jesus, unsullied by the all too-human institution called "church" and the encompassing, all too-human world in which that religion, for good or ill, has made a home for two thousand years.

Someone will retort, more or less angrily: "Hold on! You are not talking about *me*. I have absolutely no concern about the things you refer to. I'm only interested in the pure and unadulterated gospel of Jesus Christ!"

Well, it is hard to know how to satisfy such a "pure and unadulterated" interest. Because the gospel, that is, the good news about this Jesus, comes packaged in the wrappings of so many different kinds of languages, cultures, and ways of looking at and responding to reality—some ancient, some modern, and some postmodern—that not even its essential message can be extracted without an interpretive posture (something biblical scholars call *hermeneutics*) that obtains preliminary to comprehension and involves so much more than reading a series of words on a printed page.

Both in ordinary conversation and in technical writing we use the word *Christianity* to connote the particular system of beliefs, ritual practices, and sociological characteristics of the religion about Jesus as understood in various contexts. When we speak of Early Christianity, we refer to that system or systems in the first two or three centuries A.D.; when we speak of Western Christianity, we mean that system or systems which developed with Rome as the center instead of Constantinople; when we speak of black or African American Christianity, we refer to that same system or systems as they predominate in African American churches and communities rather than in European or in predominantly white American churches and communities.

Thus, in the first instance, we are focusing on the religion of Christianity from the perspective of time; in the second, from the perspective of geographical or geopolitical characteristics; and, in the third, from the perspective of race, ethnicity, or culture. All are useful and permissible, depending on what we are trying to understand or communicate about this religion called Christianity.

Note well, incidentally, that in none of these contexts can we pretend that the Bible is the primary or exclusive source of the information we seek or intend to communicate. We may, of course, consult Scripture about the particular features of the church in, say, the late first century A.D. But what we learn in the text will tell us very little about Christianity in the Middle Ages in Great Britain or in Puritan New England at the time of the Salem witchcraft trials or among Negroes in the United States at the beginning of the Civil War. Let us not ask the Bible to do for us what it was never intended to do!

A Social and Cultural Fact of Life

So it makes little sense to insist that a black or an African American Christianity does not exist. Even if you want to argue that we really ought to be talking about Jesus Christ and not about Christianity, and that Jesus Christ is "the same yesterday and today and forever," as the writer of Hebrews 13:8 tells us, we must concede that the way the religion (or faith, if you prefer) about him developed in different times, in various parts of the world, and among diverse peoples is a cultural and societal fact that most reasonable people will want to take seriously.

We may profess that we are interested only in some unadulterated form of the faith that takes no account of these matters, but on an honest investigation we would find it practically impossible to describe that form of faith without certain social and cultural accretions clinging to our description.

We may as well be honest about it. Both the sins and the virtues of humankind are all too obvious in any study of Christianity. There is really no point in being so coy about why and how it developed among African Americans as to reject out of hand the idea of a black or African American Christianity among other forms of the faith that have been adopted through the ages. Is there any reason to doubt that the Holy Spirit, sent by Jesus to lead us into the truth, has been able to use *our* form as well as other forms? The Apostle Paul confessed, "I have become all things to all people, that I might by all means save some" (I Cor. 9:22).

To speak or write about an African American Christianity is to refer to a social and cultural reality among several million believers for more than four hundred years in what used to be called the New World. And during most of those years—like it or not—83 to 90 percent of all black Christians have worshiped with their own race in all-black conventicles or congregations. Certain characteristics of faith and life, belief and behavior, worship and work have resulted from that simple (we probably should say complex, *highly* complex) fact. To acknowledge those characteristics and study them is neither to condemn nor commend them. Here we attempt only to establish the reasonableness, even the correctness, of employing this terminology.

The Christianization of Africans in America

The major credit for getting a revival started among the slaves in the South must go to the Separatist Baptists. They were rough-hewn, evangelistically minded frontier preachers, many of whom came originally from New England, who built many churches in the plantation country of the Carolinas and Georgia. There was also a group called "Methodist societies" that broke away from the Church of England after the Revolutionary War and encouraged the slaves to join them, and even gave them leave to preach to white people. These two denominations, the Baptists and the Methodists, made the most consistent and enthusiastic effort to Christianize the Africans in North America. After 1750 they were attracting increasing numbers of slaves to their services—to the displeasure of many slave owners who correctly suspected that only mischief could come out of this kind of imprudent evangelism by overzealous Bible-thumpers. They were right.

Scholars are now fairly confident that the first slaves to become Christians, and many who came after them, held on to certain features of the religions that they or their foreparents had practiced in Africa. In Africa they had recognized a Supreme or High God. The concept of a high or supreme deity was not new to them when they encountered it again in America. They also had practiced assembling for prayer and ritual worship, a form of water baptism, the bringing of offerings or sacrifices, and believing in angels or holy messengers of the High God. It is clear that several aspects of Christian belief and practice were not difficult for them to accept.

Where they adopted new ideas and rituals that were similar to the ones they knew back home, the African forms were strengthened rather than discarded, although it is more accurate to say that they were gradually "transformed." The Africanized Christianity that flourished on southern plantations, often to the dismay and disgust of the white missionaries, included some characteristics that were unfamiliar to white Christians. For example, there was much dancing and singing in the African style of "call and response"; drumming (whenever permitted, for the masters were afraid that drums might signal uprisings or revolt); elaborate nighttime funeral processions and burial customs; spirit possession (or what black folk later called "getting happy"); and spectacular conversion experiences that involved dying and coming back to life, flying, traveling great distances, or encountering spirit guides of one kind or another, in fantastic dreams and visions.

Bishop Daniel A. Payne of the African Methodist Episcopal Church found the "ring shout," a shuffling dance in a circle to a pounding beat, an unmistakable retention from the African past, being practiced in the urban AME congregations of the North well into the late nineteenth century. It is now the twenty-first century, but we would not have to search very hard in most American cities to find something very close to the ring shout today.

Black Christianity continued to retain African features, particularly where the whites granted black preachers the freedom to organize "independent" congregations which, in some areas had to have a certain number of whites present by law in order to assemble. The African Baptist or Bluestone Baptist Church appeared in 1758 near Mecklenburg, Virginia; and in 1773 slave preachers David George and George Liele had a slave congregation at Silver Bluff, South Carolina, just across the Savannah River from Augusta, Georgia. There was a flourishing congregation in Williamsburg, Virginia, as early as 1776. We can assume that these were all Christian churches that had a decided African American twist, with an emphasis on that part of belief and practice that came over from the continent.

In the North, African American Methodist and Episcopal churches were founded in Philadelphia by the former slaves, Richard Allen and Absalom Jones before 1794. A group of African Methodists had split from the white St. George's Methodist Church in Philadelphia seven years before and were quickly followed by black members of white congregations in Baltimore, New York City, Wilmington, Delaware, Charleston, South Carolina, and other places. A fever for independent churches, under the leadership of black pastors, was abroad in the free African American communities of the North and West. Such freedom was, of course, violently repressed in the South for many years before the Civil War, although a few autonomous congregations flourished under white surveillance. But in the North most African American converts increasingly became members of congregations led by preachers of their own color. In the plantation country, where the slaves continued to worship with their masters in segregated pews, many unordained black preachers carried on an "invisible institution" behind the backs of the slave owners and were ready to claim their brother and sister church members as soon as emancipation came and all of them could be brought over into the black denominations that were eager to have them.

A Church of the Oppressed

From the beginning the African Americans adopted a form of Christianity obsessed with the idea of freedom from slavery. That is probably the most significant characteristic we can point to with regard to African American Christianity. The AMEs began with a revolt against white religious control that could not obscure their dissatisfaction with their general civil condition in the cities of the North. In the deep South three of the four earliest black Baptist preachers—David George, George Liele, and Amos Williams—fled slavery and founded new congregations in Nova Scotia, Jamaica, and the Bahamas respectively. That is why we must insist that in its basic theology, as well as in its liturgical style, African American Christianity was a religion of freedom; the church was the center of a partly religious, partly secular movement the basic intention of which was to bring about the total abolition of slavery and overall improvement in the lives of the freed people.

After the Civil War and during Reconstruction the churches were at the forefront of the effort to complete the work of emancipation from which northern whites were swiftly retreating. Many African American preachers became involved in politics in the temporarily repressed states of the former Confederacy and were active in the so-called Freedmen's agencies that were initially created by the churches and the federal government to help Congress administer the Reconstruction Acts. The three great concerns of the black churches during the remainder of the nineteenth century were missions to the recently freed people; education, particularly the kind Booker T. Washington introduced at Tuskegee Institute in Alabama; and, surprisingly, African missions, including selective emigration to Africa that was being promoted by such clergymen as the AME Bishop Henry M. Turner; Alexander Crummell, an Episcopal missionary; and Edward W. Blyden, a black Presbyterian minister and educator who was born in the Virgin Islands.

In no other period did the masses of African Americans need the church more desperately than between the turn of the nineteenth century and the Great Depression of the 1930s. Whatever civil rights they enjoyed immediately following the Civil War had eroded by 1914, on the eve of the First World War. Indeed, blacks were more segregated and discriminated against during and after the war than they had been in 1850. The South was striking back with a vengeance, and the North supinely imitated its former enemies. Racism became rife in all parts of the nation. In the South and border states the Ku Klux Klan and other anti-Negro hate groups were involved in a wave of lynchings and race riots. In the North almost three million impoverished agricultural workers and tenant farmers from rural Dixie had their hopes for a better life dashed in the overcrowded urban ghettos of the northern industrial areas between 1890 and 1929. They were part of one of the greatest mass migrations in the history of the Western hemisphere, but it was a migration from one oppression to another.

During the Great Depression black city churches were under severe pressure. They braced themselves to receive the migrants but were finally overwhelmed by the need of social services for people who often arrived in Baltimore, Chicago, or Detroit with all their earthly possessions in a burlap sack. Moreover, the established churches found themselves losing out in competition with new sects and cults that sprang up in the slums to feed the spiritual and sometimes physical hungers that the mainline black denominations seemed powerless to satisfy. In the case of quasi-secular movements such as Father Divine's Peace Mission, Bishop "Daddy" Grace's House of Prayer for All People, Bishop Ida Robinson's Sanctified Church, the Moorish Science Temples, and the Universal Negro Improvement Association of Marcus Garvey, some of the economic and political, as well as social and spiritual, needs of the newcomers were met. And riding high on the crest of the concentric waves of black Pentecostalism that poured out of Los Angeles in 1906 were both jazzy storefront congregations and, indirectly, the hard-eyed cultic movements whose charismatic leaders attracted more of the people at the bottom of the heap than were drawn to what Carter G. Woodson called the socially and community conscious "institutional churches."

Whether a storefront or a renovated Gothic cathedral, the church of the masses was a church of an oppressed race. In every city a few mainstream congregations tried to meet the needs of the migrants and projected an image of racial pride and self-help. Those churches became an important base for politics when organizations like the National Association for the Advancement of Colored People gradually took over the leadership of a rising middle class. But between the two world wars, African American Methodists, Baptists, Congregationalists, Presbyterians, and Episcopalians were to see a steady diminution of their influence. Although their power over the people was never entirely destroyed, mainstream religious institutions in the North all but collapsed before the unremitting onslaught of anticlericalism, secularism, and nihilism in the black urban communities during the first half of the twentieth century.

The Era of Martin Luther King Jr.

At the lowest point of its influence, the institution that had become the custodian of African American Christianity, namely, the black churches, was suddenly jolted into a new maturity when an AME laywoman, Rosa Parks, refused to sit in the segregated section of a city bus in Montgomery, Alabama. The year was 1955. A young Baptist minister from Atlanta named Martin Luther King Jr. took up her cause by mobilizing blacks to stay off the buses. The Montgomery bus boycott demonstrated that despite the decline of church authority, when organized and inspired by their traditional religious leaders, African Americans were capable of exercising extraordinary economic and political power. The movement caught on like wildfire, and at one point, in the early 1960s, the Southern Regional Council reported the existence of sixty or more local organizations in various towns across the nation, led by black clergy and committed to nonviolent direct action in affiliation with King's Southern Christian Leadership Conference.

Out of this new mass movement, the first one since the decline of Garveyism, came, by a circuitous route, the widespread civil disorders of the North in the mid-1960s and the Black Power movement of 1965. Although many northern churches were implicated in what happened, Dr. King and other mainstream leaders dissociated themselves from the call for black power. But there were other men and women of the cloth, as well as their lay followers—particularly in the hardened cities of the North and West—who supported the young revolutionaries and black self-determination without condoning the anarchy expressed in the slogan "Burn, Baby, Burn!" On the heels of the northern city rebellions of 1964–68, the National Conference of Black Churchmen (NCBC), a northern group of black power–oriented religious leaders, moved many black church people from a moderate social gospel form of Christianity toward a new black theology, a robust political radicalism, and a reinvigorated Pan-Africanism. Dr. King, without meaning to or even realizing it, had created a new African American consciousness in the churches and the communities that was to continue for the rest of the century.

Conclusion

The term *African American Christianity* conjures up all these and many other developments, trends, and tendencies among black Americans in the nineteenth and twentieth centuries. Why? Quite simply because its major institutional forms of expression, the organized black congregation and its parent black denomination, are the engines that powered this specimen of human life, this distinctive way of being Christian in the particular society that is the United States of America.

The Christian churches, of course, cannot claim to be the exclusive custodians and disseminators of the peculiar culture and ethos that we identify with African American people during these turbulent 250 years in North America. Nor will they necessarily be in the future. But the role the churches played in the past is so important, and their battle cries of "Abolition," "Freedom Now," and "Black Power" so closely identified with communities across the nation where the masses of black people reside, that it is not possible to speak of Christianity in the United States without recognizing *African American Christianity* as a unique gift of black folk, a Christianity that is the same and yet different from the North American modality of the religion and civilization that claims to revere and model the life, death, and resurrection of Jesus Christ.

7 African Beginnings

> Always Africa is giving us something new or some metempsychosis of a world-old thing. On its black bosom arose one of the earliest, if not the earliest self-protecting civilizations. . . . Nearly every human empire that has arisen in the world, material and spiritual, has found some of its greatest crises on this continent of Africa. . . . As Mommsen says, "It was through Africa that Christianity became the religion of the world." —W. E. B. Du Bois, 1915

In 1973 the Abuna, or Patriarch of the Ethiopian Orthodox Church, Theophilus, visited Boston where he was the honored guest of the African Studies Program of Boston University. The African American clergy of the city were especially invited to attend one of the meetings at which he spoke, and about fifty came on campus to receive him warmly. In the course of his remarks the Abuna reminded the black ministers that the church over which he presided in Addis Ababa was founded in the fourth century A.D. and was one of the oldest in Christendom. Since its establishment was second only to the Coptic Church of Egypt, it antedated all the Christian communions of Europe and the Americas except for the Church of Rome itself. For that reason, he said, not to mention others that had to do with the needs of black people on both sides of the Atlantic, African Americans ought to recognize Ethiopian Orthodoxy as the parent of all baptized Christians of African descent, "so then, come home to your Mother Church—she stands ready to welcome you!"

The offer was neither unreasonable nor novel. For more than a hundred years various gestures had been made suggesting that a union between the descendants of the African slaves and the ancient churches of Africa was not only appropriate in the eyes of many African Americans but was earnestly sought by Coptic and Ethiopian Christian leaders. The

Confession of Alexandria, issued by the General Committee of the 114 member churches of the All-African Conference of Churches in February 1976, recognized the priority of the churches of Egypt and Ethiopia, which was gratefully acknowledged by many African and African American Christians before and since.[1] References to "the God of Ethiopia" and Psalms 68:31 which, in the Authorized Version, prophesies that "Ethiopia shall soon stretch out her hands unto God," abound in the early writings and speeches of black leaders in North America and the Caribbean. In the nineteenth and early twentieth centuries African Americans closely identified with what was then the only independent black nation in their Motherland, with the exception of Liberia.[2]

It was not surprising, therefore, that over the years some black Christians in North America and the West Indies, whether wisely or unwisely, would dream about settling in Ethiopia or that some who elected not to emigrate would consider aligning their churches with either the Coptic Church of Egypt or the Ethiopian Orthodox Church (EOC).

After the Garvey movement reawakened African American interest in Ethiopia and after the EOC freed itself from the control of the Alexandrian Patriarchy in 1948 and became a member of the World Council of Churches, almost every major city in the United States had at least one black preacher or self-styled prophet who organized what purported to be a branch of the Ethiopian church in the black ghetto. So when the Abuna Theophilus addressed African American clergy in Boston in 1973 he had behind him a long and complex history of vague yearnings and aspirations, on the part of both Addis Ababa and a segment of independent African American churches, to forge some kind of ecclesiastical union between the black Christians of the United States, Jamaica and other islands of the Caribbean, and the ancient church of Ethiopia over which he was an eminent prelate.[3]

The 1973 event at Boston University had no significant consequence for relations between African and African American Christians in the last quarter of the twentieth century, but it does serve to bracket the fourth century A.D., and the rise of Christianity in East Africa as a beginning point, at least in the minds of many people on both continents, for examining the history of black Christianity. It is no accident that African American spokespersons of the nineteenth century popularized the idea that the history of black religion, including Christianity, begins not among the slaves of pious whites in New England and Virginia, nor on the plantations of South Carolina and Georgia, but in Africa—with the religion of the first-century Egyptians, which had a powerful effect on early Christianity and should be regarded as the most prominent of the several African Traditional Religions that originated in the Nile Valley.[4] Black scholars of the nineteenth and early twentieth centuries sought to demonstrate tenuous connections between the first African Christian churches in North America, Egyptian religion prior to Christianity, and the ancient black churches of Ethiopia and Nubia. They did not have all the technical information and equipment that modern scholarship requires to unravel the mysteries of these putative connections, but neither do most of us today. In any case, they knew that the line of relationship did not run from the slave church on a back road of some South Carolina plantation to Rome, Wittenberg, Geneva, and Canterbury, as much as it ran to Thebes, Axum, Meröe, and Lagos.

Many have refused to accept the assumption of many white scholars that the place to commence any discussion about black Americans is their debarkation on the quays of Jamestown, Charleston, and New Orleans.

During the apogee of black consciousness and the rise of the black studies movement in the 1960s and 1970s, numerous scholars who wrote articles and books about black culture and religion returned to the earlier practice of beginning the black American story with the African story. Although some of their conclusions may have been hyperpolemic and based on less than exhaustive research, their contributions corrected the gross misconceptions of black history by others and opened up the rich vein of African and African American cross-cultural exchanges and relationships previously overlooked or disparaged.[5]

My purpose in this chapter is to explore the religious territory in which the study of an Africentric and pragmatic Christian spirituality—that is, the roots of a personal faith, intellectual commitment, and political and cultural analysis and action for contemporary African and African American Christians—ought to begin.[6] There are, undoubtedly, several ways to begin such a lifelong journey of exploration, but I recommend beginning with a discussion that traces the evolution of Christianity in Africa and its early encounters with African Traditional Religions, Judaism, and Islam (not to mention other ancient and more recent religions, faiths, and ideologies whose impact on modern Africa and the diaspora is not dealt with in this volume). Here I wish to provide a short reconnaissance of the fertile terrain of religiosity and spirituality which all these ways of believing and behaving created in the areas the majority of slaves came from to populate the New World and eventually to found the African and

African American Christian churches we have today. In that respect this discussion is obviously limited but may, in any case, be helpful to many black Christians who today are asking, "What does my faith have to do with Africa?"

African Traditional Religions

African Traditional Religions (or ATR) is the term used to designate the primal, basically monotheistic if operationally polytheistic and heterogeneous religions of Africa that stretch backward into the dim reaches of prehistory and forward, in many localized forms and languages, into modern times. It is the worship of God and gods, closely identified with primordial ancestors, tribal histories, and founders of ethnic groups and civilizations, that exist in all parts of the continent. In spite of wide variations, ATR seem to hold in common, nevertheless, some values, beliefs, and practices across the more than five-thousand-mile stretch from Dakar in Senegal to Ras Hafun and the easternmost tip of Somalia.

Generally, these religions have no sacred scriptures, no single founder, no central temple or sanctuary, neither schools of prophets nor ecclesiastical organization, and no sacerdotal officialdom in the sense that we understand these things in the West. They are family-oriented and clan-centered religions, pragmatic in their relation to and effect on the totality of daily existence, and they are firmly ecological and anthropocentric in their ontology. African Traditional Religionists regard God, natural phenomena, and the ancestors as intrinsically related to one another, and the traditionalist's primary interest in them is not philosophical but practical, that is, how together they affect the lives of human beings.[7]

Since Egypt is in Africa and, over the centuries, both contributed to and borrowed from the religions of black people in the Upper Nile Valley, we are obliged to regard Egyptian religion as an early example of ATR under the special ecological and sociopolitical conditions of the Delta, between roughly 6000 and 3200 B.C. Little is known about the evolving Egyptian civilization during that early period, but it is certain that the people were racially mixed, with both Caucasoid and Negroid characteristics, intermingled, separated, and varied in intensity from time to time and place to place depending on the migrations and settlements from both the North and the South.

The field is fraught with uncertainties and speculations, but, according to such scholars of early Egyptian religion as E. A. Wallis Budge, Norman Lockyer, and John G. Jackson, astronomy and religion were closely intertwined in Kemet (or predynastic Egypt), and worship of the moon and stars preceded the deification of the sun and the institution of sacred kingship which also developed in other parts of Africa. We are skirting the borders of an extremely complex area of study that cannot be thoroughly reconnoitered here, but two main points stand out: first, that in addition to the divinity of the kings or pharaohs of Egypt, the great sun god, Ra or Re, who personified the physical sun, was the central figure of this Nilotic ATR, and the legends that surround him cannot help but remind Christians of the Holy Trinity that was to be deified almost two millennia later. Concerning the influence of ancient Egyptian Christianity upon Christianity much later, Noel Q. King writes of the former:

> A study of the history of Coptic art reveals yet other glories of this church. She was not afraid to take over motifs from the old Egyptian religion and from Hellenism. The ideal statue-form of the Holy Mother Isis in her blue robe and her divine infant Horus, became a standard Christian nativity setting. The *ankh,* the hieroglyph for life, was combined with the cross in iconography to be a symbol of resurrection after death.[8]

Second, Budge and many black and white scholars have long been convinced that these ancient Egyptians belonged to the African race, if we can use that suspicious and outmoded classification. Egypt is inseparable from the mass of people called Africans.

> And especially [to] that portion of it which lived in the great tract of country which extends from ocean to ocean, right across Africa, and is commonly known as the Sudan, i.e., the country *par excellence* of the Blacks.[9]

The rich mythology of Egyptian religion involves many twists and turns in the story of Osiris who, in a later version reported by Plutarch, after marrying his sister, Isis, is slain by his evil brother, Set. The widowed queen-Goddess Isis gives birth to a son, Horus, and after bringing Osiris back to life, sees Horus become a king and rule the earth as the third person of the new Egyptian trinity of Osiris, Isis, and Horus. The myth of the death and resurrection of Osiris, as well as the fascination of the ancient Egyptians with the idea of life after death, has been thought by many to have been related to the death of every setting sun and its rising again in the new dawn.

The great religious reformer of dynastic Egypt was the Pharaoh Amenhotep IV, or Akhenaton (1367–1350 B.C.). Akhenaton spurned the polytheism of his predecessors and restored an earlier monotheism with the worship of "Aten, the Solar Disk." His attempt to reform Egyptian religion failed, however, and the gods of Nubia, the territory of a black people south of the first cataract on the Nile which had made a large contribution to the culture of the Delta, became even more influential in dynastic Egypt.

Judaism in Africa

Some would argue that Judaism is almost as indigenous to ancient Africa as African Traditional Religions. Certainly from the descent of the Jacob family into Egypt (Genesis 46) there must have been an intimate relationship between the religion of Israel and the religions of Lower and Upper Egypt. Given the henotheistic climate in which the Torah took shape, we are able to hypothesize the ferocity of the struggle that ensued for centuries between Yahweh and foreign deities. Nor is it always clear who won. Borrowings went on incessantly between the peoples of that time who were in contact with one another, and there is no reason to assume that the religions of the Hyksos invaders and ATR, particularly Egyptian religion, did not infiltrate Judaism to become part and parcel of the religion of the ethnically mixed slaves whom Moses led out of bondage sometime between 1290 and 1224 B.C.

Ethiopian history, steeped in an impressive biblical tradition, records that the Queen of Sheba, Makeda, came away from her visit to Solomon (I King 10:1–13) with more than royal bounty. A son born to them, called Menelik, became the first emperor of Ethiopia, the "Conquering Lion of the Tribe of Judah," the ancestor, in unbroken line, of Haile Selassie. Although the birth of Menelik is not mentioned in the Hebrew Bible and reposes in the cloudy borderland of legend, the idea that Judaism was introduced to Ethiopia through this union and the transfer of the Ark of the Covenant from Jerusalem to Makeda's home, in what later became the Ethiopian province of Tigre, has been a belief of millions of Ethiopians for centuries. The story rests on no more flimsy a foundation than some of the "historical facts" that European and American Christians take for granted.[10] It is without question that a strong Judaic presence infused the ATR that lies behind Ethiopian Christianity to this day and strengthens the contention that Judaism is semi-indigenous to Africa.

Prior to the refuge Mary and Joseph sought for the baby Jesus in the Jewish ghetto of what is today Cairo, millions of Jews were scattered all over the ancient world—from the borders of Nubia, or southern Sudan today, southeast across the Arabian peninsula and northwest across Roman Africa to what is now Mauritania.[11] The Ethiopians, therefore, had a long-standing relationship with Judaism and other Semitic religions. Some authorities who may be dubious about the story of Menelik will, nonetheless, give the early date of 300 B.C. for the emergence of the Falasha, or Black Jews of Ethiopia, who practiced an eccentric form of Judaism and possessed an apocryphal literature in the sacred language of Ge'ez.

The First "Visit" of Christianity to Africa

Christianity may be regarded as the third major religion, after African Traditional Religions and Judaism, to be so intimately identified with Africa in its first century of existence as to be practically indigenous or, as in the case of Judaism, at least semi-indigenous to the continent. The gospel made its first appearance in Africa not in the Delta region but in the Upper Nile Valley (sometimes called "Black Africa") through Judich, the "Ethiopian eunuch who was baptized at an oasis on a desert road between Jerusalem and Gaza by Philip the Evangelist (Acts 8:26–40).[12] The ancient Greeks knew all of Africa south of the First Cataract as either Ethiopia or Kush. Actually Judich came from the kingdom of Meröe, in the region of what was later called Nubia or, in modern times, the Sudan.

We know nothing about his missionizing efforts after Judich returned home, praising God for sending Messiah Jesus as his Savior, for evidently no church took root in Nubia before A.D. 600. But it is very unlikely that Judich was silent once he returned to the court of the Candace, or queen, where he was an official. It is difficult to imagine that such a distinguished person who traveled and could read the Hebrew Scriptures would not have shared his revelatory experience and have been heard by the court and others who might have responded to his grand announcement. The eunuch, barren as the desert in which Philip found him, may well have turned tables and fertilized the religious soil of the Upper Nile Valley that opened the way for ATR in that area to borrow from, if not assimilate, the Byzantine version of Christianity when it finally arrived from Constantinople. But that can only be conjecture.

African Christianity took root first in Alexandria, Egypt. That much is certain to people in that part of the world and should be graciously acknowledged by the rest of us. Records that are credible to Eastern Christians, though generally unknown in the North Atlantic community, and, if known, barely believed by most European and American Christians, report that John Mark, the author of the Second Gospel, a Cyrenian Jew and erstwhile companion of the Apostle Paul, established the first African Christian church that we know about as early as A.D. 42. In the year 68, when St. Mark was martyred in Alexandria, the first person he had converted, a cobbler named Anianos, had already been made a bishop. It was from their joint ministrations that Christianity blossomed in the Delta region and Upper Egypt before the end of the second century.[13] By the time of the episcopate of Demetrius of Alexandria (189–232), Christianity was well on its way among the Copts, the native Egyptian population that had adhered to the worship of Osiris, and the story of its tortured expansion through the next three centuries involves many Nubian and other black African converts whose martyred blood enriched the soil of the Egyptian desert.[14]

Blacks from Africa served in the Roman army in the first years of the Christian era, and many were evidently converted to Christianity. Black Roman Catholics today like to recall St. Maurice, a black Christian African general who, while stationed in Switzerland in the latter part of the third century, refused to lead his legion against the Bagaudae—a small tribe of "vagrant rebels" against the Roman Empire in Gaul—after discovering that the Bagaudae were also Christians. Maurice and his soldiers were executed by Augustus Maximilian for their insubordination to the Roman's command to slaughter the Bagaudae and for their refusal to offer sacrifices to pagan gods. After that part of Switzerland became Christian, a basilica, later the center of the monastery of St. Maurice-en-Valais, was built on the site of the martyrdom. This St. Maurice (not to be confused with St. Maurice of Apomea, immortalized in the El Greco painting) has always been portrayed in many European cathedrals and churches with black African features. He is still the patron saint of infantry soldiers and swordsmiths in Savoy, Sardinia, and Cracow, Poland.[15]

Christianity in Ethiopia

In Egypt and the rest of the Graeco-Roman world Christianity was confined to the lower levels of society for three centuries. Just the opposite happened in Ethiopia. There, according to the contemporary church historian Rufinus, it was introduced to the royal court by two young men of Tyre who fell into the hands of hostile Axumites when their vessel put ashore for provisions on the way to India. The entire crew and accompanying travelers were put to death, but the young men, Frumentius and Aedesius, were taken to the king of Axum who befriended them and appointed Aedesius, the younger, to be his cupbearer and Frumentius his private secretary. When the old king died, the queen-mother prevailed on the two youths to remain in Axum and assist in administering the kingdom and raising her son, destined to become the famous Ezana, king of Axum, the first Christian ruler in Africa—the African Constantine.

When they were free to depart the kingdom, Aedesius returned to Tyre, but Frumentius remained behind to help establish a small Christian community at court and among a few traders along the coast. Sometime later he reported its existence to Bishop Athanasius in Alexandria and was consecrated bishop himself, between 341 and 346, by Athanasius and sent back to Axum to continue the evangelization of the Ethiopians. The date of Ezana's conversion is given by most scholars as 330. There seems little doubt that the king adopted the Christian faith and brought his entire kingdom into the church. A Greek inscription belonging to him has been discovered. It begins: "In the faith of God and the power of the Father, the Son and the Holy Ghost." Also, coins that were minted in the early part of Ezana's reign bear the pagan symbol of the crescent and disk, whereas those minted later in his reign carry the sign of the Cross. Thus did Christianity become the state religion of a black kingdom, Ethiopia, a mere four centuries after the birth of Christ.[16]

Not without a struggle with paganism did the Christian faith finally replace the cults of the Sabaeans and other immigrants in Ethiopia during the next two centuries. Real resistance was encountered from the Agaw section of the population, some of whom worshiped water, trees, and certain idols, and from another segment that had been drawn to Judaism; but the faith spread rapidly in both Ethiopia and Yemen. One group of ancient chronicles speaks of the propagation of Christianity as the work of certain monks such as Abba Yohannes, who founded the monastery of Debra-Sina, or Abba Libanos, who is said to have been sent to Ethiopia at the instigation of St. Pachomius, with whom he had been associated in Upper Egypt. Linanos was only one of many Ethiopian hermit monks who withdrew from the world to almost inaccessible monasteries and churches that were hewn out of the high cliffs in the wastelands where they subsisted on a meager fare, including bitter herbs and unripe bananas.[17]

Early monasticism in both Egypt and Ethiopia involved many black Christians who upheld the new faith in Messiah Jesus with a fervor and dedication unmatched in any church outside Africa. A rivalry forever grew up between various monasteries, each vying with the other for greater holiness, recounted in a series of biographies of the so-called Nine Saints, to whom the later development of the Ge'ez liturgy and literature is attributed. The Nine Saints were anti-Chalcedonians from Syria and Constantinople who had been persecuted by the Roman emperor, harried in the Egyptian desert, and thence to Ethiopia where they undertook the enormous task of Christianizing the population by producing the Ethiopic version of the Bible based on a Syrio-Greek text, probably in the sixth century.

Of special interest to African and African American historians is the strikingly black African character of early Ethiopian Christianity. The strenuous effort of the Christian nations of the West to make contact with a legendary figure, Prester John, reputed to be a Christian ruler in Abyssinia who would help them outflank Islam in Asia Minor, brought the Portuguese envoy, Pedro de Covilham, into contact with the Ethiopian church after 1487. Covilham was well received by the people, but he was not permitted to leave. Groves reports that in 1520 a Portuguese embassy, bent on uprooting the Ethiopian church from its heterodoxy and placing it under the authority of the Roman pontiff, found a form of Christianity there that had existed for more than a thousand years but that was radically different from the faith practiced by Europeans.

> The chaplain to the embassy, Francisco Alvarez, wrote an account of the country and their visit. . . . He gives a valuable account of Christian

> practice as he found it observed. . . . Thus the shouting and leaping in connexion with worship he admits may be accepted as done to the glory of God. . . . He frankly expressed to the *abuna* (the head of the Abyssinian Church) his amazement at the ordaining of children and even infants in arms as deacons, to which the old man replied that they would learn, and that he was very old and it might be long before his successor could be appointed from Cairo.[18]

The Jesuits tried their best for more than a hundred years to win Ethiopia for the Church of Rome but without notable success. Many of them complained about the "corruptions" that had crept into the church as a result of its separation from Roman Catholicism. Jerome Lobo, a Jesuit who remained in the country after his order had been expelled by Emperor Fasiladas in 1633, gives an even more graphic picture of the tumultuous public worship he witnessed.

> They sing the Psalms of David of which as well as other parts of the Holy Scriptures, they had a very exact translation in their own language. . . . The instruments of music made use of in their rites of worship, are little drums, which they hang about their necks, and beat with both hands. . . . They begin their consort by stamping their feet on the ground, and playing gently on their instruments, but when they have heated themselves by degrees, they leave off drumming and fall to leaping, dancing, and clapping their hands, at the same time straining their voices to their utmost pitch, till at length they have no regard either to the tune, or the pauses, and seem rather a riotous, than a religious assembly. For this manner of worship they cite the Psalm of David, "O clap your hands all ye nations." Thus they misapply the sacred Writings, to defend practices, yet more corrupt than those I have been speaking of.[19]

Father Lobo's misapplication of European norms and customs to the Africanized Christianity he found in Ethiopia underscores both the divergence of the faith in black Africa from what Iberian Catholicism regarded as authentic New Testament religion, and the impossibility of any easy reconciliation that would render the Jesuits' arrogant and militant incursions acceptable to the Ethiopians. A mission of six Capuchin friars soon followed them, but it, too, failed when four of the missionaries were killed. The Muslim Turks, at the request of Emperor Fasiladas, successfully cut off any priests who attempted to reach the country. Groves adds, with cryptic understatement, "The net result of the Jesuit mission was to render the Abyssinians bitterly hostile to the Roman Catholic Church, and this attitude lasted long."

The Church of Nubia

As noted earlier, Judich, the "Ethiopian" eunuch, was the first Christian convert to enter the region the ancients knew as Kush or Nubia—the lands lying south of the First Cataract of the Nile. It was to the city of Meröe that he returned to his queen around A.D. 37 and, presumably, brought her the exciting news that the God of Israel, whom he came to Jerusalem to worship, had a Son whose name was Jesus, and that his Father had raised him from the dead. If the Meröe royal family and nobility had been persuaded by Judich and a church organized at that time, it would have antedated both the Coptic Church of Egypt and the Ethiopian Orthodox Church. What the early existence of such a church in the heart of Africa might have meant for the evangelization of the continent, the subsequent resistance thrown up against Islam, and the interdiction of the overland and trans-Atlantic slave trade, challenges our imagination. But as far as we know, the Meröitic kingdom was not Christianized by the eunuch, and it was not until the sixth century that the church was to be founded in Nubia by Byzantine missionaries.

In A.D. 500 the land that Arab authors knew as *Bilad an-Nubia,* or the country of Nubia, included Nobatia, lying below the First Cataract; Makuria, not well defined but located somewhere between the Second Cataract and Kabushiya—its capital being Dongola; and Alodia, or Alwa, the land extending from Kabushiya or Meröe to the confluence of the Blue and White Niles—its capital being Soba, a few miles east of present-day Khartoum. Perhaps the most important of these black people were the Nobatae because, in order to protect the southern border of Egypt at Aswan from a warlike people called the Blemmyes, a branch of the Beja tribe, the Roman Emperor Diocletian (284–304) invited the Nobatae to settle down as a buffer state between Egypt and the Blemmyes raiders.[20] It was therefore to the Nobatae that the first Christian missionaries, in the form of an imperial delegation from Constantinople, anti-Chalcedonians by confession, came to Nubia sometime around A.D. 543.

The Nobatae and other people inhabiting the Upper Nile Valley were adherents of an African Traditional Religion not unlike that found in other parts of the continent. They had a multiplicity of gods and goddesses, chief among whom was the Egyptian goddess Isis. According to one authority, however, an even greater god among the people near the border between Egypt and Nubia was the sun-god Mandulis, and, in Upper Nubia, Amon, the god of fertility whose cult originated in Pharaonic times. Other divinities of the Nubians included Horus, represented by a man's body with the head of a hawk, and Arensnuphis, depicted as a hunter and worshiped by both the Nubians and the Beja.

A historian of the times, Bishop John of Ephesus, wrote in his *Ecclesiastical History* that the Empress Theodora in Constantinople dispatched to the Nobatae, around 543, one Julian, an elderly presbyter of the Patriarch Theodosius of Alexandria. Julian had heard of a black people beyond the frontier of Egypt and was filled with a great passion to take the gospel to them. The Empress, who happened to share with Theodosius and Julian a Monophysite Christology, was almost thwarted by her husband, the Emperor Justinian, in her determination to be the first to bring the message about Christ to Nubia. Justinian, not to be outdone, tried to send a rival Orthodox mission with rich gifts for the king and people of Nobatia, but his wife succeeded in having the mission delayed until after Julian and his entourage could reach the country. Having failed to supercede the Monophysite embassy to the Nobatae, the Orthodox mission turned to the neighboring kingdom of Makuria with the result that the Makurians adopted the Chalcedonian or Melkite faith.[21]

After the death of Julian, a pious missionary called Longinus was made bishop by the Monophysite Patriarch Theodosius and sent to Nobatia to succeed Julian. Longinus was received with great celebration and remained in the country for six years. It was he who organized the Nubian church. He introduced the liturgy in Greek, the language of Byzantium, and, after crossing over neighboring Mukuria at the risk of his life at the hands of the new Chalcedonian Christians there, he entered the third of the Upper Nile kingdoms—Alodia, or Alwa—where he successfully founded a church which, along with the church in Nobatia, was loyal to the Monophysite see of Alexandria.

Thus the early evangelization of Nubia was marked by a see-sawing and sometimes violent competition between the episcopal proponents of the two prevailing views of the nature of Christ. In any case, by 580, Christianity had become the official religion of the three Nubian kingdoms, and a Byzantine form of the faith triumphantly raised the cross over the holy places and shrines of the former ATR in the heartland of black Africa. Perhaps no part of church history has been more neglected in Europe and North America, and, unfortunately, by Africans and African American believers, than the story of the faith in Nubia. That story is an essential element of what we might call the "first visit" of Christianity to Africa—extending across a period of six hundred years, from the conversion of the Ethiopian eunuch in about A.D. 37 and the coming of John Mark to Alexandria a few years later to the courageous mission of Longinus to the people of Alwa in Upper Nubia during the second half of the sixth century.

Despite incursions from the East by the Axumites and from the North by Persians, and the virtual encirclement of Nubia by Arabian Muslims in the seventh century, Christianity took root in the Upper Nile Valley, and the black churches and monasteries of Nubia flourished for more than eight hundred years! Scholars do not give a definite date for its final demise, which was the result of internal weaknesses, the failure to develop a native clergy, and the persistent onslaught of Islam, although dissension among members of the royal families in the thirteenth century was aggravated by the conspiracy of some of them with the Sultan Baybars in Egypt. This brought on the replacement of a series of Christian kings by Muslim kings in Dongola. Several crises after 1260 precipitated the collapse of Nubia and the virtual disappearance of Christianity over the next two or three centuries.

Even so, the longevity of Nubian Christianity is a remarkable fact of black history. Between 1974 and 1976 documents were discovered at Ibrim that mention Christian kings, bishops, and other officials of several Christian principalities that continued after the fall of Dongola to the Muslim Kanz family. These and other data suggest that perhaps one of those kingdoms, Dotawo, may well have existed as late as 1464—only twenty-eight years before Columbus sailed to the New World.

According to Fantini, the Portuguese Francisco Alvarez traveled to Ethiopia and Nubia in 1520. After returning home in 1527, he wrote a report that contained the following remark of John, a Syrian, who accompanied him on the Nubia leg of the long journey: "There are in it [Nubia] one hundred and fifty churches which still contain crucifixes and figures of Our Lady and other figures painted on the walls, and all old. He also reported," writes Fantini, "that the inhabitants had lost their faith, but had not yet become Muslims. 'They live in the desire of being Christians.'"[22]

Islam in Africa

The fourth great religion of Africa is Islam, which, from its inception, encompassed significant elements of the other three—African Traditional Religions, Judaism, and Christianity—and, on that account, presented itself to the world as the final and most complete revelation of God, known by his true name as Allah, with the Prophet Muhammad as his preeminent representative on earth. Islam's relationship to Africa was fundamental and instantaneous. One of the first converts to the new faith was a black man named Bilal, an African who lived in Mecca and became the first muezzin of Islam—the person who calls the faithful to prayer. Concerning the critical period before the hegira from Mecca in A.D. 622, Ibrahim Abu-Lughod writes:

> Muhammad counseled about forty of his disciples to seek refuge in Ethiopia, a country whose economic, cultural, and political links with Arabia are historic, and where they would be tolerated by its emperor and would preach the new faith as well. This very early coincidence of the Islamic presence in Africa made it possible to view Islam as a religious belief-system as indigenous to Africa as it was to West Asia.[23]

After the death of the Prophet in 632, when Muslim armies swept everything before them in Persia and Syria-Palestine, one of his generals, Amr Ibn al As, stormed into Egypt. The conquest was sudden and widespread. Shortly after 640 the Nile Valley, from Alexandria to the First Cataract, was in Muslim hands, although the Coptic Church in Egypt was tolerated because Christians and Jews were considered "People of the Book." Coptic remained the language of the liturgy; Arabic gradually became the language of many of the common people and Islam became their religion. In 641 Amr Ibn al As sent a military expedition across the southern border of Egypt, passing through Nobatia and reaching as far as the plain of Dongola before his army had to retreat in face of the unerring accuracy of the Nubian archers. Intermittent warfare and temporary peace settlements, requiring the Nubians to pay tributes of slaves to their Arab overlords, existed for five hundred years. With the beginning of the dynasty of King George I in Dongola, which lasted well into the eleventh century, a period of relative quiet prevailed in Nubia, despite the uneasiness of the church as many Christians converted to Islam.

One bishop, Abba Kyros, who occupied the episcopal see of Faras from 862 to 897, during the reign of George I, even bore the prestigious title "Metropolitan," indicating, among other things, that Islam did not greatly interfere with ecclesiastical organization (the Nubian church continued under the Patriarch of Alexandria) and showed more willingness to permit Christians to go on with their normal church life than European Christians were ever willing to grant the followers of the Prophet Muhammad.

The story of Islam's dramatic sweep through Cyrenaica to Morocco and ultimately across the Mediterranean to Spain is well known and need not be discussed here. It still comes as a shock to many African Americans to discover that "black Moors" not only conquered Catholic Spain, but they "blackenized" it and established outposts in Europe that lasted almost to the end of the fifteenth century. The softness and resilience of Iberian Catholicism (compared to Dutch or German Protestantism) can be partly accounted for by the long residence of a thoroughly Africanized Islam in Spain and Portugal.

Islam proceeded south of the Sahara with a markedly different strategy from the one the Christian crusaders of Europe used against the Muslims in Asia. In the first place, its straightforward and uncomplicated theology, resting on the so-called five pillars of duty,[24] made Islam easily understood by ordinary people. While powerful rulers like Mansa Musa of Mali and Askia Muhammad of Songhai were great patrons of Islamic culture as well as exemplary military leaders, the conquest of the western Sudan was accomplished by a relatively small army of the faithful who made peaceful and perhaps more effective proselytizers.

> They lived their own social life, marrying women of the countries where they were, but making them into Muslims and bringing up their children as good Muslims, educated to Muslim learning. They did not interfere in local politics to any great extent, and had a kind of special position when any local wars broke out. They traded over a vast area, exchanging the goods of the more northerly areas for gold, cola nuts, and slaves of the south. Oral tradition in northern Ghana still tells how the Gonja conquerors were met by a family of Muslim clerics who agreed to go forward with them, calling for God's blessing on what they were doing and advising them as they went along.[25]

African Traditional Religions, in those areas of the western Sudan where the Muslims carved out a foothold from which they have not been dislodged to this day, rarely experienced at the hands of Islam the bitter antagonism they received from Protestant Christianity when the evangelical missionary societies arrived near the end of the eighteenth century. Islam sometimes blended imperceptibly with ATR, content to permit Africans to call themselves Muslims without demanding more than minimal changes in belief structure and lifestyle. Much of West African culture, in terms of totem, rites of purification and invocation, reverence of ancestors, and the use of amulets and talismans, was left undisturbed as long as the pillars of Islam were upheld and Allah was entreated to make a person "a better Muslim." It may be said that the result was that ATR was enriched by the Arabic language, the Arabic emphasis on education, and the universal brotherhood of a highly diverse humanity, rather than rudely stamped out by stern and often racist expatriates bent on condemning everything African and saving the souls of the heathen.

The Second "Visit" of Christianity

Christianity made its second appearance in Africa in the same century that Columbus thought he had discovered a new route to India across the western sea. It was Portugal, a small country with fewer than two million inhabitants, that essayed to explore the coastline of Africa beyond the Canaries and Cape Bojador and carry the banner of Catholic Christianity to the "black Moors" they might encounter along the way. Prince Henry, justifiably dubbed "the Navigator," directed this enterprising Portuguese exploration, voyage by perilous voyage, between 1430 and his death in 1460, until the Senegambia had been reached and the sea lanes opened further south to Sierra Leone, the Gold Coast, Benin. And thenceforth, in rapid stages, the Cape of Good Hope was rounded by Vasco da Gama on 25 December 1497.

By 1442 some two hundred African slaves and a quantity of gold dust were already brought back to Portugal by Gil Eannes, one of Prince Henry's captains, and after forts had been established on the Guinea coast the influx of slaves increased with each voyage. When the Congo was reached and Diego Cam returned home in 1485, he brought with him slaves who were baptized. Later they boarded ship again and returned with Eannes and a large number of priests to begin the evangelization of the Congolese.[26]

By 1492 the mission to the Congo was proceeding apace. At the capital, two hundred miles inland from the coast, the king and queen were baptized under the Christian names of John and Leonora. The bishop of Sao Tome, an island off the Guinea coast, was probably the first black African to become a Roman Catholic bishop. Some authorities believe that the young man was none other than Alfonso, the crown prince. In any case, it is reported that his son, Henry, was educated in Lisbon and Rome, and was ordained to the priesthood. In 1518 the son became titular bishop of Utica and was appointed Vicar Apostolic of the Congo by Pope Leo X.[27]

Thus the Congo became the first Christian state in West Africa, but the faith was little more than a thin veneer that barely covered the royal family and a few nobles. No more so, of course, than it was in parts of Europe during the same period when animist worship of trees, stones, and springs existed alongside and under a patina of Christianity.[28] During the Roman Catholic effort in the Congo an appeal came up from the chief of a people further south, a vassal of King John of the Congo. Sometime later an expedition set out and established the faith in Angola by 1574, but with no greater depth of penetration among the populace.

Notwithstanding these deficiencies it appears that the Portuguese were able to plant Christian churches in West Africa in the fifteenth and sixteenth centuries, and many young African boys were sent to Europe to train for holy orders. But the roots were always shallow. The commercial interests of Portugal and the political machinations of the kings, contesting with one another for ascendancy, the demand of the missionaries for monogamy which threatened traditional marriage, the paltry instruction the people received before mass baptisms, and the subsequent lack of pastoral attention to guide them, and—most of all—the beginning of the Atlantic slave trade conspired to falsify and undermine the evangelizing effort.

By the end of the sixteenth century both Christian and Portuguese influence in West Africa had practically disappeared, albeit, as also happened in Nubia after the triumph of Islam, the faint afterglow of Iberian Catholicism suffused the attenuated memory of succeeding generations well into the nineteenth century. Holman Bentley, on arriving in the Congo in 1879, reported that he found "the sad relics of failure" used as fetishes by African Traditional Religionists. The chief and people paraded a large crucifix and images of saints around the town in times of drought. Some of the older people were called *minkwilizi* (believers) and functioned at great funerals using some of the relics of Christian worship.[29]

The Third "Visit" of Christianity

The third and definitive encounter between the Christian religion and Africans came in the late eighteenth and early nineteenth centuries. In that period African American slaves, who had fled or been evacuated from the American colonies with the British during the Revolutionary War, were rewarded with their freedom and, together with native African Christians, undertook the task of evangelizing their "heathen" brothers and sisters. One African historian calls the second visit of Christianity to Africa, which began with the Portuguese effort in the fifteenth century, "the era of frustration," and the third visit and more hospitable reception given to the faith between 1787 and 1893, "the era of promise."[30] Certainly the founding of the British colony of Sierra Leone for the repatriation of slaves from England and those intercepted by the British navy on the high seas was the most significant factor ensuring the success of the Protestant effort. It began when 411 former slaves, including 60 or 70 white women prostitutes from London who were to be their wives, sailed from Plymouth and landed at what was called the Province of Freedom on May 9, 1787.[31]

But the promise of the Sierra Leone settlement, conceived by Granville Sharp and other British abolitionists as a bulwark against the continuation and proliferation of the slave trade, was moot until the arrival of the former American slaves from Nova Scotia—under the leadership of the former black British army sergeant Thomas Peters and the highly regarded white abolitionist and naval officer John Clarkson. An evangelistic campaign was the primary motivation for bringing the group of black Methodist settlers, who embarked under the spiritual leadership of Boston King, and a smaller group of black Baptists under David George, a former slave who had fled with his congregation from Silver Bluff, South Carolina, to Savannah, Georgia, and from there to Nova Scotia. The fleet of 15 ships carrying 1,190 passengers, including 450 children, lowered anchor in the Sierra Leone River on March 16, 1792.[32]

The dream that Christians in England had that Sierra Leone would one day become a beacon of evangelical light for the Dark Continent was never fully realized, but the gospel did go abroad from the colony, preached by black men and women. This time the church took root, as also occurred almost simultaneously in the United States as black preachers gradually took over congregations that had been started or supervised by white men. It can be said, therefore, that Christianity found a permanent home in West Africa and in black America at about the same time, under black leadership in both places. In 1820 Christian churches were established in Liberia by African American ex-slaves who had been liberated by one means or another and who had returned to their motherland, for one purpose or another.

The major burden of this successful third "visit" of Christianity, this time to West Africa, was borne by native African sons and daughters themselves—converts like William Wadé Harris, a Grebo of Liberia; Thomas Birch Freeman, who was born in England of a mixed marriage; Samuel Adjai Crowther, who had a tragic career as the first African bishop of the Anglican Church; James "Holy" Johnson, a Yoruba, who became a bishop of the Anglican Synod of Nigeria; and Mother Martha Davies, of Freetown, Sierra Leone, who gathered a group of nine other Creole mothers and founded a "Confidential Band" in 1907 restricted to married women, to pray for, teach, and convert African people.[33]

Since the 1960s African Americans have been interested in what they might learn about their African Christian heritage from research into the nature of the groups in Africa that rejected missionary Christianity from Europe and North America, and established their own independent churches. In that direction may lie the answer to questions African American theologians and church leaders are asking about God's revelation to Africa prior to the arrival of whites and how what theologians call "common revelation" can be made coherent with biblical revelation. Instead of the history of missionary Christianity in West Africa, more relevant to the black churches of the United States may be the history of such independency or "instituted" movements as the Church of the Lord (Aladura) of Nigeria, the Kimbanguist Church of the Congo, the Cherubim and Seraphim Church of Nigeria, and the Army of the Cross of Christ Church of Ghana.[34]

West Africa and African American Religion

More research is needed before we can determine the extent to which both Judeo-Christian and Muslim ideas and practices were mixed, if only on the surface, with the ATR of West Africa. Many of the slaves who were brought to America had already been introduced to Islam, and some may well have brought some attenuated knowledge or wisps of faded influence from Christianity's three visits to the continent. Given the longevity of Nubian Christianity and its decay and leaching, via ancient caravan routes, into Darfur, Bornu, and possibly as far as Northern Nigeria and the eastern bank of the Niger, the cultures and religions of the western Sudan were probably not as isolated and quarantined as some have supposed. After all, even contacts that were more distant than Nubia were known.

"Roman beads," writes H. H. Johnston, "are dug up in Hausaland and are obtained from the graves of Ashanti chiefs," and "Christianized Berbers from North Africa even carried Jewish and Christian ideas of religion as far into the Dark Continent as Borgu, to the west of the Lower Niger."[35] Given that Johnston was infected with the "Second Hamitic hypothesis" which held that any evidences of high civilization in the Western Sudan must have come from outside Black Africa, we should be suspicious of some of his claims, but it comes as no surprise that there were and continue to be borrowings back and forth between Christianity, Islam, and ATR from at least the eleventh century on. The three great faiths accommodated themselves to one another both in West Africa and in America. "God," claimed some of the Muslim slaves imported to Georgia, "is Allah, and Jesus Christ is Mohammed—the religion is the same, but different countries have different names."[36]

The assimilation of Islam and Christianity into ATR should no more prejudice the primal values inherent in the traditional religions of West Africa than the other way around. Students of West African societies insist on an independent development of many religious ideas in the traditional religions that found their way into both ancient and new churches on the continent and today can enrich both Christianity and Islam outside Africa. Kofi Asare Opoku, a critic of missionary Christianity and European anthropologists who continue to march around the countries adjacent to the Gulf of Guinea in search of material for doctoral dissertations, writes:

> The West continues to hold up to Africa its perverted image of the African past, and anything that does not fit into that image is dismissed or attributed to non-African sources. Westerners attributed the Yoruba statues to Egyptian influence, the art of Benin to Portuguese creation, and the architectural ruins of Great Zimbabwe to the Arabs. . . . In recent years, Carl Sagan could write, in connection with the astronomical knowledge of the Dogon of West Africa: "I picture a Gallic visitor to the Dogon people. . . . He may have been a diplomat, an explorer, an adventurer, or an early anthropologist."[37]

The African Inheritance

We cannot delve into the complexities of ATR during the last five hundred years. It should be sufficient here at the end of this discussion to note that our study of African beginnings not only shows the antiquity of the black Christian church but also indicates that many of the great religious ideas and spirituality of Judaism, Christianity, and Islam arose spontaneously not only in Egypt but, at about the same time, also far to the West. Within the great bend of the Niger and Congo rivers the indigenous ATR revealed to the black inhabitants of that region some of the same answers to the deep-seated questions of human existence that other peoples have sought in other times and places. Yet it seems also irrefutable that, despite significant differences, the essential truths of African Traditional Religions, Judaism, Christianity, and Islam have reinforced one another in diverse times and places across the broad stretch of sub-Saharan Africa. Thus we acknowledge the mystery of the universal revelation of God. Some knowledge of the true God, the Creator and Sustainer of the universe, was given to the African people long before the "arrival" of Judaism from Palestine, the three "visits" of Christianity from Palestine and Europe, and the conquest of Islam from Arabia. With particular reference to Christianity, it is not too rash to speculate that the relative ease with which these later introductions were able to mix with the belief systems of ATR had something to do with the alacrity with which many of the slaves who were taken to the New World were able to convert and syncretize their new faith in Jesus with the religious traditions they brought with them across the Atlantic.

Monotheism or "monarchial polytheism"; the concept of a High God and lesser divinities who open the way, serve, or are the messengers of

God; the voluntary recession or forced separation of God from his/her creation which requires appeasement through blood sacrifice, redemptive suffering, and other means of reconciliation and reunion; the necessity of rites of purification, glorification, thanksgiving, and supplication; the gradations of visible and invisible power—from personal charisma to impersonal spiritual forces that can do good or evil and ultimately to the omnipotence of a Supreme Being—all these more or less characteristic aspects of many African Traditional Religions find correspondence with aspects of the Judeo-Christian tradition.

From Senegambia, around the Gulf of Guinea, to the Congo and Angola (not to mention peoples within Equatorial and Southern Africa) devotees of ATR have found in both Christianity and Islam sufficient cognizance of the God and gods of their ancestors to make it possible and desirable for them to adhere to both religions simultaneously, keeping one or the other in reserve ready to be called for as the changes of life occur. The tremendous proliferation and popularity of the independent or "instituted" Christian churches in these areas since the latter half of the nineteenth century bear eloquent testimony to the affinity between the traditional religions and the religion about Jesus and the latter's ability to penetrate and enrich the people's devotional life. Many observers recognize the possibilities inherent in this affiliation and its implications for the future of an Africentric form of Christianity disengaged from Euro-American cultural and religious hegemony.

> The love affair between Christ and the church on the African continent goes back two millennia. At the present time the church has a future and possibilities more dazzling than anything we can imagine, if only she can dissociate herself from some of the misdeeds of her rascally self-appointed friends of the past (and of the present in southern Africa). Perhaps, at last we may be allowed to discern her as she really is, in all her beauty, black and comely and arrayed as a bride for her Lord.[38]

Having explored the taproot of Christianity as it emerged, disappeared from sight, and returned to Africa again to be reconstituted and reinterpreted under a sometimes racist European and sometimes compliant Islamic proselytization, the Atlantic slave trade, native evangelism, and the fluctuating resistance today of African Traditional Religions and a money-mad and materialistic secularism, we should have some appreciation of the contention of some Africentric scholars that it is wrong to separate the history of black religion in America from its African crucible.

Today, more than ever, it needs to be made clear to African American Christians, and to white American Christians as well, that the distinctive spiritual gifts and sensibilities of black people that were melted and molded prior to the Middle Passage, and that underwent resurgence in the "invisible institution" of the brush arbor churches of the antebellum period, the Azusa Revival of 1906, and the movements for civil rights and countervailing power in the 1960s, are still available. They are ready to be used by those who want to challenge the deficiencies and excesses of conventional Christianity and proffer to the world that "something new," if not that mysterious "metempsychosis" of which the great Du Bois spoke.

We need to celebrate the fact that, despite ignorance, prejudice, and suppression, African spirituality found refuge in the religion of the slave—until liberation came and the essence of that ancient spirituality reasserted itself in the African American churches of the twentieth century. It is a precious inheritance that we still have but that can too easily dissolve into nothingness if black Christians fail to be self-critical, to be wary of corruptions, inauthenticity, and trivialization, and determined to use the gifts that God has given us for the edification and healing of the world.

The Protestant theologians of Europe and America will doubtless go on rummaging the legacies of Luther, Calvin, and Wesley and the insights of Barth, Brunner, and the Niebuhrs. There is nothing wrong with that except they may never understand what Pope Paul VI was talking about when he told the African bishops assembled in Kampala, "You must now give your gifts of blackness to the whole church."[39]

8

The Black Messiah

Revising the Color Symbolism of Western Christology

In *An Introduction To African Civilizations,* Willis N. Huggins and John G. Jackson write, "One of the earliest flares of the race and color question" is recorded in hieroglyphics on a hugh granite stele erected about 2,000 B.C. by the Egyptian Pharaoh of the Twelfth dynasty, Usertesan III. It stood like a modern highway sign on the boundary with Nubia and contained the following advertisement:

> No Black man whatsoever shall be permitted to pass this place going down stream (the Nile) no matter whether he is traveling by desert or journeying in a boat except such Blacks as come to do business in the country or traveling on an embassy. Such, however, shall be well treated in every way whatsoever. But no boats belonging to Blacks, shall in the future be permitted to pass down this river.[1]

In India race prejudice may be as much as five thousand years old. Here we see blackness, believed to be a contemptible color, being rejected by Indra, the God of Aryas. The Rig-Veda describes an invasion of the land of a dark-skinned people by the Aryas or Aryans. The God Indra is described as "blowing away with supernatural might from the earth and from the heavens the black skin which Indra hates." The account goes on to tell how Indra slew the flat-nosed barbarians, and after conquering the land for the Aryas, he ordered the Anasahs to be flayed of their black skin with whips.[2]

During the Middle Ages Talmudic and Midrashic sources sought to explain blackness with such suggestions as "Ham was smitten in his skin" or that Noah told Ham "your seed will be ugly and dark-skinned" or that Canaan was "the notorious world darkener."[3]

Frank M. Snowden makes the following observation concerning the ancient Greeks and Romans:

> There was a belief in certain circles that the color of the Ethiopian's skin was ominous, related no doubt to the association of the color black with death, the underworld, and evil. It was noted, for example, among omens presaging disaster that ill-starred persons were known to have seen an Ethiopian before their misfortune. An Ethiopian who met the troops of Cassius and Brutus as they were proceeding to battle was considered an omen of disaster. Among the events listed as foreshadowing the death of Septimius Severus was his encounter with an Ethiopian.[4]

These and other evidences of color prejudices from ancient times, no matter how naive and blameless, seem to cast doubt on the allegation of some Western historians and cultural anthropologists that "real" prejudice against black skin color is of very recent origin.

It is true that not until justification was needed for the African slave trade did what scholars today call racism develop as such. But to regard racism as only the highly reasoned, pseudo-scientific theory of the natural superiority of whites over blacks and other people of color that arose in the nineteenth century seems much too limiting. Some people evidently assigned a pejorative meaning to blackness long before the beginning of African slavery—for whatever reason—and if the Bible itself seems relatively free of this bias (which is questionable) another explanation is available. The Jews, after many years of residence and intermarriage in Africa, were themselves a dark-skinned people by the time the Hebrew Bible had been written. Victims of prejudice themselves, the medieval Jews simply consigned black people to a lower status than themselves. It was not the Jews of the Old Testament period but the Jews and Gentiles of medieval Europe—particularly those of northern Europe and Great Britain—who were repelled by black skin color and African physiognamy and gave renewed vigor to the prejudice that had been sporadic and peripheral in the ancient world. Hence the Hamitic hypothesis in the Babylonian Talmud of the Middle Ages.

We should not be surprised, therefore, when we come to the nineteenth century and find such low opinions of black people by an American divine, the Reverend Buchner Payne.

> Now as Adam was white, Abraham white and our Savior white, did he enter heaven when he arose from the dead as a white man or as a negro? If as a white man, then the negro is left out; if as a negro then the white man is left out. As Adam was the Son of God and as God is light (white) and in Him is no darkness (black) at all, how could God then be the father of the negro, as like begets like? And if God could not be the father of the blacks because He was white, how could our Savior "being in the express image of God's person," as asserted by St. Paul, carry such a damned color into heaven, where all are white, much less to the throne?[5]

There is no point in wrangling over what is meant by racism, either ancient or modern. Its victims know immediately what it is. If one prefers one skin color over another, whether white over black or black over white, with the implication of aesthetic, genetic, or cultural superiority, the seeds of racial prejudice are already present. Racism waits in the door. And when that preference is not simply a natural, subconscious ethnocentrism but a self-justifying, egregious concomitant of economic, political, and cultural domination and exploitation, color prejudice is raised to the level of an ideology that stretches from a rather benign form of "racial thinking" to full-blown racial hatred, brutality, and potential genocide. That is an all too human phenomenon—a perfect example, from a biblical perspective, of original sin. It exists with or without sophisticated theories and systematic theological rationalizations. It may be conscious or unconscious, continuous or sporadic. But it is racism and it originated far back in human history, although its prototypical and classic expression is found in white European and North American societies where it attained its most developed and malicious form during the period of the enslavement of Africans in the New World.

One might suspect that the argument of the anthropologist Ruth Benedict that white racism is of recent origin and must be limited in classification to the late pseudo-scientific theories of racial purity in Europe is a well-intentioned attempt by liberal scholarship to make the historic rejection of blackness and African ancestry a secondary and even peripheral characteristic of Western civilization that will soon lose its beguilement of enlightened minds. White people, in other words, are not as prejudiced as they seem and have been so only a short time. But the dychotomy of whiteness and blackness, despite the incursion of a whole new spectrum of colors and ethnicities in multicultural America of the twenty-first century, is still with us. The imputation of positive value to light skin color and negative value to darker skin continues to be deeply embedded in the consciousness of the white people of Western Europe and the Americas, and has been elevated almost to the status of an ontology. God himself is white for most Western Christians, and the Christian faith itself, as inextricably bound as it is to the history, culture, and power of the predominantly white North Atlantic community, is unmistakably a white religion.

That is not a fantastic claim concocted by black storefront preachers after the turn of the twentieth century to persuade their ghettoized and impoverished followers to resist white domination and exploitation. It is not a wild allegation dreamed up by the Rastafarians, the Black Jews, or the Black Muslims during the highly popular ministry of Malcolm X. It just happens to be the simple, unadorned truth about what was given out to African Americans with their chains. The Christianity of the slave owner and his preacher was a shamefully distorted and corrupt religion that was believed by most white Euro-Americans and accepted by many blacks.

Roger Bastide, in a brilliant analysis of color symbolism in Western Christianity, writes:

> Although Christ transcends all questions of race or ethnology, it must not be forgotten that God incarnated himself in a man of the Jewish race. The Aryans and the Gentiles—even the most anti-Semitic—worship their God in a Jewish body. But this Jewish body was not white enough for them. The entire history of Western painting bears witness to the deliberate whitening or bleaching effort that changed Christ from a Semitic to an Aryan person. The dark hair that Christ was thought to have had come to be rendered a very light-color, and his big, dark eyes as blue. It was necessary that this man, the incarnation of God, be as far removed as possible from everything that could suggest darkness or blackness, even indirectly.
>
> His hair and his beard were given the color of sunshine, the brightness of the light above, while his eyes retained the color of the sky from which he descended and to which he returned. The progressive Aryanization of Christ is in strict accordance with the logic of the color symbolism. It did not start, however, until Christianity came into close contact with the other races—with the African race, in particular. Christian artists began to avoid the darker tints in depicting Christ in order to remove as much as possible of their evil suggestion.[6]

Eulalio R. Baltazar makes this further comment implicating Calvinism and later white Protestantism as a whole in this conspiracy of color symbolism in Euro-American racism:

> To see the transference of the black-white symbolism from the theological to the economic, the key concept is that of election. In the theological sense, white skin came to mean the possession of grace and spiritual poverty, the "voluntary and stubborn abandonment of race in sin." Under the influence of Calvinism and later Puritanism, however, the notion of election became secularized to mean economic and material success. The whiteness or blackness of the skin accordingly came to have a secular meaning also. Thus whiteness of skin came to symbolize material, scientific and technological successes while blackness of skin came to be equated with a prescientific mentality, with economic poverty and with ignorance.[7]

More recently African Americans, with the more sophisticated tools of scholarship in languages, ancient Christian history, theology, and biblical studies, have returned to W. E. B. Du Bois, Rufus Perry, William L. Hansberry, and other black writers of the late nineteenth and early twentieth centuries to question the uses and abuses of Egyptian, Ethiopian, and Nubian ethnicity and black skin color in early Christian discourses. Such discourses reflect theological and cultural inclusion or exclusion related to the exigencies of orthodoxy.

This renewed interest in how ancient peoples regarded color differences arises from several different motivations. Some arise from Africentrists interested in uncovering the neglected role of black people in the early Greco-Roman civilization for the purpose of building black pride and self-esteem; other motivations belong to racial justice activists searching for evidence of racism in Western culture in order to attack contemporary white racism at its roots; still others come from scholars intent on learning more about early Christian writings and how "ethno-political rhetorics" shaped sociopolitical ideologies in the past and influence the way we relate to one another today. Together they represent a new countervailing scholarship against the facile assumptions of some liberal whites who, still remembering the progressive stances of Ruth Benedict, Ashley Montague, and other cultural anthropologists of an earlier period, insist that race prejudice is of recent origin and is ephemeral in advanced societies. Gay L. Byron, who has studied symbolic blackness in the rhetoric of the early Christians, describes the result of contemporary research in the field:

> No longer can one claim that the early Christians were oriented around a universalist worldview that extended its arms to the ends of the earth. No longer is it acceptable to dismiss the possibility that ethnic and color differences played a significant role in the Greco-Roman world, in general, and in early Christianity in particular. No longer is it possible to claim that the references to ethnic and color-coded language are sporadic and exceptional in ancient Christian literature.[8]

Some contemporary African American scholars are loath to identify what they find in this literature as racism. But it is not stretching the point too much to refer to the rhetoric of the early exponents and defenders of the faith as preracist ideas and sentiments that would have humiliated and angered black folks today. Whatever historians of antiquity want to call it, few would deny that those ideas and sentiments helped to provide insulting discourse and legitimation for the later denigration and subjugation of people of color. What Africans and African American Christians have suffered at the hands of their Caucasian brothers and sisters in the faith cannot be divorced from rhetorical habits that were formed in the first few centuries of the Christian era, simply on the excuse that the early white Christian writers were innocent of the kind of color prejudice that can be considered malicious or racist. It seems naive to suppose that the calamities African peoples have suffered in this world are not related, in some significant ways, to the various combinations of feelings of superiority, fear, sexual attraction and repulsion, guilt, contempt, and hostility that many white Christians have long experienced in the presence of blackness.

As a young boy running around the streets of North Philadelphia I used to hear some of the older boys quote the lines:

> Dark man born of a dark woman sees dark days,
> Rises up in the morning like a hopper grass,
> Cut down in the evening like asparagas.

This harsh truth in the mouths of children is repeatedly authenticated every day for the masses of African Americans. It forces us, in our striving for a way out of the meaninglessness and absurdity of the connection between blackness and oppression, to search at the most profound depths of our religious sensibilities for something that contradicts that historic coherence. Instead of creating for ourselves the sentimental illusion that the coherence does not really exist (for the sheer intensity of what it takes to exist in a white-dominated world makes that assumption hard to sustain), black Christians can create a new meaning for the interpenetration of color and calamity. Rather than trying to whitenize blackness by deculturating or bleaching our inheritance and obliterating our memory of "how we were," and thus becoming—as many of our race have already become—a "dark white people," we can make blackness positive and enhancing for those who continue to struggle against the evil and degradation it has symbolized to many white Christians. We can perceive it as a symbol of the age old human warfare against the sterile, oppressive whiteness of the principalities and powers that oppress us all. Blackness can then take on ideological and theological meaning that is grounded in the experience of the universal human struggle for liberation and redemption.

This reinterpretation of the color symbolism of Christianity has been a consistent principle of radical black religion. But radical black religion has seldom been the choice of the majority of African American Christians. Only a few black leaders, such as Robert Alexander Young, Bishop Henry M. Turner of the AME Church, Bishop George Alexander McGuire of the African Orthodox Church, Marcus M. Garvey, and Jaramogi Abebe Agyeman (Albert Cleage), had the intellectual courage and prophetic zeal to speak of a Black Messiah and attempt a fundamental revision of the color symbolism of Christianity. Most were so intimidated by the powerful white symbolism of Euro-American cultures that they could not personally authorize a structure of religious belief that gave blackness a constructive theological meaning without falsifying daily experience.

But in the last few years, as the masses of black people in Africa and the Caribbean basin experience, however imperfectly and painfully, political independence and self-determination for the first time in almost five hundred years, and as African Americans still search for the meaning of the culture and religion that once sustained them, a new possibility opens up. A new structure of meaning for blackness is now accessible and is able not only to transform the external or physical features of economic, political, and cultural landscape but can also transform the inner life of the people through a reinterpretation of Christian symbolism. Newbell N. Puckett was no friend of ours, but he spoke a truth that was more of a theological boomerang than he realized.

> The mere fact that a people profess to be Christian does not necessarily mean that their Christianity is of the same type as our own. The way in which a people interpret Christian doctrines depends largely upon their secular customs and their traditions of the past. . . . Most of the time the Negro outwardly accepts the doctrines of Christianity but goes on living according to his own conflicting secular mores, but sometimes he enlarges upon the activities of God to explain certain phenomena not specifically dealt with in the Holy Scripture.[9]

If indeed the God of the oppressor is a different God than the God of the oppressed, it is high time for black Christians of today to place at the center of their understanding of the gospel the affirmation that the God whom they worship and glorify did in the past and still does identify with their suffering and yearning for liberation. Black theologians and black denominations have not yet made that unmistakably clear enough to impact the normal acts of worship, study, and action at the congregational level. When Moses and Aaron went to the people to relate the message that Moses had received in the land of Midian, the Bible tells us, "And the people believed; and when they heard that the Lord had visited the people of Israel and that he had seen their affliction, they bowed their heads and worshiped (Exodus 4:31).

God reveals himself in solidarity with the affliction of the oppressed by the revelation of his Son, Jesus Christ, as the Oppressed One or Oppressed Servant of God. Although the slaves did not articulate this belief as a *black theology* in the sense that we understand that term today, they did recognize themselves in the description of the Lord's Servant in Isaiah 53. Generations of the oppressed have pondered the meaning of the Suffering or Oppressed Servant in relation to their own condition but none more consistently than the sons and daughters of Africa and the diaspora. They were struck not only with the similarity of what seemed to be their inexorable fate as a race and the Messianic vocation of redemptive suffering. They recognized the strange, if not exact, correspondence between their experience of blackness in the societies of white people and the description of the Messianic figure in Isaiah 53:1–3.

> He had no form or comeliness that we should look at
> Him, and no beauty that we should desire him.
> He was despised and rejected by men;
> a man of sorrows, and acquainted with grief . . .
> And we esteemed him not.

Only the story of the Exodus from Egyptian captivity, the scriptural prefigurement of black emancipation in the nineteenth century, compares with the suggested identity of biblical prophecy and the historic experience of black women and men in the West. Unless, of course, we are speaking about the Jews themselves, and, in that connection, one can appreciate what has been a deep affinity that existed for many years between the two peoples in the United States. Here are other relevant passages from Isaiah 53.

> He was oppressed, and he was afflicted,
> Yet he opened not his mouth;
> like a lamb that is led to the slaughter,
> and like a sheep that before its shearers is dumb,
> so he opened not his mouth.
> By oppression and judgment he was taken away;
> and as for his generation, who considered
> that he was cut out of the land of the living.

It is the symbolic meaning of blackness in relation to redemptive suffering, and not the claim that Jaramogi makes for the actual skin color of Jesus, that gives warrant to our designation of Jesus as the Black Messiah. To call Christ the Black Messiah is not to infer that he looked like an African from south of the Sahara, although he may have been darker than many African Americans, considering the likelihood of the mixture of the Jewish genetic pool with those of people from the upper Nile valley. Nor are we implying, by calling Jesus the Black Messiah, that other people may not find it meaningful to speak of him as the White Messiah, the Yellow Messiah, the Red Messiah, or, indeed, the homosexual, lesbian, bisexual, transgendered, or physically challenged Messiah! There is no basis for exclusion here. Nevertheless, African American men and women have been among the first American groups, again after converted Jews themselves, to claim this special affiliation with Jesus, the Crucified Messiah.

To speak of Jesus Christ as the Black Messiah is to invest blackness, particularly in the United States and South Africa, with religious meaning expressing the preeminent reality of suffering in the historical experience of blacks in Africa and the diaspora. But more than that, it is to find in the mystery of Christ's death and resurrection a theological explanation of all undeserved suffering and oppression, and an ultimate liberation. To speak of the Messiah figure in terms of the ontological significance of the color black is to provide both black and other people with a way of understanding the relevance of the Person and Work of Christ for existence under the conditions of humiliation, subjugation, and subordination. It is to call both the black and the white churches to the vocation of sacrificial involvement in the liberation of the poor, the outcast, and the oppressed in history.

The symbolic power of this Christological formulation has not yet been fully disentangled from all the various difficulties it poses, nor has its possibilities been fully explored. That is the future work of black and womanist theologians who are attracted by the potential of this radical way of thinking and what it can mean for Christians in situations of social and political submersion.

In the meantime, perhaps the most serious challenge to the implications of this concept is presented by humanist philosophers. In his still provocative book on theodicy, the black theologian William R. Jones contends that any theology which presumes that black suffering is redemptive either denies the existence of God or makes him a demon.[10]

I do not think that the Christian nonviolent love philosophy of Martin Luther King Jr., or a specific interpretation of black suffering such as the one offered by Joseph R. Washington,[11] satisfies the demands of the symbolic Christology I am proposing here. Jones's objections are telling with respect to all of us; nevertheless, what I have to say about the theology of the Black Messiah will briefly engage the position he takes. In the remainder of this chapter I intend to suggest that my own approach to the concept of the Black Messiah is the most meaningful way to understand the cross as the eternal presentation of the judging and gracious presence of the poor, outcast, and the oppressed in the world that God loved and to which He gave His only perfect incarnation of His self.

Jesus comes to us as the Oppressed One or as the Oppressed Servant of God. He comes not only to atone for our sins but to destroy the powers of evil that rule the world, and to bring an end to the contradictions and conflicts that have been introduced into human affairs since the Fall. That was the Messianic work of reconciliation and peace-making to which the Apostle Paul referred when he wrote, "For in him all the fullness of God was pleased to dwell, and through him to reconcile to himself all things, whether on earth or in heaven, making peace by the blood of his cross" (Colossians 1:19–20).

One reconciles with that from which one is estranged or in conflict. Throughout the New Testament there is testimony to the fact that the conflict is not merely personal and interpersonal but is cosmic in scope. Liberation and reconciliation has to do with more than the plight of the poor and oppressed and our feeble striving. In II Peter 3:13 we read that "according to his promise we wait for new heavens and a new earth, where righteousness is at home."

Where did this cosmic estrangement and conflict come from which is taken up, experienced, and canceled out on the cross? It comes from our perennial disobedience, which has caused all of us to pretend to be God instead of the fallible women and men that we are. Even the law was not able to reconcile the creation. It was rather God's gracious judgment upon our finite, sinful human existence that in both its highest moral attainments under the Law and its most miserable sinfulness, except for God's redemptive intervention, we would remain frustrated, incapacitated, broken by an intrinsic imperfection symbolized in biblical language by the difference between heaven and earth, the creature and the Creator.

> So I find it to be a law that when I want to do right, evil lies close at hand. For I delight in the law of God, in my inmost self, but I see in my members another law at war with the law of mind and making me captive to the law of sin which dwells in my members. Wretched man that I am! Who will deliver me from this body of death? (Romans 7:21–24)

Here the Apostle Paul is not speaking merely of the physical form of flesh and blood. This "war," this "body of death," are symbolic representations of human experience itself; of existence in conflict with itself, of a universe in "bondage to decay." It is in this world of conflict and contradiction that the guiltless will suffer equally with the guilty, thereby revealing a fatal deficiency in all human virtue and the indiscriminate applicability of the law of sin and death. In this world evil must prosper, if only to destroy itself in the end by the very consequence of its momentary subversion of the orders of creation and the plan of redemption.

This aspect of the doctrines of creation and redemption reveals the inescapable anguish and doom that is the inevitable harvest of both human powerlessness and power, misery and exaltation. The Bible tells us that this is what life is really like in the world—for all people, black and white, saints and sinners alike. It is written, "Everything before them is vanity, since one fate comes to all, to the righteous and the wicked, to the good and evil, to the clean and the unclean. . . . This is an evil in all that is done under the sun, that one fate comes to all (Ecclesiastes 9:1–3). Such is the nature of the inexplicable conflict that the Apostle Paul saw in his own life and found etched into the very structure of the universe which groans in travail waiting for its redemption along with the sons and daughters of God.

Of course, there is a great mystery shrouding human responsibility or irresponsibility for the condition of earthly existence which the Apostle describes. The problem of moral guilt and finitude has been debated for centuries, and there is still no easy solution. This is the paradox of the Book of Job and even before Job, of Adam and Eve, who, as human creatures made in the image of God who gave them all that they needed for life and happiness, yet lusted for the fruit of the tree of the knowledge of good and evil—a tree, let us remember, whose fruit was good for eating and a delight to the eyes. And yet tempted by Satan rather than overcome by the evil designs of their own hearts, they taste the tree's good fruit only to receive banishment and death (Gen. 3:6). Paul wrestles with the paradox and mystery of this strange contradiction of life under law and grace.

> What then shall we say? That the law is sin? By no means! Yet, if it had not been for the law, I should not have known sin . . . the very commandment which promised life proved to be death for me. (Romans 7:7–10)

So it is that in this life of unresolvable contradictions, where both goodness and evil, sin and virtue, oppression and liberation seem to cancel each other out, it is precisely in this hopeless condition, this closed circle of futility, that God, for a little while, has made us humans a little lower than the angels and crowned us with glory and honor, subjecting all things under our feet (Hebrews 2:7–8). Into this life the Messiah comes in human flesh, choosing blackness as the condition of his incarnation in order to be in solidarity with the most abused and wretched of his brothers and sisters. He entered into their historical existence at a given time and place—during the reign of Emperor Caesar Augustus, when Quirinius was governor of Syria and Herod the king of Judea—and henceforth struggles alongside of them on the stage of real history, in good days and bad days, until he wins the final victory.

By becoming black, which is to say, by suffering humiliation, oppression, and death, God revealed to humankind the nature of its existence in a fallen world and God's decision to be identified with both our willful self-assertion and our sometimes virtuous but always frustrated hopes. Jesus took upon himself our blackness as a badge of his own forsakeness, and thus, by being the extreme antithesis to what the world esteemed, he dramatically demonstrated his determination to save to the uttermost, to share his victory with "the least of these" (Matthew 25:45).

If blackness is made to symbolize endangerment, bondage, suffering, and death, then we can say that God became black! Black liberation Christology affirms that the God of the universe became black in order to show us human beings that blackness is the ultimate reality for life in a fallen and unjust world. The crucified and risen Christ reveals that the final reconciliation of blackness and whiteness, of the slave and the slave master, of those in prison and those who stand guard over them, of the oppressed and the oppressors, of death and life, though not within the bounds of our puny power, is within the boundless possibilities of God, through the grace of the Black Messiah, who is the incarnation of the invisible Creator, our Lord Jesus Christ.

What then is the meaning of the historical struggle of the oppressed for liberation? Is it only a stage play whose illusions dissolve with the fall of the last curtain, a divine hoax? No, because it is not only in victory, but in the anguish of *the struggle itself* that the oppressed come closest to realizing the meaning of their existence and gracious union with the Oppressed Servant of God: "to make all men see what is the plan of the mystery hidden for ages in God who created all things" (Ephesians 3:9). And, on their part, the oppressors begin to realize the judgment God has pronounced upon their sin-saturated efforts to become gods over their brothers and sisters whom God gave them to love and care for, not to humiliate, subjugate, and destroy. Yet in that very judgment lies the possibility of their redemption: "for this is why," writes the Apostle Peter, "the gospel was preached even to the dead, that though judged in the flesh like men, they might live in the spirit like God" (I Peter 4:6).

The meaning of the liberation of the oppressed is inclusive. Its message is that all of us will become conscious of the fact that the humanizing struggle for life, hope, and true freedom in the world shows that God created all of us for freedom in God's self. Perhaps that is the meaning of Christ's words from the cross. "Father, into thy hands I commend my spirit." In God's hands is perfect freedom. The stage is set for our freedom by the manifestation of the liberation of the Oppressed One in the event of the resurrection and in his exaltation. That event becomes the ultimate liberation, for without diminishing the significance of historical struggle for political, economic, and cultural liberation, our one and only hope is the resurrection of the Black Messiah. It was his victory that guarantees that defeat and death have no final dominion over the poor and oppressed who will share his triumph.

In the suffering of the struggle both the oppressed and the oppressors are given warning of the judgment and an intimation of the grace sufficient for salvation. But we are not talking here about a secular struggle presumed to be exclusively the business of politicians, scientists, and the experts in governmental affairs. The gospel must be preached to the powers as an accompaniment of the struggle itself. For when the church proclaims the gospel and acts on the strength of its promises, it makes clear that the struggle is a part of God's liberating action in Jesus Christ, not merely a contest of opposing forces that have no relation to Jesus Christ. In such a struggle not only are the oppressed uplifted and emboldened by the good news of their incorporation into the Oppressed One on the cross and the victory they already share with him but the oppressors, witnessing the power of the Word themselves, may also be drawn into the ambience of God's purpose to save to the uttermost by the blood of the cross.

In the resistance of those who are oppressed and the proclamation of God's refusal to permit their misery to be more than they can bear, the oppressor can discover that the downtrodden cannot be destroyed forever, because God forever stands against those who exercise unauthorized mastery over the least of his children. This is the essence of the good news we must believe and proclaim. Historically this has been the message of the African American churches. But, as Martin Luther King Jr., one of the two or three greatest Christian theologians of the twentieth century, always made plain, the oppressor who seeks to dehumanize his sisters and brothers is himself humanized by their faithful resistance, by the realization of the limits of his own power, and by the dawning realization that he needs to turn around and be forgiven. When the gospel is proclaimed and demonstrated as an accompaniment of God's liberation of the oppressed, its power frees the oppressor from his delusion of omnipotence and, through the agency of restitution and reparation, gives him or her the assurance of mercy and reconciliation as the consequence of true repentance.

By this theological framework for understanding the significance of the cross for the struggle of the oppressed I have attempted to show how the title of the Black Messiah is consonant with the experience, faith, and hope of African and African American Christians and other struggling people for whom blackness may symbolize oppression and whiteness the arrogance of dominating power. This turning of the color symbolism of Western Christianity on its head is the distinctive characteristic of black theology in the United States.[12] It is perhaps one of the most important reasons why many of us have not called what we are doing "African American theology" but insist that ours is still a "black theology."

Just as the truth of Good Friday had to await the event of Easter morning, the transhistorical truth of the liberation of humankind from the oppression of blackness and the delusion of whiteness awaits the consummation of God's purposes for the whole creation. In the meantime black liberation is real and God is on our side. That, I think, is where William R. Jones's otherwise compelling critique of black theology is in error. Precisely in the midst of conflict and suffering, the wretched of the earth, typified in black theology by the dehumanized and oppressed people of color, experience liberation by the power of God's saving Word. This liberation is not dependent for its realization on the cessation of conflict and suffering. It transcends political, economic, and social freedoms while nonetheless including them. That is why African Americans joyfully celebrated their freedom in Christ long before January 1, 1863, and ever since have understood that emancipation is both a historical event and a continuing process.

Racism has been one of the most endemic features of the white societies of the West. Despite all the research done and all the words that have been written we do not yet fully understand why black skin color and calamity have been so inseparable in white civilizations, but, authenticated by the concept of the Black Messiah, the struggle against that historic coherence appears to us as a victory already confirmed. What we do know for certain is that God has not forsaken black people nor rendered their struggle meaningless. Indeed, it may well be that God has given us the key to the real meaning of the gospel for all struggling people through our peculiar identity with the doom and resurrection of the oppressed and liberated Son of God.

9

Black Consciousness

Stumbling Block or Battering Ram?

African American theologians, no less than others in the United States, worry about the corrosive effects of extreme pluralism on the theological fidelity of the church. Indeed, part of the vehemence of black theology was in response to the allegation that there was no theology worthy of the name among black Christians, and that the low level of biblical and doctrinal understanding in the mainstream black denominations is deplorable. In response I would venture to say that black Christians have been more willing to consider the hopeful and redemptive possibilities of culture—particularly the possibilities of our African American subculture, infused as it is with black pragmatic spirituality and corporate action for justice—than are many of our friends and colleagues on the other side of the color line.

This more positive and hopeful view of culture, found in the writings of James H. Cone, J. Deotis Roberts, Diana L. Hayes, Dwight N. Hopkins, Jacquelyn Grant, and even younger black theologians and scholars in religion, stems from a disinclination to erect too thick a partition between the black church and the black community. These scholars are not prepared to sacralize black culture—particularly today's weakened model of an authentic African inheritance and the trivialization of African American urban culture by the hucksters of gangster rap and hip hop. Too many people, black and white, are getting rich today exploiting black youth who are on the verge of desperation. But black theological scholars do perceive a strong spiritual bond between poor and disprivileged African Americans, including some of the hip hoppers, and the religious institutions that first gave them the soul force to resist dehumanization.

Black and White Theology

The primary carriers of black culture have always been ordinary church folk—especially church women; the poets, playwrights, and novelists; the artists and musicians; and the street people who joined the others in support of religious leaders like Bishop Henry M. Turner, Rev. Adam Clayton Powell Jr., Minister Malcolm X, Dr. Martin Luther King Jr., Rev. Jesse Jackson, Dr. James H. Cone, and Rev. Al Sharpton.

The question that concerned white friends of the Black Church movement, like Frederick Herzog, Edward Huenemann, Benjamin Reist, Peter C. Hodgson, and several others,[1] was whether black theologians were stretching their radicalism beyond the pale of interracial coalition building and cross-cultural collaboration by emphasizing blackness rather than social justice. In other words, they wanted to know if the "ethnic-specificity" of black and womanist theologies turned out to be merely expressions of an outmoded religio-cultural tribalism. They feared that the putative unity of the church across racial and ethnic boundaries was about to be sacrificed for an ambiguous emphasis on blackness for which no white person could be expected to qualify. The very fact that the Society for the Study of Black Religion (SSBR), organized in 1970, had not yet opened its doors to white scholars may have given some credence to the suspicion that black theology had indeed been seduced by a racial narcissism.

A few members of the SSRB never agreed that white seminary professors, if admitted to the Society, would inevitably reshape its mission and "take it over." Although I considered that fear exaggerated, I did, nonetheless, understand the uneasiness of some of my colleagues toward the limitations of interracial organizations. We all wanted to be sure that well-meaning white friends like Paul Lehmann and Fred Herzog, who had publicly recognized the importance of the work we were doing, were really committed to lifting up the distinctive contributions of African and African American religion and culture, and not simply interested in buttressing their own political position *vis-à-vis* the white religious establishment with which they were embattled.[2]

It was not easy then nor is it easy today for white theologians to rid themselves of the notion that Americans live in a color-blind society or one that has reached a point where it ought to be blind to color and ethnicity. The failure among some white scholars to concede that racial prejudice in the United States, if not in the whole Western world, still impedes the general valorization of black life and culture, as well as the distribution of justice to all, is partly related to their conclusions about what the Civil Rights movement actually accomplished—as illustrated by the successful middle-class blacks they read about in *Ebony* and *Jet,* and the deceptive images of racial integration they see on prime-time television. The other part may be their inability to face up to the racism in themselves, hidden in denial. The aplomb with which many white academics and church bureaucrats seem to have regarded Proposition 209 in California, and the rejection of affirmative action against our appeals to be relieved of the disabilities still conjoined with growing up black in America, indicates where some of our former friends in the academy and the white church have gone. Alas, many have gone back to the cold, cold world which believes that any continuation of the fight against racism only coddles the black poor, divides the society into warring camps, and ultimately will do more harm than good.

The Meaning of Blackness

White scholars in theology and religion who were born and raised in the United States should know something about the symbolic meaning of blackness in the consciousness of both white and black Americans. The shame is that few of them have given enough attention and study, or have had enough genuine experience in the African American community, to have cultivated the ability to grasp the profound symbolic meaning and the psychosomatic depths that are plumbed and stirred up by the idea of blackness.

When I was a little boy growing up in the Negro ghetto of North Philadelphia during the Great Depression, there were sayings that were a part of the folklore of the post–World War I generation—the street pedagogy of the black oppressed. I particularly recall this one, which reveals the same sentiment of self-denigration and forsakeness, with a baneful allusion to sex with white women.

> Oh Lord, will I ever, will I ever?
> No nigger, never! Never!
> Well, where there's life there's hope.
> Yes, and where there's a tree
> there's a rope.

And all black people of my generation can recite that gloomy adage of our childhood consciousness of the undeniable importance of skin color:

> If you're white, you're right,
> If yellow, you're mellow,
> If you're brown, stick around,
> But if you're black, get back.

Of course, there was another side of blackness expressed in sayings like "the blacker the berry the sweeter the juice" and, later, "black is beautiful." But these more self-esteeming proverbs were rarer and did not prevent most of us from wanting to fight anyone who had the temerity to call us black. Young African Americans living today cannot imagine the force of the cultural revolution that, like a flood bursting through an obsolescent dam, swept over their parents and grandparents when blackness became a metaphor for militant humanization and ultimate liberation. It was the period of the 1960s and 1970s that brought about the transition from Negro to black. The growing alienation of the Student Non-Violent Coordinating Committee from the Southern Christian Leadership Conference following the Meredith Freedom March in June 1966; the summer rebellions in scores of cities cited in the Kerner Commission's report on civil disorder; and the rise of the Black Power movement, the National Committee of Black Churchmen, and the demand for black studies in the nation's colleges and universities—all these developments mark a historic change in the consciousness of African Americans that has not run its full course as we enter the twenty-first century. As always, for good or ill, as the black community goes, so goes the black church. C. Eric Lincoln saw clearly why the Negro church *had* to become the black church and the depth of the revolution that brought about that change:

> The Negro Church is dead because the norms and presuppositions which structured and conditioned it are not relevant norms and presuppositions. . . . The Black Church is or must become the characteristic expression of institutionalized religion for contemporary Black Americans because it is the perfect counterpart of the Black [person's] present self-perception and the way he sees God and man, particularly the white man, in a new structuring of relationships.[3]

This "new structuring of relationships" required a new theology that perceives the hand of God in the concerted effort of the masses for political action by valorizing blackness as a symbol of personal and collective liberation. Thus, for all the problems and ambiguities that accompanied a change many whites regarded as superfluous, *blackness* and *whiteness* as color terms became critically important for the way that some African American Christians began to think theologically. Most white European and American theologians and ordinary church members were baffled by this "obsession with color," which they presumed the black theology movement was about. Even Latin American liberation theologians were vaguely uncomfortable with the language of color symbolism and felt that it mistakenly wrapped the gospel up in a cultural husk that, as well meaning and justified as it might seem, obscured the universal political requirements of a liberation praxis.

To accuse African Americans of being obsessed with color is like accusing fish of being obsessed with water, or human beings with air and sunlight. When one's environment has been saturated for centuries with the substantiality of color, to be concerned with how to live and move and have one's being in such an environment, what to do with it, how to make it work for health and life rather than sickness unto death, is not so much to be obsessed as to be forced to grapple with skin color as an inescapable responsibility of one's humanity. Anyone who has not grown up in a culture in which color is deeply etched into the fabric of his or her consciousness will be unable to feel or understand the full impact of blackness and whiteness in the experience of being human in America. Blackness and whiteness are so germane to what it means to be an American that in the United States the terms have become items of responsible theologizing, sources and norms for thinking about and ordering the life and behavior of the Christian churches under the claims of the gospel. It may not always be that way, but that's the way it is today.

The Apostle Paul reminds us that, inasmuch as it has to pass through earthen vessels, the treasure of Christian revelation is never delivered from heaven pure and unalloyed (2 Cor. 4:7). For African Americans, to speak of a black theology is just as natural as to speak of a German or a Japanese or a Latin American theology. It has not always been so for us. But during the last thirty years—since the black revolution of the last fifty years of the twentieth century—we have been more aware of being, in some senses, a nation within a nation. All these contextual theologies have to do with a collective identity, a sense of peoplehood, a matter of time, place, language, and custom, through which the gospel has always been filtered as it makes its way from the throne of God to the hearts, minds, and lips of believers.

Religion and Color Symbolism

As we have seen, the color symbolism that permeates the consciousness of African Americans antedates the Atlantic slave trade and colonialism; it goes back to ancient times. I cannot accept that there were no negative psychological consequences among African Christians south of Egypt during the first four centuries when they were consoled by their lighter brothers and sisters that "though you may be black on the outside, you have been made white on the inside by the blood of Christ." I am not convinced that they were unaware of some sneakily ambiguous connotations in this petition they were encouraged to make: "May God wash us that we may be whiter than snow." While it is true that some African peoples attach no opprobrium to such injunctions, it is hard to believe that there was no invidious color consciousness hinted at in these sayings we find in the literature of the early church. We have here a suggestion of what was basically a flawed self-image imposed on dark-skinned Africans: the sense of an imputed color pollution and deprivation of whiteness. If the Bible itself seems to equate whiteness with purity and blackness with sin, some African Christians (but not traditional religionists) must have felt that there had to be something unaccountably wrong with being black—even on the outside! If the Hamitic hypothesis did not offer an acceptable explanation, it at least suggested to believers of both colors that it was no mere accident of nature that Europeans were born with light-colored skin and Africans and Asians with skin of a darker color. Some Africans would surely have wondered if some preternatural design had been at work. The question must have occurred to blacks in their contact with European Christians, "If I had a choice before I was born to be one color or the other, which one would I prefer, and why?"

The pejorative connotations continued in the English vocabulary where we continue to speak of "blackmail," "blackguards," black sheep of the family," or of having one's reputation "blackened." All these, and many more found in the dictionaries, are negative images that reflect on Africans and their diasporic descendants. On the other hand, whiteness has been consistently presented to the world as something positive—something connoting goodness, cleanliness, beauty, holiness, and purity. It would be much fairer to make the case that we are *all* somehow "obsessed" with color than to single out the psychology of black people as unfortunate. As much as we may deplore it, the color symbolism of our language in Great Britain and North America gives the whiteness/blackness dichotomy ontological significance—at least, up to the end of the twentieth century. We must wait and see what happens now in the twenty-first, but do not look for any startling changes.

Unless something happens that we cannot foresee, almost all the visual media in the United States will continue for some time to remind us of the degradation of dark skin color—in books, newspapers, magazines, paintings, billboards, movies, and television. Even though the employment of natty black newscasters, handsome actors, lovely actresses and fashion models, beauty contestants, and talk-show hosts and hostesses has reduced the old debasement of an earlier period, many children still grow up with the feeling that they are lacking something critically important for happiness and success if they are not white or at least of a light skin color. Many of us, both black and white, have tried to avoid the embarrassment, but even the pictures of Christ hanging on the walls of our Sunday School rooms suggest the superiority of whiteness, for this Lord, who calls us to imitate and follow him, is presented to the world as a white man with flowing, "blow" hair, and the features of a Hollywood star. Since the 1960s more and more black Sunday School children cannot help but ask themselves, if not their teachers, "If he is *that* white, with blond hair and blue eyes, and I am as black as an ace of spades, with kinky hair, a flat nose, and brownish eyes, I can't help but wonder what this Jesus really has to do with me. Does he even *like* me?"

In our country, let us admit it, there continues to be this nagging sense of something being wrong, of some kind of deprivation, some kind of inferiority and unworthiness connected to the fact of color. Many African Americans still harbor a feeling of an indelible infection that one can only be rid of if God will "wash us and make us whiter than snow." Since nothing visibly changes on the outside after such "washing," one might have some doubt about what can possibly happen on the inside.

I recall that once, during my teen years, I got into a fight with a white boy on the Benjamin Franklin Parkway in my hometown of Philadelphia. It started when I accidentally bumped into a boy in a crowd of white people who were massed along the sidewalk watching a patriotic parade marching, with bands blaring and flags waving, toward the commanding heights of the Philadelphia Art Museum on a bright, sunny day. Immediately on my bumping into him, the kid yelled something at me, backing away in fake horror and screaming at the top of his lungs, "Don't touch me, you black nigger! Now I gotta go home and wash your black offa me!"

I realized then, possibly for the first time, that my color was an offense to white people. That I polluted them. Of course, I had known for a long time that there was something not quite right about me, that I had been treated differently in elementary school and in certain public places. But that jolting experience on the Parkway made it clear why. It was my color! My dark skin was the thing that white boys and girls, men and women, feared and avoided coming into contact with, because they believed that somehow it stained, contaminated, made whatever it touched impure.

That early experience was soon reinforced by the explanations of black parents and church school teachers (I had no black public school teachers) about the prejudice and discrimination we young people would inevitably encounter in life. I do not recall that it was particularly traumatic to hear their stumbling explanations, probably because we lived in a more or less black world, even in Pennsylvania, and as children our contacts with whites, except at school, were infrequent and shallow. But I do remember what it was like to have to explain color prejudice to my own children after I myself became a parent.

Anyone who has never had the experience of being a black parent will have difficulty appreciating the agony of having to explain to a child why he or she cannot go here or there, or do this or that, because of color. Blackness, whether we like it or not, has been a mark of oppression and, although the situation has changed since my boyhood, skin color continues to affect one's daily existence in myriad and inexplicable ways. W. E. B. Du Bois never spoke more truly when he declared in 1903 that the problem of the twentieth century would be the color line. I am tempted to enumerate the instances of racial prejudice that are being reported in the press and talked about in the black barber shops and beauty salons even as I write, but let it suffice that one can scarcely open a newspaper or magazine published in the African American community (do not expect an accurate picture from the white press) without reading about acts of racial hatred that still ebb and flow in our nation.

What is this all about? What is it about the white man or woman of the United States that makes them hate African American blackness with such a passion that sometimes they seem to want to banish it from the earth as one would a pestilence or plague? Other races, it seems, can be assimilated. Even new immigrants from other nonwhite nations are readily received in our country today and can become honorary members of the majority group. But for many older white Americans, and for many who are still young, the blackness that is associated with African Americans who were born and raised in this country ought to be blotted out of existence as if it were an affront to nature. No question, such an attitude sooner or later incites violence and, at worst, genocide. How these deep-seated feelings can exist alongside the adulation of the sensuous black female body, the celebration of sports figures like Magic Johnson and Michael Jordan, the hysterical acclaim of a Queen Latifah or an Oprah Winfrey is a mystery. Some have theorized about the deep psychological source of this madness, alluding to subterranean feelings of unredeemable guilt or some ancient, archetypal preference for the lightness of the daylight sky and fear of the darkness of the night which held unthinkable terrors for primitive humans. But that does not explain why some African and Caribbean black people are more acceptable to whites than a black person born in the good old U.S.A.

I have no facile explanations for either the norm or the exceptions. I only know that color prejudice and racism are endemic in American society, and no one should, for the sake of courtesy and affability, give up the right and duty to speak out about them, to strive to understand them, and to oppose them with all one's might.

Where We Are Now

Since the first African disembarked on the wharfs of the New World, religion has been one of the major forms of opposition he has chosen to counteract racism. It devolved upon highly trained African American churchmen and women of the last half century to unearth a rich and deeply laid vein of resistance in the quarry of black religious belief and folklore. Out of this source, African American Christians have hewn a monument of theological criticism. In the face of ridicule and rejection from white academicians, black systematic theologians like Cone,

Roberts, Jacquelyn Grant and Kelly Brown Douglas hammered out the main outlines of a black liberation theology, which drew wisdom and emotive power not only from the Bible but from the living traditions of African American history and culture. That work is still going on, but today it is in younger, more tender hands that have not yet become calloused and sufficiently dirty with the grime of the rundown housing projects and rural slums of America to mobilize a mass movement.

It was important in the early, formative years to listen to the left wing of the civil rights organizations and later to the grass-roots leadership of the Black Power movement. First and foremost, we had to do something about the way black people thought of themselves and what they understood to be the meaning of their experience in the light of the revelation about Jesus. It was not so much a matter of creating a theology as of retrieving one that had been concealed beneath a patina of pulpit-thumping evangelicalism. Before the Civil War black Christian writers and thinkers had already rejected the spiritualization of the message of the New Testament by the mainstream churches that robbed it of all political salience. Then came the inundation of the South during Reconstruction by courageous white missionaries and teachers from the North, the rise of an apolitical Holiness and Pentecostalism, and the mesmerism of urban revivals under gifted preachers like Dwight L. Moody, Billy Sunday, and later Dr. Billy Graham.

These developments on the right flank of the American religious front served to blunt the radicalism that characterized a good part of the black church during the two decades leading up to the Civil War. But by the turn of the century many black churches in the larger cities were taking the implications of the Social Gospel seriously. Even more important, powerful new resources in the renaissance of black culture helped theologians like Benjamin Mays, Howard Thurman, and George Kelsey to reinterpret the message of Jesus in terms of the struggle for justice and liberation for all people. Hence the remarkable ministry of Martin Luther King Jr., who laid the foundation for the work of the National Committee of Black Churchmen and the black caucuses of the major white denominations, which opened the floodgates of cultural and theological self-esteem and anti-racism among the middle class. Many in the black community, if not immediately in the churches, expressed a rage that spilled out into the streets of the ghetto. They believed that it was past time to reverse the color symbolism of the nation—to turn it on its head, so to speak—in order to divest themselves of the self-abnegation and feelings of powerlessness that had been foisted on them for generations.

By now, the early years of the twenty-first century, many of us have gone through a process in which we experienced, first, a paralyzing, secret feeling of inferiority; second, a profound hatred of white people and everything that belonged to their world; third, an exaggeration of the intrinsic worth of blackness, expressed in such phrases as "Black is beautiful" and "blacker than thou"; and, finally, a stage in which we came into a realistic acceptance of self and others, a candid appraisal, in theological terms, of who we are and how we came to be what we are. There have been different descriptions of this transition from Negro to black, but the process is essentially the same. With it comes the ability to look unblinkingly at white people for who they were, who they are today, and what they will be tomorrow; an indifference about those whites with whom we are still playing games; and a new appreciation for those who are striving to be what God created them to be.

This fourth and final stage in the journey to black maturity is not yet complete in any black person I have ever met. It is provisional, conditional on the unique experiences of each day, and ongoing into an unpredictable future. But in these opening years of the twenty-first century it is our best chance for mental and emotional equilibrium and for a progression with eyes wide open, into a new interracial and multicultural world that can bring as much black heartbreak and tragedy as it can bring exhilaration and triumph, but a new world and new relationships we cannot avoid.

Reconciliation Prematurely?

The problem with some of our white friends is that they wanted, twenty years ago, to move us more swiftly and, I would say, prematurely through these stages of black consciousness toward their poorly understood and fuzzily defined goal of racial reconciliation. They were in too much of a hurry. They wanted to see us do theology *beyond* blackness before we had scarcely discovered what it meant to *do* black theology. Notwithstanding Victor Anderson's provocative demurrer,[4] I believe that one must go through blackness in order to get beyond it, and that even beyond it one will still feel its gravitational pull until the demonic power of racism has been dethroned. In other words, we must somehow confront and reconstruct the symbolism by which we have been wounded in order to heal and to be capable of healing others. In some way that black theologians have not yet made entirely clear, it is at this point that the suffering and victory of Jesus of Nazareth become meaningful for the contemporary African American Christian, a point at which she or he is able to speak more boldly and confidently about the "Black Messiah."

There is no need for an apologia, even if this may sound like one. We have, I think, made it quite clear that blackness has to do with more than skin color, although skin color is not beside the point. As Paul Tillich taught, the symbol partakes of the reality it partially conceals and partially discloses, but it is never that reality in any totalistic sense. We cannot entirely expunge the relationship the symbol bears to our experience of being of a color that denotes subordination in America, but blackness has to do with more than the color of our skin. Blackness can symbolize, for both blacks and others, the struggle and suffering necessary to transcend negativity. The fundamental theological meaning of blackness is its appropriate representation of what Jesus suffered and, through the resurrection, what he overcame as the Oppressed Messiah of God who sits at the right hand of God and will come again to judge the earth.

One of the most powerful expressions of this connection between blackness and Jesus as the Oppressed Messiah is found in a poem written by the South African theologian Gabriel M. Setiloane. I quote only a few verses here.

> A wee little babe wrapped in swaddling clothes,
> Ah, if only He had been like little Moses, lying
> Sun-scorched on the banks of the River of God
> We would have recognized Him,
> He eludes us still this Jesus, Son of Man.
>
> His words, Ah, they taste so good
> As sweet and refreshing as the sap of the palm
> raised and nourished on African soil,
> The Truths of His words are for all men, for all time.
>
> And yet for us it is when He is on the cross,
> This Jesus of Nazareth, with holed hands
> and open side, like a beast at a sacrifice:

When He is stripped naked like us,
Browned and sweating water and blood in the heat of the sun,
Yet silent,
That we cannot resist Him.

How like us He is, this Jesus of Nazareth,
Beaten, tortured, imprisoned, spat upon, truncheoned,
Denied by His own, and chased like a thief in the night.
Despised, and rejected like a dog that has fleas,
For NO REASON.[5]

When our slave ancestors sang, "Were you there when they crucified my Lord?" the ringing answer was in their hearts if not on their tongues. "Yes, we were there because we were with him all the time. We are like him and he is like us!" Perhaps not all people can make the transference as squarely as that, but all oppressed people can appropriate the spiritual meaning and power of that agonizing declaration, "Yes, we were there in our blackness!"—blackness understood as weakness, degradation, and rejection through that dark experience whose mystery has not yet been pierced by our enlightened theologies but also understood as the symbol of strength in struggle, salvation in damnation, resurrection from the dead, and exaltation in the final world to come. The brilliant, enigmatic, shining blackness of the Negro Spiritual, "I'm so glad, trouble don't las' always, Oh my Lord, oh my Lord, what shall I do?"

African American Christians are not ready to surrender this richly laden symbol, which carries all the mystery and illumination of our historical vocation. Since it was not created by our theologians but arose out of the life of the people, we will continue to try to understand it, to wrestle with it, to make it useful for the humanization and liberation of all people who want to be somewhere other than where they are right now in a world somebody else imposed on them.

That such a transfiguration is necessary in this country is too obvious to argue about. Look at the Senate of the United States, at the court system, at the assemblies of the intellectual elite of the nation. Look into the board rooms and executive suites of corporate America. Turn on C-Span and other public affairs programs on your television set. How often do you see blacks on the distinguished panels, at the head tables, or even in the audiences in the rarefied atmosphere at the summit of the scientific, economic, political, and world affairs totem pole? There are more, indeed, than fifty years ago but still not enough to suggest racial equality. We are there at times in the flickering limelight, but not as frequently as on the basketball court, the football field, the music videos, or the vulgar, self-deprecating TV sit-coms and comedy hours.

Why is this so? Why are most of the people who live on the top floors of this world house white Americans and European males, although in recent years one does see an increasing number of white females? Why have some white females become so satisfied with their new status that they can no longer protest the absence of others whom they know full well ought to be enjoying what they enjoy?

Who built this house? Did God? Decidedly not. And here we have no need for inclusive language. Men built this world house! White men built it more than a thousand years ago, then renovated it after the Industrial Revolution, repaired it after the First World War, and today are desperately trying to maintain and defend it against the incursions of women and "ethnic minorities." Its weight-bearing pillars and superstructure, fashioned over many centuries, are held in place by white power, and that makes it almost impossible for millions of other people to have access to the building's upper floors. And to pursue the metaphor a bit further: notice that stairways suddenly run out; doors that should open into hallways open, instead, into airless closets; and intricate passageways wind haphazardly from one level to another. If you happen to live in this house where most of us do, you cannot find those passageways but, if you do, you will discover they are blocked. Glass ceilings and mirrored partitions abound, creating the illusion of entrances and exits that simply do not exist.

Deep in the basement of this world house, on the lower floors, generation after generation of occupants live and die in chambers resembling prison cells. There is little space to grow, to maneuver, or to be able to rise to the upper levels. Thus a rebellion, sometimes noisy but mostly quiet and desperate, rumbles in the bowels of this world house. It never sleeps; it is ongoing. Its pressing goal is to tear down all the walls, shatter the fake ceilings, and break through the locked doors and blocked staircases in the name of justice and equality. Fred Herzog eloquently reminded us that Jesus said that in God's mansion there were many rooms, but he knew that the Lord was not referring to anything like this egregious world house we live in today.

The theology of blackness is a critical thinking and praxis designed to dismantle this house in order to erect something more like what Jesus was talking about. But it is a theology that cannot be foreshortened or prematurely universalized. It is a thinking and praxis that must draw its sustenance and energy from a specific culture that was fused long ago out of the bits and pieces found in a special corner of the basement where black and other colored people have languished too long. That is what the second generation of Africentric and womanist theologians, like Delores S. Williams, Cain Hope Felder, Dwight N. Hopkins, Forest Harris, Jacquelyn Grant, and Diana L. Hayes, are trying to draw from when they research African Traditional Religions, the slave narratives, the spirituals and the blues, the possibilities of Islam in the West, or the impertinence and toughness of black mamas who not only have stopped working in Miss Daisy's Buckhead kitchen but also would not be caught driving her through Atlanta's Piedmont Park.

Of course, we still do not know how these younger black thinkers can use this basement culture without being seduced by it. The United Church of Christ document, "Sound Theology," which Fred Herzog had a large hand in shaping, is helpful when it declares, "The church can be engaged with culture without being co-opted by culture as court chaplain . . . the church is people working for an obedient culture in keeping with God's will—an unending task."[6]

Today some liberal Protestants who are engaged in that "unending task" are exploring the possibility of a pluralistic culture in America and the world that will wipe out all invidious distinctions while still being obedient to the will of God. Albeit some of us still believe that we cannot effectively contribute to that multiform culture without first shoring up our own consciousness and self-understanding. That may not be true for all groups coming to America from the Two-Thirds World these days, but the future of the African American church, and perhaps of African Americans generally, depends on deepening and enriching the culture that helped us survive "the stony road and the bitter chast'ning rod" and, as Fannie Lou Hamer used to say, that makes us "keep on keeping on."

It is not helpful to point out that black identity and consciousness are futile in a world that is becoming smaller every day at a time when each day the world is moving in quite a different direction from where it ought to be going. The world has not yet arrived at a place where the particularities of race, color, class, gender, sexual preference, and ethnicity have been effectively neutralized by an awesome technology and an enveloping global economy. As long as these ancient divisions are exacerbated by structural inequalities and injustices those people housed in the basement will either stumble over them in the imprudent pursuit of their own vested interests or use them as battering rams to break down the walls that other vested interests have selfishly erected.

I believe that African American Christians want to join with others who are struggling to emerge from their own sub-floors and basements and are not so much concerned about their own vested interests as to stifle the hopes and aspirations of others. It is better, in any case, if we all join hands. But on the way to that much desired collaboration, we cannot help but work in our own bumbling ways with whatever God has given us in the spaces we happen to occupy, and with the comrades nearest at hand.

Our ancestors would say, "In that great gittin' up morning" we can all move out of this earthly house that is already condemned, to enter "a building of God, a house not made with hands, eternal in the heavens" (II Cor. 5:1). But until that glorious day we have a lot of remodeling to do, and African and American Christians who understand the deeper meaning of their symbolic blackness have an indispensable role to play.

PART III

Black Theology

History and Major Motifs

10

What Is Black Theology?

In conversations with white scholars on the subject of black theology, a question invariably arises: "If your black theology is really valid, why haven't the ministers and members of the black churches embraced it more enthusiastically?" The answer is not easily framed, and any attempt to deal with the question thoroughly would require delving into several disciplines such as public opinion research, history, sociology, psychology, cultural anthropology, and perhaps others. Such a question has the same complexity as certain other questions, such as "Why did the Jews in Germany permit the Holocaust?" or "Why do such large numbers of black people refuse to register and vote in local elections?" Such profound questions have no simple answers, as Pilate must have realized when his question to Jesus, "What is truth?" was met by silence.

The truth about why black theology, after ten years, has not made a greater impact on the black churches is hidden in the subtleties and paradoxes of black life and black consciousness in our American society and the church. It is related to what I have called "the crisis" of the black church in America. For the present I wish only to acknowledge, with keen regret, that the term *black theology* is rarely heard in most African American congregations and more rarely understood by either our clergy or our laity. It is therefore appropriate to ask, "What does black theology mean, and does it have any significance for us today?"

According to the date on the original typescript this chapter was first presented at a conference on June 1, 1968. It was revised for a lecture in the late 1970s, but it was never published. I offer it here, with only slight revision, as an interesting piece that shows what we were saying about this new way of doing theology in the African American churches during the 1960s and 1970s. The absence of any reference to Womanist Thought gives the lie to the liberation perspective some of us touted before our belated enlightenment in the 1980s.

In my view it has considerable significance, and my intent in this chapter is to answer the question, "What is black theology?" I will then suggest why it is important not only for theological scholars but also for ordinary preachers, congregations, and poor and oppressed people in the African American community.

Two Black Theologies

It is important, first and foremost, to differentiate between black theology, in the first instance, as an academic discipline occupying scholars and theological students on seminary campuses and, in the second instance, black theology as a term that expresses what African American Christians in the local church, who have no particular interest in theology of any kind, believe about God, human beings, nature, and the world we live in. This does not mean that the two kinds of black theology have nothing in common. They are, I believe, trying to answer the same questions but at different levels of abstraction and with different vocabularies. Both levels are necessary for a full inquiry into, and a rational development of, the faith of African American Christians in North America.[1] To the extent that African American academic theologians ignore what is or is not happening in local congregations, we ministers and our congregations are irrelevant. And to the extent that black ministers and their congregations ignore what the theologians are writing and teaching these days, they are theologically impoverished—and that is bad news for the black community and for America in general.

What is black theology in the first instance described above? Professor Charles S. Brown of the United Theological Seminary in Dayton, Ohio, explains that academic black theology is "an intellectual phenomenon . . . a new, normative understanding of theology" that was created to oppose the prevailing form of theology in America, namely, white theology, because of the latter's inability to seriously address the realities of black life in the United States since 1960.[2] The research, study, and ordering of the theological concepts and ideas that go on at this first level of what we are calling "black theology" is committed to breaking through the defenses of the historic Western synthesis of theological and philosophical presuppositions that have been used to humiliate and subjugate black people, in order that we might establish the priority of a very different theological and ethical insight into the nature of Christian faith, namely, that "God, in Jesus Christ, always stands with the oppressed in their struggle for freedom."[3]

To use the term *black theology* to describe a way of thinking about the Bible and Jesus Christ that emphasizes this doctrine as the essence of the faith as it relates to our existence as a people ought not to be as threatening to intelligent white men and women as it appears to be—even though they may not be persuaded by the academic credibility of our argument.

I suppose that everyone who attended a seminary in my generation was asked to read H. R. Mackintosh's *Types of Modern Theology: Schleiermacher to Barth,* in which Mackintosh speaks confidently of the preeminence of German theology over British theology since the nineteenth century.[4] I don't recall that, as seminary students, we found anything so strange or misguided about speaking of a German or a British theology. Later, when I did further graduate studies and read Henri de Lubac, I learned about "Gallicanism" and a French Roman Catholic theology that differed, for example, from Iberian Catholicism. No eyebrows were raised in my Temple University theology classes, where almost all my fellow students were white, over the idea of such theological schools existing in Europe. Still later, when I became active in the World Student Christian Federation (WSCF) and M. M. Thomas of India was our favorite theologian of ecumenism, I learned of the Indian theology being developed at his center in Bangalore where much later I had the privilege of giving a lecture. And when Emil Brunner became interested in the new Christian movements in Japan, we talked in the WSCF about a Japanese theology.

No one questioned the possibility or legitimacy of these theologies shaped by the unique character and circumstances of nationality. Why, then, all the uproar and head-wagging over black theology in the United States?

Professor William R. Jones, formerly of Yale Divinity School, writes:

> As a teacher of black theology, I am often asked, "What is black theology?" I have found that the question, most often, is not a request for a definition, nor is it usually a call for the statement of the *raison d'être* that is demanded of every new discipline. Rather, the questioner is generally asking: "Is black theology, theology?" . . . The term black theology

> is still, for many, a theological and semantic monstrosity. [I]s this yet another instance where the quality is suspect because it is black or is its novelty at issue?[5]

Black scholars in religion have thrown down the challenge to our white colleagues. Although black scholars do not all agree on the fine points, we do concur that it is possible and important to the whole Christian church for black people to conduct theology from a black perspective. As do we agree that something is stirring on the American scene that may be called black theology and that it is no less valid than German theology or Japanese theology. Eighteen million African Americans in the United States, 90 percent of whom are organized in predominantly black denominations and congregations, will be deprived of the intelligence and ingenuity of their own scholars as long as black ministers fail to investigate and speak to their people about black theology as a relevant approach to the meaning of Jesus Christ for African American Christians. We would go further to insist that many millions of white Christians, both here at home and in Europe, will be deprived of a distinctive way of thinking about the nature of our common faith if they are not apprised of the insights and passion of black liberation theology.

It must be clear, nevertheless, that the way James H. Cone, Charles S. Brown, William R. Jones, and I do black theology in our seminaries and in books and articles is only one kind of black theology, and not the most important. As much as we may try to make it otherwise, it is essentially a black theology of schoolmen, an academic, intellectual enterprise—a polemic against the predominantly white, Anglo-Saxon interpretation of the Christian faith that failed to perceive what God was about in our struggle for liberation and justice. As a concern of black folks in the pews it may be somewhat remote, but we are not happy about that, and some of us are trying hard to bring it nearer to ordinary church people. But we should not forget that it was the effort of professors of theology, working with a few pastors, that produced the intellectually cogent and politically strategic definition of black theology which was adopted on June 13, 1969, by the National Conference of Black Churchmen at the Interdenominational Theological Center in Atlanta. That first statement on black theology still stands as a quasi-official description of the approach that many African American scholars, and some clergy who do not claim to be scholars, make to what has evolved over the last few years as the essential meaning of the Christian faith for African Americans in struggle.

> Black Theology is a theology of black liberation. It seeks to plumb the black condition in the light of God's revelation in Jesus Christ, so that the black community can see that the gospel is commensurate with the achievement of black humanity. . . . [It] is not a gift of the Christian gospel dispensed to slaves; rather, it is an appropriation that black slaves made of the gospel given to them by their white oppressors.[6]

A Second Level of Understanding

This brings us to the second level of understanding the term *black theology*—one that has no interest in developing a polemical response to the Euro-American synthesis of Christian truth in the context of Euro-American experience but has another purpose instead. At this level we are not concerned about the ontological and soteriological meaning of blackness but rather about recovering the simple truth about God, Jesus Christ, and the Holy Spirit which African American Christians have taken for granted in relation to themselves from slavery to the present day.

It is important to remember, however, that the questions black church members have asked about the faith, questions they would not ordinarily think of as relating to something called "black theology," are not substantively different from the questions theologians are asking. Without using the term, black church members have been practicing black theology for a long time but on their own level. Generally they have been less interested in sources and norms, abstract rationalization, Scriptural justification, and philosophical cogency and coherence than in whether God is *their* God, namely, the God who is against segregation and discrimination, the God who is concerned about their health, welfare, and liberation. They care less about whether their beliefs offer an acceptable alternative to the thinking of Barth, Niebuhr, and Tillich than whether their faith is something they can sing and shout about because it is true and sensible and makes a concrete and immediate connection with their lives as they live it every day in the sight of God.

Black theology, in this quite ordinary and basic sense, means simply the belief system of African American Christians as shaped and conditioned by their experience in the American racial ghetto, and by their membership in an ethnic church that, for at least two hundred years, has been separate from the mainstream of white Protestantism in the United States. We cannot pretend with any absolute certainty to fully understand this second level of black theology. We in the academy have only some tentative ideas about it based on our incomplete study of our own history, our experience of ministering to black congregations and listening to what they say they believe, and observing how black people worship in our mass-based churches in America.

We are speaking here of a *folk* theology, of the religion of the people. That does not make it any less or more true, any less or more faithful to Scripture and Christian tradition, nor any less or more reasonable than the theology of the scholars among us; what we can say, however, is that it is indeed another aspect of black theology inasmuch as it, too, is God-talk, God-belief, and the God-action of many—unfortunately, not all—African Americans who call themselves followers of Jesus Christ.

We have recently learned that it is just as much the task of black scholars to understand and be able to interpret this black theology of the folk as it is for us to be able to understand and interpret the theology of Karl Barth, Reinhold Niebuhr, and Paul Tillich. I dare say that we have an even greater responsibility to deal with the former. But, by the same token, black preachers and the people in the pews have a responsibility to study and to understand what we are trying to say in their behalf.

Black theology in this second and most important sense began when the first slave asked the question, "What does this God I believe in have to do with my bondage as a slave?" The literature of the black church in the nineteenth century shows that preachers and church members alike were puzzled about why they were enslaved—particularly by a people who called them their brothers and sisters in Jesus Christ but yet would not go to the communion table with them, segregated them in church balconies called "nigger heavens," and refused to ordain their chosen exhorters and preachers.

An unnamed member of the African Society of Boston, which was the matrix for the first black churches of that city, wrote, in 1808:

> Yes, many have had so great a desire for power, that it seems to have been their delight to oppress and distress their fellow men, which the Africans, I say, the poor Africans, have too often felt the dire effect of, by being made subservient to the will of other nations . . . however wise or ignorant; all appear to be affected with one blood. . . . If so, why this division? Why these discords between nations? Why is the thought so disgustful to many that they cannot bear it? And why should it raise the

> indignation of many to such a degree that they would enslave all those nations which they viewed inferior to themselves?[7]

African American Christians, both slaves and free, asked these questions of God, and they must be understood as theological questions demanding theological answers. These Christians were smitten by the sheer incongruity of their lives with the belief in a just and benevolent Creator. By what inscrutable plan of God had they been snatched from their homes in Africa, herded into the stinking holes of slave ships, and carried thousands of miles in chains, less cared for than animals in transport, to be sold as chattel so as to provide uncompensated labor for the rest of their lives to people who called themselves Christians?

Some decided that it was an unfathomable mystery. Others suspected that slavery was a penalty for the sins of paganism in their African past. Still others felt that physical bondage was not to be compared with spiritual bondage and that the internal freedom of the soul was more important than the external freedom of the body. And still others recalled the story of Joseph and his brothers in the Bible and surmised that God must have destined black people for some great mission, and slavery was only to refine them in the fires of suffering. But the majority of those first, humble black lay theologians believed that slavery was opposed to the will and purpose of God; that the God and Father of Jesus Christ was a God of justice and Lord of Hosts who wreaked vengeance upon his enemies. His loving providence over all people, however, may be frustrated for a time by the machinations of evil men, but in his own good time and way he would overthrow the thrones of injustice, for "the last will be first and the first last."

This was the basic tenet of the seminal black theology of both illiterate slave preachers and the more educated leaders of the northern black churches and community organizations created by members of the churches before 1861: God is a God of truth and justice. He will vindicate the sufferings of black people. The Reverend Nathaniel Paul, pastor of the First African Baptist Church of Albany, New York, is a good example of the way, in 1827, many black Christians articulated their misgivings about the faith as presented by the white churches.

> Did I believe that [slavery] would always continue, and that man to the end of time would be permitted with impunity to usurp the same undue

> authority over his fellows, I would ridicule the religion of the Savior of the world . . . I would consider my Bible a book of false and delusive fables, and commit it to flames. Nay, I would go still further: I would at once confess myself an atheist, and deny the existence of a holy God.[8]

Anyone who seriously studies African American religious history will probably be convinced that the black preachers and lay people of that early period had considerably more theological starch than many of our preachers and laity today. They wrestled with the fundamental issues of black theology, with the meaning of their Africanness or blackness. They finally came to the widely shared conclusion that the God of the oppressed cannot be the same God they worshiped, for their God was identified with them in the condition of their suffering and had revealed to them that every nation on the face of the earth would be the beneficiary of freedom through Jesus Christ. Those dusky Christians saw an identity with Isaiah's picture of the Suffering Servant of God in their blackness, their alleged depravity, and their lack of beauty by the Eurocentric standards of their day.

> He had not form or comeliness that we should look at him, and no beauty that we should desire him. He was despised and rejected by men; a man of sorrows and acquainted with grief . . . and we esteemed him not (Isaiah 53:3).

And when they looked into the New Testament, black Christians saw themselves in the humble birth, the humiliation, rejection, and crucifixion of Jesus, and in his mother, Mary's description of the purpose for which he came into the world—this strange baby who leapt in her womb.

> He has shown strength with his arm, he has scattered the proud in the imagination of their hearts, he has put down the mighty from their thrones, and exalted those of low degree; he has filled the hungry with good things, and the rich he has sent empty away (Luke 1:51–53).

For many slaves who sang "Were You There When They Crucified My Lord?" Jesus was like a first-century nigger, spat upon, beaten, lynched on a tree, who understood what they were going through because he had been there first. Yes, they were there, preternaturally, when they crucified the Lord! It was no accident to them that Simon, the Cyrenian (after whom, incidentally, several black Episcopal churches were named), was forced to carry the cross for Jesus on that first Good Friday. Simon was, after all, an African, and his identity with Jesus on the road to Calvary was a prefigurement of the fact that black people were forever to be bound to the Savior in his suffering and struggle, and by his glorious resurrection they were assured of also being bound to his triumph over the powers of sin, oppression, and death.

White Christianity has never known this profound Christology that can affirm, in the words of Bishop Henry McNeal Turner, George Alexander McGuire, Marcus Garvey, and Albert Cleage, Jesus of Nazareth as the Black Messiah. This form of black theology is as old as black Christianity in this country, and it began not with James H. Cone and J. Deotis Roberts but in slavery. I believe that ordinary African American believers, living today, instinctively understand what we mean when we use the title "Black Messiah," even if they are, shocked and embarrassed, unable to articulate its full meaning for themselves. This is the primal black theology of the masses who know the experience of suffering and victimization. And if black preachers and teachers cannot elicit it from their congregations today, this probably has something to do with their domestication in the modern equivalent of the Big House and their people having been suckled on the teat of the moralistic and de-radicalized verbiage of nineteenth-century revivalism, shorn of its original affinity for social justice.

The Present Situation

It should be readily acknowledged that the black theology of the masses has been deeply penetrated in our own day by the accretions of conservative white fundamentalism. What happens in many of our churches on Sunday mornings is not very different from what occurs in any poor rural white Southern Baptist Church, with the American flag in the chancel and the Ku Klux Klan hood and robe in the pastor's study. To the extent that African American Christians believe that God is an old American white man with a long white beard and that the church is nothing more than a haven of safety from the troubles of the world until we all get to heaven, to that extent the primal black theology of the pre–Civil War church has been extirpated.

What do black Christians really believe? That is the point at issue in the quest for the theology of the masses, and only intensive and extensive study and research can give us the assurance that we really know the answer. One factor seems fairly certain, namely, that black religion and the theology of the people cannot be separated and that, as James H. Cone continues to remind us, the power of black religion is in telling a story whose truth and verifiability are rooted and grounded in the peculiar experience of being black in America.

> The truth of the story was dependent upon whether the people received that extra strength to go one more mile in their struggle to survive and whether they received the courage to strive one more time to right the wrongs in this world. The message was the passion for affirming the truth of their lives, a truth not recognized in the white world. . . . That is why the people inquired of every minister: "Can the Reverend tell the story?"[9]

Although here is not the time to fully develop this idea, I only wish to suggest here that an adequate explication of black theology today will involve not only the story as it is told in the pulpits of our all-black denominations but also the story as it is told in the black churches of the predominantly white Protestant churches, in the black Roman Catholic churches, in the temples of our black Jewish brothers and sisters, and in the mosques of our Muslim brothers and sisters, and—perhaps more than we realize—in the streets of our de facto segregated communities. In other words, what black people have to say from other religious persuasions about what it means to be the people of God, what our novelists, poets, and musicians are saying about black consciousness and the arts, what is being said by black Marxists and other political radicals about our political destiny, are all interwoven parts of our ceaseless quest for the Eternal God who made us, bound us together with our African ancestors, and wrapped us in that peculiar amalgam we call African American culture.

Only that holistic, Africentric culture and worldview, hammered out in the strife and struggle for survival and liberation, can give us the secret of what it means to be black, and how to go about building a New World for all oppressed peoples on the shambles of the Old World of Euro-American racism, capitalism, imperialism, and their concomitant phobias and hatreds.

The black churches, temples, and mosques, in their entirety, are inseparable from the entire black community. Our other non-Christian religionists may not be able, at first, to concede that we are bound together by a single cord of faith, but some of us are ready to say that the God who revealed himself to us in Jesus Christ during our sojourn in Egyptland also reveals himself in and through the totality of our African American history and culture: in the Free African Society, as well as in the African Methodist Episcopal and the African Baptist churches; in black abolitionism as well as in black denominationalism; in the Blues, as well as in the Spirituals; in the excesses of the Universal Negro Improvement Association, as well as in the deficiencies of the National Association for the Advancement of Colored People; in the National Committee of Black Churchmen, as well as in the Southern Christian Leadership Conference; in the radicalism of James Forman's Black Manifesto and Angela Y. Davis's old-fashioned communism, as well as in the urban Gospel-driven revivalism of Tom Skinner and C. L. Franklin.

Everything that black people have hoped and feared, struggled and striven for with bitter tears of anger and shouts of joyous exultation, belongs within the orbit of black theology, not as the knit-picked lineaments of a confessional statement about Jesus Christ or the Prophet Muhammad but as the raw data of life from which we can learn to tell the story, and formulate the agenda, of our dialogue with ourselves and with all people "who ain't been done right by." For it is in that ragged dialogue with oppressed folk like we *used* to be, enriched with the inheritance of the past and the unimaginable possibilities of the future, that we shall hear the voice of God, calling to his black diaspora to tell us what we ought to be doing in behalf of all people.

This is what I take to be the baseline—or, better, the spirit and content—of the latest analysis of black theology by the Black Theology Project of Theology in the Americas (TIA), in August 1977, in Atlanta, Georgia.[10] That analysis, which, unaccountably, was never publicized but deserves careful study by all scholars, ministers, and congregations interested in the maturation of black theology, represents widely variant elements of the academic community and the black masses, the black church and the black secular community. It is a remarkable consensus of spiritually sensitive and politically conscious black men and women from all walks of life and from all over the country who look to the church, as the major repository of African American culture, to lead them in the kind of theological reflection and dialogue that can give us the solidarity and direction we so desperately need today. Significantly it reads, in part:

> We embrace all of God's children who hunger and thirst for justice and human dignity. We rededicate and recommit ourselves, and the black churches in whose leadership we participate, to the struggle for freedom from injustice, racism, and oppression. This we declare to be the essential meaning of Black Theology.[11]

A new and more relevant contemporary faith for African American Christians is being constructed by the collaboration of seminary professors, lay theologians, and ordinary black people committed to liberation. It seeks to build on what we have always believed, that the God of the new Exodus has broken the bonds of our Egyptian captivity and is leading us into the Promised Land in the company of all people who value humanity and want to be free. That is essentially what the new black theology is about, and African American ministers and congregations of today will ignore it only at the risk of marching to a white and oddly muffled drum that does not beat the authentic rhythm of the black religious experience.

11

Eschatology in Black

Many years ago a dear friend, the late Joseph E. Coleman, who served several distinguished terms as a councilman for the City of Philadelphia, co-authored a small book with his sister, Mary E. Walls, entitled *Another Chosen People—American Negroes.* I doubt that many people outside the extended Coleman family tree, which was planted in Mississippi shortly after the Middle Passage, ever read this book. But I find myself going back to it again and again in my senior years. It sounded a clarion note about the distinctiveness, if not the uniqueness, of the African American journey that has reverberated in my heart and mind ever since I first read it as a fledgling professor at Pittsburgh Theological Seminary. Joe and Mary recounted the history of black people, against the background of the history of Israel, to show that African Americans did not accidentally discover the God of the Old Covenant and the New Covenant in Jesus Christ but were actually, alongside the Jews, another *chosen people,* a people whose history shows, for all nations to behold, that God elected them to play a particular role and redemptive purpose in the world from the beginning of modernity until now. An excerpt from the book follows:

> Their birth; their growth; their religious fervor, matched only by early Christians; their gift of the soul-stirring spirituals; their miraculous liberation from physical slavery; their phenomenal and unparalleled progress without human leadership, and the accelerated build-up of momentum and expectancy that surround American Negroes are more than mere unrelated, unguided, and purposeless incidents of time. They are all part of this great unfolding miracle, which may be another demonstration of God's dealings with another chosen people, as is suggested by the similarities and identities which they have in common with other chosen peoples of the past.

For the same reasons, and others we need not discuss here, I have frequently spoken of African Americans as *another eschatological* people, which is, I think, one example of that "choseness" of which the Colemans wrote. Perhaps the Puritans of New England were the first people with that notion on American soil, but black people had an eschatological vision so close to their black *being-ness* that they must have been right behind the English Puritans, and actually antedated those who, by 1619, had not yet landed. I think of my ancestors as another eschatological people in the New World.

That is all the more remarkable because the Puritans, of course, were already Christians when they arrived. Not many of the African slaves brought to British North America became Christians during the first 150 years after their arrival. But those who did receive baptism at the mission stations or joined white congregations were deeply impressed by the revival preaching of the Great Awakening of the 1730s and 1740s. The preaching of New England Congregationalists such as Jonathan Edwards about the coming millennium, and his conviction that Christians were called to prepare for it, reached the slaves through the far-ranging missionary work of white evangelists such as Shubal Stearns, Wait Palmer, and Matthew Moore—all of whom left Congregationalism and became Separatist Baptist preachers in the plantation country of Virginia, North and South Carolina, and Georgia.

The eschatological orientation of the slowly evolving independent black churches took a different turn from that of late Puritanism. It is not surprising that black Christians, who would remain in bondage for the next 133 years, could not share the heady feeling that they were helping to build the Kingdom of God on earth that was at the heart of Puritan eschatology. They were, in fact, puzzled by how they could be expected to participate in that great enterprise when they were kept in chains. During the Revolutionary War period several groups of Christian slaves expressed that very concern in petitions to the colonial legislatures.

The eschatology of the black church, therefore, took on a more "otherworldly" character. The hope that was commended to them in white preaching was the hope of a life beyond the grave, beyond the misery and hardship of their daily existence—the hope of another world, in short, the hope of heaven. But, strangely enough, this was not a tranquilizing but a disruptive other-worldliness. Black preachers, ordained and unordained, took up the theme of deliverance from the woes of this world in their at first clandestine, and then increasingly above-ground, churches. But there were other factors at work that were to make the slaves another eschatological people on American soil who had a somewhat different perspective on "the last things" than what they had been taught or what they had heard expressed in the postmillennialism of white Protestantism in the Second Great Awakening. Some of these factors were also present on the continent of Europe in what has been called the "left wing of the Protestant Reformation," especially in seventeenth-century Puritanism in both England and on the continent. But we must not forget that the black slaves in America were an *African* people—and that makes it necessary to begin our discussion of their eschatology from a different point of departure.

The African Factor

In recent years a careful study of slavery from the perspective of the slaves themselves and the investigation of neglected sources of black history have tended to support the view that the slaves did not disembark as tabula rasa but that their ways of looking at themselves and the world, their forms of recreation, religious practices, and other functions of daily life, were combined in various ways with the culture of colonial America to produce what soon became a new and distinctive African American culture. Most scholars today agree that this African Americanization took place mainly between "sundown and sunup" in the slave cabins after the working day, and represented something different from either a pure African or a pure Euro-American culture. What happened was the engrafting of the white society's ways on an African base to produce not an *American* African but an *African* American community.

Melville Herskovits, a white anthropologist, and W. E. B. Du Bois, a black sociologist, held independently the conviction that this could be seen most clearly in the powerful human institution we call religion. Although the African gods did not survive more than a brief time on American soil, the indigenous African worldview and traditional African spirituality did continue for a considerable time in the slave community. Worldview and spirituality were partly selective and partly unconscious factors in the new religion of the black converts to Christianity up to and including the early twentieth century.

Some Implications for Eschatology

If blacks became another eschatological people under the impact of Christianization in the New World, how did this happen? How did their eschatology, or understanding of "last things," differ from that of the Calvinistic and Wesleyan churches of America? Here, again, although we cannot go into great detail, some basic explanations are necessary.

In his book, *New Testament Eschatology in an African Background*, the African theologian John S. Mbiti shows how traditional African concepts among his own Akamba people (of Kenya, but also among certain tribes in West Africa) related to the eschatological preaching of European missionaries and how the hope in Christ was understood by their hearers. Most important was the difference between the three dimensions of time in the New Testament (past, present, and future), as interpreted by the white missionaries, and what are essentially only two dimensions of time for black Africans—the dynamic, intense "present" and the long, myth-laden "past." The concept of an extended future, many years hence and going on into infinity, is virtually unknown to Africans, says Mbiti. Consequently, when the white missionaries translated the New Testament into the Akamba language and preached, "Jesus will come," they were understood to be saying (depending on the tense of the Akamba verb) either (1) that he would come in a few months; (2) that he would come immediately; (3) that he would appear at any time but surely before one's death; or (4) that he is "just outside the house, right on the road, and can even be seen approaching the homestead." There were no other possibilities in the language or worldview of the African traditional religionist.

John Mbiti points out many of the misunderstandings and distortions of the eschatological message of the gospel that resulted from this encounter of the two different ways of understanding time and the *Parousia*. His study gives us some valuable hints for understanding why the eschatology of the African American church turned out the way it did—quite apart from all we have heard about its other-worldliness and escapism. It helps us to understand what happened when African American slaves heard the New England Edwardian eschatology being preached to their masters or when the missionaries tried to translate it into the pidgin English of recently arrived Africans—being careful to emphasize a future heaven over the possibility of their gaining their freedom and experiencing social progress here on earth.

Using Mbiti's analysis, even with due consideration for the differences between the situation of the Akamba in Kenya and the mixed tribal groupings in, say, tidewater Virginia or along the Savannah River, we can see why the "other-worldliness" of black religion in America is far more complex than we imagined and that it contains glimpses of depths that go beyond the millennial perspectives of frontier revivalism. It is possible that they even go beyond what Mbiti would consider a mature and appropriate expression of Christian hope, given his thoroughly Anglican critique of Christian eschatology as reinterpreted by African traditionalists.

The historic black churches of the eighteenth and nineteenth centuries succeeded in getting rid of most of their African inheritance in the interest of becoming what they thought were "respectable ecclesiastical institutions" for the rising middle class. As Du Bois noted, however, some traces of the African worldview and spirituality continued to cling to their practices. We know, for example, that Daniel Alexander Payne, the great senior bishop of the African Methodist Episcopal Church, had difficulty stamping out the "spiritual songs" and the African "ring shout" from the AME worship services as late as the 1870s. The tenacity of the African practices was noted not only in isolated rural parishes but also in some of the better known and "respectable" AME congregations in Baltimore and Washington, D.C.

It is in the beliefs and practices of the later sects and cults, well into the twentieth century, that we can see most clearly how the African inheritance that Mbiti investigated may have influenced eschatological ideas that continue to pervade black folk culture and make African Americans another eschatological people—with a difference. What we need to do is uncover some of the responses of the slaves to the millennial eschatology of the white church by tracing the early development of black religion in the United States. In this way we may be able to see what the differences are between the hope embedded in African American religion and culture, and that same hope as expressed in white Christianity, particularly in Protestant fundamentalism.

"Last Things" in Black Contexts

It should be well known by now that the Christian slaves were a people who believed that Christ was coming again and that there would be a radical transformation of the world and relationships between people. This, unfortunately, is not the case. Most people are not aware of the nature of slave religion. Religious history is written primarily by the dominant group, and very little is passed down about other groups. When we look at the story of the faith from the "underside," a different picture comes into view.

In the Negro spiritual, that is, the religious folk songs created by spontaneous combustion in the fields and cabins of the plantations during the latter part of the eighteenth century and into the nineteenth, there is much talk of the great impending event of the Final Coming:

> Yes, one o' dese mornin's bout twelve o'clock,
> Dis ol' worl' am gwinter reel and rock,
> I want to be ready, I want to be ready, I want to be ready,
> To walk in Jerusalem just like John.
> Great day! Great day! Great day! The righteous marching,
> God's goin' to build up Zion's walls.

Literally hundreds of spirituals like that one could be quoted to show, without a doubt, that the religion of the slaves contained strong elements reflecting various apocalyptic passages of the Bible, particularly from the Book of Revelation. Consider, for example:

> Come down, come down, my Lord come down,
> My Lord's a-writin' all de time;
> And take me up to wear the crown,
> My Lord's a-writin' all de time.
>
> O what a beautiful city,
> O what a beautiful city,
> O what a beautiful city,
> Twelve gates to the city, hallelu!

But what was the timetable of Jesus' appearance for the slaves? How did they deal with the delay, and what was the significance of their expectation for the development of black religion in the Americas?

John Mbiti tells us that the African converts in Kenya sang many similar songs and hymns stressing the Final Coming, even though, as he ruefully concedes, the absence of an appropriate verb tense to suggest the possibility of a long waiting period made for some misunderstanding and distortion of what Mbiti believes to be the true meaning of the biblical symbolism. I shall return to this later, but first consider this question: is it possible to see some of these same "misunderstandings and distortions" corrupting African American slave Christianity?

In view of what Mbiti has written concerning the traditional African concept of time (as pervasive in West Africa as in the East), a conjecture can be ventured that the first slaves to hear the gospel in the New World must have had some of the same reactions as the Akamba in Kenya. The short future of the worldview—no more than five or six months hence—must have intensified the expectation of "Massa Jesus" whenever the missionary preaching included the millennial ideas that were articulated during the two Great Awakenings—one before, one after, the Revolutionary War. The poetry of the spirituals, with their strongest accent on personal experience, makes it reasonable to believe that the intensity was even greater—stretched almost to the breaking point—by the brutality of the slave system. The backbreaking labor from sunup to sundown without wages, the humiliation and the beatings, the constant fear of being sold farther South into even more intolerable conditions, all these were ever present goads to millennial anticipations.

The Slaves' Three Basic Responses

Generally three basic responses to the preaching of the end of the world and the *Parousia* can be illustrated by experiences of slave conversions reported by some missionaries and found in autobiographical slave narratives. These responses roughly correlate with what sociologists call the passive and the aggressive, or the accommodating and resisting modes of behavior of an oppressed group. Two additional factors, however, have not always been considered in analyzing how black Americans responded to millennialist preaching: first, the absence of any concept of a long, indefinite future in the culture of African slaves; and, second, the way the desire for immediate gratification as a characteristic of that culture was intensified by the unusual brutality of the institution of slavery.

To begin, there was a turning away from Christianity altogether. We know that many slaves reacted to eschatological preaching with disbelief when it became obvious that nothing was going to happen within the time period that made sense to them. We also know that millions never became church members and that many who were backslid from their "conversions," much to the astonishment and chagrin of the missionaries. In their reports of evangelization efforts, many missionaries speak of apostasy on the plantations as a common occurrence. Some slaves were never convinced that the white preachers were telling the truth. Others believed and were baptized, but it seems that many, perhaps the majority, drew back from their original commitment and either returned to the remnants of their ancestral religions or refused to believe anything.

In any case, when the ministers and teachers of the northern-based black denominations went south in the wake of the Union armies, they found thousands of former slaves who had heard about Christianity but had not practiced it. These were soon to swell the ranks of the African American churches. Those thousands who were drawn into the Methodist and Baptist churches following the war were undoubtedly attracted by hearing the Word out of the mouth of someone of their own color. But we know that there was also a different message from what they were accustomed to hearing from both the white southern preachers and the white northerners who frequently competed openly with the missionaries from the AME and AME Zion churches for new members among the recently freed people.

It is important to realize that even during this triumphant period many continued to stay outside the organized church (which is not to say that they did not have their own religion) and went into the twentieth century unchurched. Mbiti reports that some Akamba converts concluded Christ may have "changed his mind" and will never come and that they shout "eat and drink, for tomorrow we die." Some former Christians certainly felt the same way in the United States. Some of them joined non-Christian or marginally Christian sects and cults in the ghettos of the northern cities during the First World War and the Great Depression. This has been, of course, a common phenomenon in Africa since the 1870s, when scores of independent or "Ethiopian" churches grew up beside the missions—evidence of disappointment and dismay over the imported religion of Europe and America. Many independent black sects and cults sprang up in this country during the last decade of the nineteenth century and the early twentieth for the same reasons.

The second response of the American slaves that parallels the experience of converts in Africa was the internalization of the excitement about the immediate return of Christ by the intensification of charismatic phenomena and spirit possession. Before the Civil War, Presbyterian minister

Charles C. Jones, of Liberty County, Georgia, and other whites reported that many converts were given to wild visions, dreams, "rousements," and other signs of altered states of consciousness. Spirit possession, having lost its identification with native African deities, was interpreted by black Christians as the visitation of the Holy Spirit and often occurred at the time of baptism.

Baptism, as Mbiti asserts, does not simply wash away sins but "temporal limitations are neutralized, so that the soul arrives at its spiritual 'Promised Land,' and is enabled to derive sustenance from the powers of the Age to Come." Hebrews 6:4 ff. expresses this idea, and slaves reinterpreted baptism against the African background of spirit possession. The eschatological hope of the gospel and the heightened desire to be delivered from the painful realities of the present age were compressed into a single, dazzling moment of transcendence when the slave was transported to the Promised Land "across the Jordan, wide and cold" (as the spiritual says), into the presence of the risen Lord. This Lord and Savior who did not come *in fact* therefore came *in truth*—in the overpowering experience of the Holy Spirit in communal worship. The emotional quality and so-called other-worldliness of slave religion was, at least partly, a way of squeezing into the dynamic present an expectation and excitement that could not be projected into a remote future, given the traditional concept of time among many African peoples.

The way that the new African American urban working class related to Pentecostalism, with its strong premillennial flavor in the early twentieth century, supports this contention. The black Pentecostal experience was more of a dissociation experience, more of an alteration of identity and perception than its white counterpart. It was, in other words, an African more than a Euro-American experience. The black Pentecostal historian Leonard Lovett brings this out when he describes the great Asuza Street Revival in Los Angeles in 1906, when the whites withdrew (a year later) because of what they considered to be offensive and pagan "Africanisms" in the way black members received the baptism of the Holy Ghost.

My point is that one of the typical responses to eschatological preaching on the part of the slaves and their near descendants was the abandonment, at least temporarily, of the futurist idea about the advent of the Messiah and the adoption of an "immediatist" orientation. Christ came to the black Christian community in the ecstasy of communal worship, and many of the spirituals echo this idea, as in the following refrain:

> I know my Lord has set me free,
> I'm in Him and He's in me!

The third response of the slaves to eschatological preaching is closely related to the second. It is another aspect of the immediacy of black spirituality in the interim between the episodes of spirit possession. Mbiti points out that the basic notion of "the next world" is a feature of all African societies. This does not contradict the absence of a remote future, but it does indicate that the future is sometimes pushed back into the present and mythic past where it makes a connection with the "living dead"—the belief that our ancestors are still with us and involved in many aspects of our daily lives. Mbiti writes: "The next world is the hereafter beyond physical death . . . pictured exclusively in materialistic terms which make that world more or less a carbon copy of the present."

Put another way, it is the present world turned upside down—a world in which "the evil cease oppressing" and the "last shall be first." But it is also a world "not far from the physical world" in the sense that it is where the natural gestures, affections, and relationships of this present world are validated and fulfilled. Mbiti has some difficulty with this idea, as we shall see.

In both African and African American religion the idea of the next world, that is, "the Kingdom of God," is not some highly mystical, spiritualized realm that floats over the real world and has no business with it. It is peopled with the ancestors who are ever near, with people we have known and loved, and it contains the things of this world, wonderfully transfigured. In that sense it is the *criterion* of the present world, a model of perfection that stands always in judgment upon this world. What we have too glibly called the other-worldliness of slave religion was in fact the eschatological vision that made it possible not only to experience that world ecstatically in worship but to make it visible and tangible in pragmatic ways in the daily realities of the believer's life. Thus, as Miles Mark Fisher and other interpreters of the slave bards tell us, "Steal Away to Jesus" was often used as a signal on the Underground Railroad. "Crossing the Jordan" and "Wade in de Water, Children" sometimes meant getting across the Ohio River to free territory; "Goin' to de Promised Land" not only suggested heaven but also the dawn of Emancipation Day and the final achievement of liberation.

The hope that is expressed in the spirituals and in some of the later gospel songs of the black church is related to the desire for freedom and a better chance here in this world that has been judged and found wanting by the next one. The images called forth, therefore, are materialistic and reminded the slaves of the palpable deprivation of their bondage, as well as representing a profound realization that there is a different experience available in this life when Christ is Lord, notwithstanding the machinations of evil men.

Marc Connelly's parody of a black heaven in *Green Pastures* is fatuously extravagant, but certain aspects of the play creatively convey the worldliness and materialistic concreteness of the black religious imagination. Considering the thin line between the sacred and the profane that is characteristic of African and African American cosmology, it is not surprising that Father Divine, Daddy Grace, and other "black gods of the metropolis," with their heavens and retinues of flesh-and-blood angels, had mass appeal in the black urban communities during the 1920s and 1930s. The familiar spiritual "All God's Chillun" is an example of the down-to-earth concreteness of black eschatology.

> I got a robe, you got a robe,
> All God's chillun got a robe,
> When I gets to Heav'm, goin' put on my robe,
> Goin' to shout all over God's Heav'm,
> Heav'm, Heav'm,
> Goin' to shout all over God's Heav'm!

The spiritual speaks of robes, shoes, crowns, wings, harps, and songs. With the exception of the crowns and wings, all these images used by the slave poet refer to worldly things. They are not mystical accessories to a heavenly status. To the contrary, they are understood to be basic to it—the fundamental earthbound rights and requirements of personal fulfillment, of justice, freedom, and self-determination. "Goin' to shout all over God's Heav'm!" With these quite ordinary things in his or her possession the believer can shout without the inhibitions experienced in daily life. But represented here is not only what the believer has been denied in this world but also the values by which the world is weighed in the balance and found wanting, by which the world is called to account for not being what God intended it to be in the first place—fulfilling, just, free, and contributing to a happy and autonomous existence; read: "life, liberty, and the pursuit of happiness."

During the Civil Rights movement the people marching and attending the rallies sometimes added votes, schools, and seats, that is, acceptance in places of public accommodation, to the traditional list of robes, shoes, and crowns. It was perfectly consonant with the proleptic vision of the slave poets. The notion of using votes "when I get to Heav'm" cannot be mistaken as an example of "compensatory religion" when those who are doing the singing are walking a voter registration picket line in open defiance of enraged whites with guns. Obviously something else is at work here.

A Distorted Eschatology?

All this presents a problem for my old friend John Mbiti, but that problem, I suggest, may have more to do with his Anglican education than with his African roots. In his discussion of the Akamba concept of "treasure in heaven," he is sharply critical of how the traditional worldview has "distorted" the lofty and magisterial symbolism of the gospel writers.

> It is relatively easy to transfer one's wishes for material benefits from the immediate environment of deprivation and want to a dreamland which in this case is identified with heaven. . . . Thus, the whole concept of heavenly treasure or riches is entirely divorced from Christ except insofar as He conveys people from the world of material deprivation to that of rewards and riches. What seems to be happening, therefore, is that the extension of the future is not possible in terms of Time, *per se,* but only in a materialistic projection of people's experiences and wishes in this life. Even God is oriented toward the production or creation of that type of future—an intensely anthropocentric and physicalized future.

At this point we must question whether John Mbiti appreciates the full significance of the reluctance of colonized and oppressed people to draw a sharp distinction between heaven and earth, the sacred and the secular, religion and life. This division is, of course, a natural presupposition of Western epistemology, particularly since the Enlightenment. But there are other explanations for what some might consider the unspiritual and vulgar "distortions" of the Akamba converts. I would argue that this characteristic of traditional culture in Africa was, perhaps, more of a positive contribution to survival in America than it may have been for the Akamba under British colonialism in Kenya. Under the brutality of chattel slavery in America it was precisely the desperation of the slaves (as contrasted with the African converts of British missionaries) that made what might first appear to a Western-trained theologian as a "false spirituality" a more human and more authentically Hebraic and Christian spirituality in the American South. The difference between the black experience in Africa and in the United States comes to the surface in Mbiti's negative assessment of what we might consider "pragmatic spirituality."

Several factors account for this difference: (1) the institution of chattel slavery forced blacks in America to fight for their humanity with whatever they had, or die; (2) the absence of a common language that could compete with the language of their white captors; (3) the absence of a single, viable tradition of non-Christian religions in the slave community; (4) being removed to a strange land and, in most instances in North America, being a numerical minority; (5) the subversive connections made between Christianity and emancipation by a few renegade white missionaries; (6) the rapid development of a quasi-independent leadership class in the slave community with strong secular as well as religious ambitions and motivations; and (7) the centrality of the church rather than the family or clan in African American culture.

All these factors account for the unrealism of expecting the African American Christian slaves to so quickly exchange their "crude" symbolism and "vulgar" materialism for the highly refined theological correctives one might expect to find at Oxford or Cambridge. The African American religious experience, *as a whole,* should not be glibly described as regressive or given to a "false spirituality." While there is ample evidence of escapism and conservative other-worldliness in black American religiosity, that is not the main story. The general direction of this spirituality has been toward stubborn resistance, wily subterfuge, and stubborn nonconformity in the interest of survival. Such spirituality sought more frequently to transform existing reality by insisting on a materialization of eschatological hope against stone-hearted, earthly subjugation and high-sounding but perverted spiritualization. What the slaves believed about heaven was not so much in dispute of sound theology by pious white scholars as it was, surprisingly, an approximation of the Hebraic background of New Testament eschatology. What edified the slave converts was the thought that "everybody talking 'bout heav'm ain't goin' there!"

Slave Religion and the Black Church

In concluding this discussion of the responses of slave religion in America to eschatological elements in gospel preaching, I offer the following observations:

1. The three major responses we have analyzed are not related exclusively to carrying over the African concept of time into African American culture. Other influences must be taken into account, including elements of Native American religions (with which many slaves had a close acquaintance), white revivalism, and elements from the slaves' own perception of their situation and what was required to deal with it.

2. Whatever may be true about Akamba Christianity in Kenya, it would be a mistake to think of African American spirituality as being either crassly materialistic or hopelessly other-worldly. The authentic faith of the black folk community brought together this world and the next one in a creative tension that produced such sentiments as were expressed in these four spirituals.

> I'm so busy serving my Jesus,
> That I ain't got time to die.
>
> Marching up the heavenly road . . .
> I'm bound to fight until I die.
>
> Singin' wid a sword in ma han', Lord,
> Singin' wid a sword in ma han',
> In ma han', Lord,
> Singin' wid a sword in ma han'.
>
> O Freedom, O Freedom, O Freedom over me,
> And before I'd be a slave,
> I'd be buried in my grave,
> And go home to my Lord and be free!

It was the acquaintance of African Americans with "a fight for life," because of their experience with suffering, and struggle that gave them an eschatology that took the message of liberation in the Old and New Testaments and welded them to the base of an African spirituality, and to fading but still vital elements of the African worldview. The result was a new perspective for Christianity in America. It arose in the sanctuary as the ecstasy of a vision of paradise at one moment, and, in the next, it drove believers into the streets to give that vision material reality in the structures of the society. In the worship experience of the African American congregation Jesus Christ came every Sunday as the guarantor of a new reality "for all God's chillun"—bringing to naught the things that are and bringing into existence the things that do not yet exist (I Cor. 1:28).

3. Finally, it is no accident that Dr. Martin Luther King Jr. chose the "I Have a Dream" speech for the great March on Washington on August 28, 1963, to articulate the eschatological meaning of the black struggle for "jobs and freedom." Nor is it surprising that he died in Memphis, where he had set up his headquarters in Mason Temple, the "cathedral" of the Church of God in Christ, the largest of what some scholars would mistakenly call the other-worldly black Pentecostal denominations. King was in Memphis to support a garbage workers' strike of a union made up primarily of members of the Church of God in Christ, shouting spirituality on Sunday, but pragmatic spirituality on Monday.

King was, after all, a Baptist preacher who had grown up in the culture and religious tradition of the black folk community. Although he had varnished it with the erudition and sophistication of a Boston University Ph.D., he knew the power of the vision that excited and motivated his people. It was a vision of the Kingdom of God as liberation from sin, slavery, and second-class citizenship. But it was, he knew, also freedom from bigotry, genocidal hatred, and the alienation of people from one another in the land of their birth. And so he preached that hot August afternoon in Washington just as he preached at the Dexter Avenue Baptist Church in Montgomery or in his father's pulpit at Ebenezer Baptist in Atlanta:

> I say to you today, my friends, that, even though we face the difficulties of today and tomorrow, I still have a dream. It is a dream deeply rooted in the American dream. . . . I have a dream that one day on the red hills of Georgia, sons of former slaves and sons of former slave-owners will be able to sit down together at the table of brotherhood. I have a dream that one day even the state of Mississippi, a desert state sweltering with the heat of injustice, sweltering with the heat of oppression, will be transformed into an oasis of freedom and justice. . . . I have a dream that one day every valley shall be exalted, every hill and mountain shall be made low, the rough places will be made plain, and the crooked places will be made straight, and the glory of the Lord shall be revealed, and all

> flesh shall see it together. This is our hope. This is the faith that I go back to the South with. With this faith we will be able to hew out of the mountain of despair a stone of hope.

For King, and for the many others who heard him speak those words on that August day, his dream was not something impossible to realize, an oratorical flourish black preachers sometimes use as much to entertain as to edify. It was not a dream for some distant future, beyond history, when Jesus would descend with a clap of thunder and a blast of heavenly trumpets. Rather, it was a dream of the Kingdom of God in which marching people, black and white, Jew and Gentile, lined up to be registered to vote, to challenge segregated schools and lunch counters, and to overturn the tables of economic exploitation, greed, and job discrimination. It was, in short, a dream to be brought into reality by the struggles and sacrifices of the people of God. King would not have used such a symbol at this crucial event had he not known of its wide acceptance in the black community—and especially in the African American church.

Whether this dream has been or can be actualized is not the question that concerns us here. What does matter is that, in this famous address at the Lincoln Memorial, King represented the historic tradition of African American Christianity at its best—the faith of another eschatological people who had come to these shores in chains but who had not given up hope, a people for whom the promise of "a new heaven and a new earth" was taken seriously as both spiritual and physical possibilities in present time or the near future. For those who follow this tradition to say that "Jesus Christ is coming" was to make a statement that is both religious and secular, and it is within the competence of those who truly believe to experience both the spirit and the substance of this Final Coming of Jesus in the world in which their struggle is waged.

But this faith is not without its problems for both high-minded intellectuals and revolutionary activists. In its traditional form it shares with premillennialism the belief that the visible reign of Christ does not come by social action programs but rather by catastrophe. It is of the nature of African American spirituality to be suspicious of projects to "build the Kingdom of God on earth," although they may provide the motivating power for Christian political action. As one African American theologian of the 1960s, Nathan Wright, used to say, the object of black religion is not to do good or to make the world better; it is to experience the glory of God. That means, essentially, that faith in the resurrection from death is the bottom line. Rationalistic, programmatic social action rarely finds enthusiastic support in the black churches not because the people and their leaders are politically reactionary or willing to wait for some supernatural transformation of this sinful world but, rather, because black faith is humble toward God and unpretentious about human capabilities.

There is a tragic motif in black faith that comes out of a long experience of suffering. Black people know a great deal about the cross. That is why James H. Cone is correct in his contention that "black theology rejects as invalid the oppressors' attempt to escape the question of death." Cone is careful to walk the fine line between resignation as a negative response to the promises of spiritual salvation and the delusion of omnipotence that makes some Christians believe they can have heaven on earth. Cone, the major exponent of black liberation theology, writes:

> Heaven cannot mean accepting injustice of the present because we know we have a home over yonder. Home is where we have been placed now, and to believe in heaven is to refuse to accept hell on earth. . . . But there is another dimension that we must protect despite white corruption of it. Black theology cannot reject the future reality of life after death—grounded in Christ's resurrection—simply because white people have distorted it for their own selfish purposes.

It is difficult to articulate this central paradox of black eschatology, and James Cone does not altogether succeed in doing so in the discussion in his *A Black Theology of Liberation* (1970). Perhaps that is because such ineffable and paradoxical truth can only be expressed in the poetic language of the Negro spirituals. It is no accident that John Lovell Jr., in his almost exhaustive analysis of these joyful and sorrow-laden songs, places the songs that deal with the determination "to struggle, resist and hold fast" side by side with those that talk about heaven. Lovell observes that the spirituals frequently use the "soldier theme"—the call to fight for black manhood and womanhood in a mean and hostile world:

> O stay in the field, children-ah
> Stay in the field, children-ah,
> Stay in the field,
> Until the war is ended.

> I've got my breastplate, sword, and shield,
> And I'll go marching thru the field,
> Till the war is ended.

But there is that other affirmation one finds over and over again in the spirituals. We may have to fight until the war is over, but the time will surely come when "I'm going to lay down my sword and shield, down by the riverside, to study war no more!"

The true eschatological hope of black faith is sounded in the latter spiritual, which looks for the glory of God to be revealed, in all its healing and transforming splendor, for all flesh to see it together when the gates of heaven are flung open for all faithful people to enter. And that hope is most confidently and triumphantly expressed in that plainly spoken but magnificent spiritual that we hear more and more frequently these days in African American churches.

> I've a crown up in that Kingdom,
> Ain't that good news!
> I've a crown up in that Kingdom,
> Ain't that good news!
> Goin' to lay down this world,
> Goin' to shoulder up my cross,
> Goin' to take it home to Jesus,
> Ain't that good news!
> Good news! Good news!
> *Ain't that good news!*

WORKS CITED

Coleman, Joseph E., and Mary E. Walls. *Another Chosen People—American Negroes* (Philadelphia: Coleman Company, 1962).

Cone, James H. *A Black Theology of Liberation* (Philadelphia: Lippincott, 1970).

Du Bois, W. E. B. *The Souls of Black Folk* (Chicago: McClurg, 1929).

Fisher, Mark Miles. *Negro Slave Songs in the United States* (New York: Russell & Russell, 1968).

Frazier, E. Franklin. *The Negro Church in America* (Liverpool: University of Liverpool Press, 1963).

Herskovits, Melville. *The Myth of the Negro Past* (Boston: Beacon, 1958).

Jones, Charles C. *The Religious Instruction of Negroes in the United States* (Savannah, Ga.: T. Purse, 1842).

Lovell, John, Jr. *Black Song: The Forge and the Flame* (New York: Macmillan, 1972).

Mbiti, John S. *African Religions and Philosophy* (New York: Praeger, 1969).

Mbiti, John S. *New Testament Eschatology in an African Background* (New York: Oxford University Press, 1971).

Payne, Daniel Alexander. *Recollections of Seventy Years* (New York: Arno, 1969.

12

Black Power, Black People, and Theological Renewal

The Civil Rights movement began to show signs of serious disability when Martin Luther King Jr. and the staff of the Southern Christian Leadership Conference ran afoul of northern white power in the form of the Chicago Board of Realtors and the Daley machine during the long, hot summer of 1965. The movement managed to rally momentarily the next year, when, with symptoms of desperation, it turned its attention to launching a Poor People's March in Washington, D.C. Finally, amid great consternation and confusion, it died with the tragic assassination of its leader on April 4, 1968. During those three fitful years, from 1966 to 1968, the African American community went through a hardening process from which it did not recover during the more placid 1970s and, some might say, from which it has not recovered to this day.

When King was laid to rest temporarily on the campus of his beloved Morehouse College, a great and terrible silence descended on black communities across the nation. It was as if a vast dark shadow, an eclipse of the sun, swept soundlessly and swiftly across the broad lap of the land—from the black upper-class neighborhoods of southwest Atlanta, over the tar paper sharecropper shacks of the Mississippi Delta, to the lonely, dilapidated rooming houses of the Albina area of Portland, Oregon. African Americans everywhere turned off their radios and television sets and settled back grimly, in the gathering darkness, to think. What was the meaning of the recent events? What could be made of the last ten or twelve years that had claimed so much of the flower of black youth and now, in this sudden and terrible way, had snatched away the most beautiful flower of them all—this brilliant, articulate, God-sent young preacher who called himself a "drum major for justice"?

Nobody knew where it was going, but a new tough-minded skepticism, collective self-interest, and a fresh determination to survive slowly took over black America. At first there was burning anger, then frustration, and finally despair. But the long years of adamantine resistance and suffering had taught lessons that could not be easily forgotten. Those lessons—scarcely remembered during the almost lighthearted days of the Montgomery bus boycott—began to be dredged up from the depths of the collective unconscious of the masses. The old feelings of having to close ranks, of insularity, and of inner-directedness in the face of the overwhelming coercion and repression of the white community generated a new, almost brassy confidence that rested on foundations deeper and firmer than anything white America had ever imagined or witnessed from these sepia-colored descendants of slaves.

The year after King's death, the National Committee of Black Churchmen (NCBC) held its third annual convocation in Oakland, California, with members of the Black Panther Party and other grass-roots organizations, and, drawing from the wellsprings of King's deepest commitments, they sounded a new, more radical note about the connection between black faith and black power. Despite what now must be recognized as an embarrassing insensitivity to the role of black women, a new theological and political challenge to the white church and community somehow arose from the large group of preachers and lay people who gathered on the turf of the Black Panthers.

> By the faith of our fathers, by the faith of Nat Turner and Denmark Vesey, of Allen and Varick, of Delany, of Garvey and Du Bois, and Martin Luther King, Jr., and Malcolm X, and by the grace of God, the NCBC has undertaken, in cooperation with IFCO [Interreligious Foundation for Community Organization] and BEDC [Black Economic Development Conference], to call this nation, beginning with the white churches which have a clear and acknowledged moral responsibility, to the conference table to negotiate in good faith the transfer of power to those segments of society which have been deprived of freedom, justice, and self-determination. It *can* be done. It *can* be done peacefully. It *must* be done, in any case, or peace, brotherhood, and reconciliation will remain empty, mocking words in an American wasteland of racial hatred and strife.[1]

The Black Power Movement

The development generally described as the Black Power movement was consolidated and invigorated by the assassination of the one who had, in the hour of the movement's birth, opposed it with all his might. Black Power was, in a way, the inevitable and historic response of the community to white perfidy—this time to a series of white backlashes beginning in 1964: the retreat of the federal government from the "War on Poverty," the half-hearted enforcement of the Civil Rights Act of 1964 and the Voting Rights Act of 1965, the election of Richard M. Nixon in the fall of 1968, and Nixon's secret decision to stamp out black radicalism, both religious and secular.

These developments were interpreted as clear indications that white America had taken all it was willing to take of the drive for racial integration. It seemed clear, therefore, that it was time for blacks to join together on some other basis than the good feeling of the King and Abernathy era.

The most important contribution of the Black Power concept was the recognition of the crucial importance of the political and economic control of land. It was now clear to those who lived on this increasingly blackenized urban terrain (which whites had declared unfit for white habitation by a plebiscite of feet in the direction of the suburbs) that racial integration was an idle dream. Black Power meant that only by solidifying their ranks through a new consciousness of history and culture, by building political and economic institutions, and being willing to legitimate group self-interest, even defensive violence if necessary, could African Americans hope to survive the onslaught of repressive policies in the wake of the collapse of white liberalism and take control of their own future.

Early in July 1966 Benjamin A. Payton, the executive director of the new Commission on Religion and Race of the National Council of Churches, called a meeting at the Interchurch Center on the upper west side of Manhattan. Its purpose was to discuss the hysterical reaction of some white clergymen to Black Power, the way many whites were distorting the slogan and many blacks thoughtlessly bandying it about, and the obvious inability of King's Southern Christian Leadership Conference to respond to the new situation. It was agreed that the time had come to mobilize the increasing numbers of radical black ministers in the northern cities as a more strategic and aggressive leadership for the next phase of the struggle. The decision was made to form an ad hoc group called the National Committee of Negro Churchmen (NCNC) and then to publish a carefully written statement on Black Power that would clear the air by clarifying the position of northern church leaders and articulating some of the theological implications of the concept.

Within a few days Payton prepared a first draft. It was revised and adopted unanimously by a larger group that met at the Bethel AME Church. The "Black Power Statement" was a signal success. It was published simultaneously on July 31, 1966, in the *New York Times* and the *Los Angeles Times,* and in several other cities during the following weeks. It received widespread attention both at home and abroad. This was the first tightly reasoned, analytical pronouncement on Black Power to receive international publicity. That its signatories included some of the best known and most powerful African American ministers in the nation shocked and disquieted the white leadership in both church and state. Although the statement was intended to be read by the masses, its real target was "the leaders of America"—the white ecclesiastical and secular establishments that molded public opinion and had reacted in horror to what it considered the dangerous trend toward lawlessness and "reverse racism" among former allies. The July 1966 "Black Power Statement" declared forthrightly:

> As black men [*sic*] who were long ago forced out of the white church to create and to wield "black power," we fail to understand the emotional quality of the outcry of some clergy against the use of the term today. It is not enough to answer that "integration" is the solution. For it is precisely the nature of the operation of power under some forms of integration which is being challenged. . . . Without . . . capacity to *participate with power*—i.e., to have some organized political and economic strength to really influence people with whom one interacts—integration is not meaningful. . . . We regard as sheer hypocrisy or as a blind and dangerous illusion the view that opposes love to power. Love should be a controlling element in power, but what love opposes is precisely the misuse and abuse of power, not power itself. So long as white churchmen continue to moralize and misinterpret Christian love, so long will justice continue to be subverted in this land.[2]

In spite of its call for organizing the masses and the "rebuilding of our cities," the NCNC statement, by every measure, was a moderate document, although by the standards of the times it read like a radical jeremiad. Vincent Harding observed that it was far from that:

> Its definition of black goals was thoroughly American. The churchmen repeatedly claimed that black people wanted power, "to participate more effectively at all levels of the life of the nation." At the same time they condemned programs of either "separation" or "domination," and made a point of referring to America as "our beloved country" and our "beloved homeland."[3]

Nonetheless it is important to recognize that the theological and political definitions of the statement were considerably to the left of most black middle-class organizations and the mainstream black churches. It placed the signatories in unapologetic discontinuity with the traditional civil rights organizations and the interracial reconciliation theme of SCLC.

Dr. King had talked a great deal about Christian love, but the statement's critique of the *agape* ideal as the motivating force of the freedom movement cast a shadow of doubt across the minds of those liberals who had been comfortable with the idea that the consciences of whites could be appealed to by the redemptive suffering of blacks. The statement warned white America that power, not love, was at issue. "Powerlessness," it declared, "breeds a race of beggars. We are faced now with a situation where conscienceless power meets powerless conscience, threatening the very foundations of our nation."

There is no evidence that King took more than a glancing notice of the "Black Power Statement" or recognized in it a challenge to SCLC's domination of the liberal forces for racial justice. It is significant, however, that some of his close associates in the North and some members of SCLC's board of directors were among the signatories, though the historic black Methodist denominations and the three largest black Baptist conventions followed King in taking no official notice of NCNC. Indeed, one or two of the denominations came close to repudiating black power.

The NCNC, however, went on to establish its headquarters at the Convent Avenue Baptist Church and erected a permanent organizational structure at its first national convocation, held in Dallas, Texas, in November 1967. Although it was studiously ignored by the official hierarchy of the black churches, the black power pronouncement received enthusiastic support from nationalist groups. Stokely Carmichael quoted freely from it in several speeches he made around the nation. Street people began to take notice of their younger and more militant black preachers.

Finally, the National Council of Churches (NCC) and a few white denominations, faced with the revolt of their own African American clergy and lay leaders, found it expedient to give at least tentative recognition to the legitimacy of black power and counseled white clergy to consider the need for countervailing power and self-determination in the African American community.[4]

September 1967: A Critical Turning Point

In September 1967 the NCC Division of Christian Life and Work sponsored a national conference on the urban crisis in America. It was held in Washington, D.C., and brought together black and white church activists and race relations specialists from several denominations. The African American delegates, many of whom were members of NCNC, which was still an ad hoc group representing both all-black and predominantly white churches, insisted in the opening session that the conference be divided into two caucuses, one black and the other white. They further proposed that the caucuses meet separately for most of the three days and then come together for the final plenary session to see if a consensus report could be drafted.

This was the first time such a format had been proposed in the history of the ecumenical movement in the United States. The white clergy made a weak remonstrance, but the blacks were firm and uncharacteristically aggressive at this meeting—one in which most of the whites present were known to be reliable allies. The motion to divide was sustained, and the two groups retired, hard-eyed and tight-lipped, into separate rooms, with a strange feeling in the air that something of grave consequence was about to happen—not unlike, perhaps, the day Richard Allen and Absolom Jones walked out of St. George's Methodist Church in Philadelphia in 1784. And, indeed, the decision that was made that day in September 1967 at the 4-H Center, just outside Washington, D.C., would prove equally irreversible.

The discussions in the two caucus rooms were essentially over the feasibility of interracial alliances in the crisis that was facing the nation and the churches. After an agitated closing session, the conference adjourned with the adoption of two statements. The whites had almost broken up in confusion over the issue of the separate meetings after ejecting some of its most radical members. They were able, however, to draft a statement for the final session. The statement of the African American caucus affirmed black power, advocated the creation of black caucuses in all predominantly white churches, and called for greater involvement of church bodies in the problems of American cities. The report of the white caucus deplored the faithlessness of the white church but, in an unprecedented display of maturity, unequivocally supported the position of the black caucus by calling on white Christians to stop trying to dominate coalitions with African Americans and to return to their own communities to fight racism.[5]

This historic conference was convened two months before the first convocation of the NCNC, which changed its name to the National Committee of Black Churchmen (NCBC) in Dallas later that year. In Dallas the group committed itself to a program that went beyond the interchurch bodies' usual function of simply making pronouncements. The rapid development of black consciousness and the desire of African Americans to organize pressure groups in almost every major denomination, including the Roman Catholic Church, is directly traceable to this "Crisis in the Nation" conference at the 4-H Center. Within a year African American ministers established caucuses or revitalized them (as was the case in the United Presbyterian and United Church of Christ) in eleven or twelve national denominations, representing more than half the organized white Protestants in the nation.[6] It was a dramatic demonstration of the influence of the Black Power movement within the precincts of religion. The 4-H conference inaugurated an era of confrontation and negotiation between blacks and whites unprecedented in the annals of American Christianity.

The dynamic for this turn of events undoubtedly came from outside rather than inside the churches. It was the black folk of Watts, Newark, Detroit, Washington, D.C., and hundreds of other communities, and the young men and women of SNCC and northern-based student groups, that convinced African American clergy that the church was expendable if it proved unwilling to immerse itself in the turbulent waters of the Black Power movement.

Although Dr. King did not immediately participate in these developments in Washington, D.C., and New York City, he gradually became aware of their significance. The enormous workload of administering

SCLC, organizing opposition to the war in Vietnam, and planning the second march on Washington prevented King from joining the small group of northeasteners who were plotting the course of dissident black Christians and making new contacts with the secular radicals now alienated from SCLC.

By late 1967 King was well on his way to a basic shift in his own theological and strategic posture. He began to see merit in NCBC's attack on the entrenched power of the white denominations and the NCC. He called on NCBC leaders for help in training cadres of black ministers and lay leaders in key cities, thanks to a grant from the Ford Foundation, and he sent his own staff members to NCBC meetings. Some of his closest lieutenants—Hosea Williams, T. Y. Rogers, and Wyatt Tee Walker—became members of the New York–based organization.

In 1967 NCBC announced plans for a National Renewal and Development Corporation to enable the African Americans to establish an economic power base by controlling the selection of sites and personnel for urban renewal and community development under Model Cities and other federal programs. The collapse of Lyndon Johnson's Great Society program and the reluctance of NCC to support the approach of the Black Power movement to the urban crisis eventually forced NCBC to abandon the plan. The irony did not pass unnoticed in the board of directors that, pretensions to black power notwithstanding, it had neither the expertise nor the financial resources necessary to launch a national ghetto redevelopment scheme without massive private sector and governmental support. Neither, of course, would be forthcoming.

The logic of NCBC policies was inescapable, although, as Harding's critique of its public statements argues, the group never proved that it was prepared to "find, educate, and mobilize [its] logical constituencies around the positions taken."[7] The day King was assassinated in Memphis, the NCBC board of directors was meeting in Chicago, where it declared support for the Poor People's March on Washington and released an important statement to the white churches that was all but ignored by the white media. That statement, "Urban Mission in a Time of Crisis," raised serious questions about the mission of white denominations in African American communities. It called on the white home mission boards and agencies to surrender their hegemony over urban social welfare and educational institutions and to "come to the bargaining table" with black churches for the transfer of power to those who were the recognized leaders of the communities.[8]

A continuing frustration for NCBC during the late 1960s was the problem of encouraging the creation of black caucuses within the predominantly white denominations while simultaneously welding them together under the interdenominational banner of NCBC. For example, when the Unitarian, Methodist, and Lutheran caucuses received funds for program implementation they began to employ staffs and convene expensive national meetings that diverted already sparse resources that could have been used to strengthen NCBC. Money was desperately needed for setting up a regional structure, but the issue of loyalty to the denomination or to NCBC presented a serious problem. As a result, the new interdenominational organization was unable to produce the infrastructure necessary for a nationwide mass movement, namely, regional offices, membership drives, fund-raising, educational and action programs, and the integration of African American lay persons, particularly women, into what continued to be a male, clergy-dominated movement. Although several powerful bishops and pastors of key congregations around the country were NCBC members, the major African American churches officially stood aloof and regarded the organization with suspicion. Ironically the first Black Church movement that was able to sponsor and propagate an authentic black theology was unable to concretize and activate that theology in the places where it would have made a palpable difference. There are many reasons why this was so.

First, the NCBC was too closely identified with men and women who were pastors in the white denominations—especially the Methodists, Episcopalians, Presbyterians, United Church of Christ, Disciples of Christ, and the Unitarian-Universalists. The congregations of those denominations were made up largely of the upper crust of the black middle class, and their educational methods and styles of church work were influenced by white norms and standards. Second, the leaders of the black communions were no more willing to permit this new northern-based group of radical churchmen to encroach on their power and prerogatives than they were prepared to be relegated to a subordinate status in their own communities by Dr. King's southern-based SCLC. Many ministers who were beginning to accept black theology were unprepared to make it effective in the public square. They assumed a "wait-and-see" attitude about mobilizing black power in the community, keeping their eyes and ears open for signals from their bishops and national denominational officers.

Because the primary leadership and power of NCBC was in the white rather than the black world, the coolness of the African American churches might have been predicted. Some of that coolness was dissipated by the historic relationship of most black congregations to their immediate communities. Although African American congregations of the white denominations were somewhat active in the programs of their parent bodies, they could not escape a first responsibility to the people who lived around them. This was recognized by both the official and unofficial leadership as long as the pastors and congregations appeared to be fighting racism within their own structures. During the 1950s and 1960s blacks in the white churches garnered a few committee memberships and chairs in important boards and agencies. In some churches they even acquired an impressive number of top-echelon positions in the national headquarters staffs. In such cases, black power was more than a pretentious slogan.

Linkages between NCBC and these strategic outposts of power in the white religious establishment made it possible for the organization to continue if not thrive without the wholehearted support of the black Baptists and African Methodists.[9] The caucuses of the white churches, while enlarging their own domains, were an important political factor in obtaining, for both NCBC and SCLC, access to national and world decision-making bodies—such as the NCC Crisis in the Nation program and the Programme to Combat Racism of the World Council of Churches—and in releasing white church funds for the administration of black organizations.

Shortly after the creation of the Interreligious Foundation for Community Organization (IFCO) in 1966, a strong black caucus emerged in its interracial board of directors and took control of most of its deliberations.[10] The leaders of IFCO were active members of NCBC and the policies of the two organizations were usually in close agreement. When Lucius Walker, IFCO's director, introduced the idea of a National Black Economic Development Conference, to be held in Detroit in April 1969, he was acting out of an ideological and institutional framework that had been in place for at least three years. The IFCO National Black Economic Development Conference (BEDC), which convened at Wayne State University in Detroit in April 1969, was a direct outgrowth of trends that had been in the making in African American church circles and among mass-based community organizations for several years. But no one anticipated the black power demands that would explode from this historic conference.

The Black Manifesto

The conference at Wayne State University met from April 25 to April 27, 1969. It was attended by more than six hundred people from all segments of the African American community, many coming as delegated representatives of ghetto community organizations and local churches. The purpose was to "help coordinate black economic development and community organization efforts, and to give blacks a chance to develop an agenda for total community development."[11]

In a series of resolutions the conference rejected "black capitalism" and "minority entrepreneurship" as misleading panaceas for the black condition in America and emphasized its own solution of land ownership, cooperatives, and mass-based organizations for the political and economic control of areas where African Americans predominate. It also voted for the continuation of the conference as a clearinghouse for national strategies on economic development. Thus BEDC began a separate existence alongside NCBC and IFCO, the parent organizations that called it into existence to administer the conference at Wayne State.

By far the most significant action to come out of the Detroit meeting occurred on the night of April 26. James Forman, the international affairs director of SNCC and one of the architects of its famous Mississippi Project in which the NCC and the United Presbyterian Commission on Religion and Race were active participants, presented what he called a "Black Manifesto," which he promptly announced as the consensus of the conference.[12] Forman wrote the preamble himself and had discussed it with several persons, including some of the ministers, before making it the substance of his address to the April 26 plenary session.

The preamble was a caustic indictment of black accommodation and white racism. It called for the identification of black America with Africa, and the repudiation of capitalism and imperialism. "We are dedicated," said Forman, "to building a socialist society inside the United States . . . led by black people . . . concerned about the total humanity of the world." He broadly hinted at a plan to seize state power and to engage in guerrilla warfare. Finally, he declared that the conference was being justly "taken over by virtue of revolutionary right."

It was the preamble, rather than the action plan itself, that caused the greatest alarm and strongest rebuttal from white religious groups. Rabbi Marc Tannenbaum, president of IFCO and national director of interreligious affairs for the American Jewish Committee, which subsequently withdrew from IFCO over the Manifesto, complained of its "Marxist-Leninist doctrine" and its acceptance of the "use of force."[13] Edwin H. Tuller, general secretary of the American Baptist Convention, could not agree with "the complete elimination of capitalism" and deplored "the military and guerrilla stance taken by Mr. Forman."[14]

Although it used the rhetoric of violence, the Manifesto somewhat modified its condoning of violence as a tactic by denying "that [violence] is the road we want to take . . . but let us be very clear that we are not opposed [in principle] to force . . . and violence," and in the final paragraph of the preamble, it declared: "Our demands are negotiable, but they cannot be minimized."

The main body of the Black Manifesto called for reparations to African Americans in the modest sum of 500 million dollars, to be paid through BEDC by white Protestant and Catholic churches and the Jewish synagogues of America. Repeating the theme expressed more fully in the preamble, the document insisted that the white churches and synagogues are "part and parcel of the system of capitalism." "For the sake of the churches and synagogues," it continued, "we hope that they have the wisdom to understand that these demands are modest and reasonable."

Detailing the purposes for which sums from 10 million to 200 million dollars would be spent, the Manifesto listed the following:

- A Southern land bank to secure land for black farmers;
- Black-controlled publishing and television facilities;
- Research and training center for community organization needs and the development of various communication skills for young people;
- Funding of organizations that assist welfare recipients to secure their rights and influence the national welfare system;
- Establishment of an International Black Appeal for financing cooperative businesses in the United States and in Africa;
- Establishment of a National Black Labor Strike and Defense Fund for workers fighting racist employers;
- Establishment of a national black university.

These were to comprise the first installment on reparations owed to African Americans by the United States government and its racist religious institutions that participated in and reaped untold benefits from three centuries of uncompensated labor on the part of African American men, women, and children. On June 8, in a discussion of these programmatic items, Forman said at St. George's Episcopal Church in Manhattan:

> Those are basically the uses we are talking about. . . . They are not a total solution [to the race problem in America], but they are a new departure. It's certainly a new departure to the Poverty Program whose funds are sapped up by the politicians making twenty-five thousand dollars to thirty thousand dollars a year. It's certainly a new departure to so-called Model Cities, and it is most definitely a new departure to whatever Nixon was going to propose about bringing business into the community, which is really a tax gain, you see, because he is going to give them the same kind of favored status that many other businesses have overseas.[15]

Clearly the Manifesto went far beyond being merely a "new departure" from the Great Society program of the Johnson administration and the proposals of Richard Nixon for "Black Capitalism." What the Manifesto contained, in fact, was the organizational and communications apparatus for institutionalizing black separatism and power in the United States. It was an almost comprehensive plan for the enhancement of racial pride, solidarity, and self-determination as the initial thrust toward systematic control of the urban and rural areas where African Americans reside—in other words, control of the land, the institutions, and the human resources.

These demands were not new. Church leaders had already suggested many of them. Some of the ideas, for example, support of the National Welfare Rights Organization, utilization of black-owned land in the southern states, and development of research and training centers to teach community organization skills, had even been advocated by some of the white mission boards that were beginning to negotiate with African American communities in the South. The telling difference was that the Manifesto combined these programs in the context of black power and Third-World revolutionary rhetoric, and gave them a new urgency as totalistic approaches to liberation. Forman also backed up his demands with bold and coercive tactics that refused to permit the issue to be sidetracked by the usual bureaucratic procrastination and endless red tape of the white denominations.

This intransigence was the reason for the confrontation on Sunday morning, May 4, a few days after the Wayne State meeting. Forman walked down the center aisle of Riverside Church in New York City and hurled a series of demands at its pastor and congregation. During the ensuing months, similar confrontations took place in various parts of the country and overseas. African American expatriates in Europe took up the cry for reparations with American churches in foreign cities and the World Council of Churches at a crucial meeting in London.[16]

It was the dramatic appearance of James Forman at Riverside Church, bearded and brandishing his staff like an Old Testament prophet, that galvanized the nation and brought a storm of outrage from the white churches. The rude disruption of the Sunday morning worship at one of the most prestigious congregations in the nation alienated many liberals who could not go along with the belligerent policies of BEDC and NCBC. Not a few black church leaders outside the organization also deplored Forman's behavior as "extreme and sacrilegious." The usually militant *New York Amsterdam News* of Harlem echoed the shocked reaction of the African American middle class with the observation that "busting up church services is not our idea of how to gain any demands, no matter how righteous they may be."

The fact remains, however, that the tactics used by Forman and BEDC in other cities achieved what years of gentle prodding and begging by church executives and pulpiteers had not been able to achieve a short circuit of the "business-as-usual" footdragging of the churches. The Manifesto sounded a note of impatience and urgency that sent officials scurrying into emergency meetings at the 475 Riverside Drive Interchurch Center in New York and many other places across the country.

Yet, despite numerous expressions of penitence, no major church body or the National Council of Churches either actually acknowledged the legitimacy of reparations or publicly recognized BEDC as a channel for funding the specific projects listed in the Manifesto. The prophetic challenge thrown down by Forman—a modern-day enactment of Amos before the temple at Bethel—only momentarily perturbed America's three great religious communions. Both black and white Amaziahs rose to defend the establishment. With profuse apologies and hard eyes, white church and synagogue officials called on mayors, police chiefs, private detectives, law firms, and ad hoc defense leagues to restrain the unruly black radical who talked about millions in reparations as if he really meant it. Church boards rapidly adjusted the delicate mechanism of their bureaucracies to absorb the impact and then went on with the usual business of being the church.

As the days passed it became increasingly evident that the major problem for NCBC would be with the denominational caucuses. All of them, either dutifully or enthusiastically, supported the Manifesto, but the question was whether they could maintain credibility with their constituencies back home and the officialdom of their respective denominations if they did not insist that the funds be channeled through the caucuses rather than through BEDC's books.

Unreconstructed conservatism and a dismal failure of creative imagination are to be blamed for the depressing performance of the denominations in the Manifesto crisis. But most patently revealed are the naivete and vulnerability of black clergy when they are in competition for scarce resources—the lingering, divisive effects of a welfare mentality and denominationalism within the NCBC. The caucuses helped to bring that ecumenical organization into existence in 1967, and they were the advance guard from which a successful attack on racism in the churches had to begin. And yet the controversy taken up by NCBC with the white churches convincingly demonstrates that, unless black caucuses are prepared to surrender their individual autonomy, black Christian action cannot present a united front for social and political change. The dynamism and integrity of the African American religious tradition cannot be sustained without a struggle for justice and liberation through some kind of interdenominational collective like the National Committee of Black Churchmen, which soon became, in response to the criticism of black lay women and women clergy, the National Conference of Black Christians.

Black Theology

Between 1966 and 1976 articles and news items in the national press heralded the beginning of an unprecedented era of black theological discussion and sounded the themes that were to be further refined by a few scholars in both the black and predominantly white seminaries. The interdenominational journal, *The Christian Century,* published astute essays by C. Eric Lincoln and Vincent Harding on black power. Harding's

"Black Power and the American Christ" came to the defense of Stokely Carmichael and Floyd McKissick of the Congress of Racial Equality (CORE), declaring that, for black Christians, "Christ is the Lord of this [Black Power movement] too."[17] A Mennonite layman who chaired the Department of History at Spelman College in Atlanta, Vincent Harding brought an impressionistic but insightful view of what Nathan Wright, the black Episcopal theologian and black power advocate, called "the de-honkification of black Christianity."

Harding's equation of black religion with the eclectic spirituality of black power (which included the contribution of Islam) was the insight of an academician whose major interests were outside the sphere of organized religion. As such, it lacked the practical realism and authority of working clergy who could view the function of theology from within the institutional church and would be obliged to test it in the world outside the church doors.

Such a person was Rev. Albert B. Cleage Jr., later to be known as Jaramogi Abebe Agyeman. In the 1960s Cleage was a minister of the United Church of Christ and pastor of the Shrine of the Black Madonna in Detroit—a nationalist congregation that experienced a new birth during the rise of the Black Power movement. His first book, *The Black Messiah,* is a collection of sermons preached during the tumultuous years of the uprisings in Detroit, where one of the most devastating riots occurred in the summer of 1967. No black theologian was more passionate and controversial than Cleage. His thesis, drawn from some black preachers of the nineteenth century and the cults of the twentieth-century urban ghetto, was that Jesus is the Black Messiah—a descendant of the nation of Israel that became black during its sojourn in Egypt and Babylon. Cleage argued that Jesus was a member of a small underground movement, a Zealot whose revolutionary message of racial separation and liberation from Roman imperialism was corrupted by the Apostle Paul and later by the theologians of the white churches of the West. He told his Detroit congregation, which included many young people from the movement:

> So then, I would say to you, you are Christian, and the things you believe are the teachings of a Black Messiah named Jesus, and the things you do are the will of a black God called Jehovah; and almost everything you have heard about Christianity is essentially a lie.[18]

Like other radical theologians, Cleage attacked the traditional Christian concept of selfless love and redemptive suffering. He boldly declared that only the Old Testament was canonical for the black nation. He pressed on his congregations, emerging in several cities, the idea of African Americans as God's chosen people, called to purify the religion of Israel that whites had despoiled, and to undertake revolutionary action "to build one Black community, one Black Nation, all stemming from the hub which is the Shrine of the Black Madonna."[19]

Intimately involved in the Black Power movement and much sought after as a spokesman and organizer, Cleage worked to weld the radical, anticlerical elements of the movement into a reconstructed black church that had divested itself of the theology of white Christianity. "Jesus was black," he wrote, "and he did not preach universal love. . . . God is working with us every day, helping us to find a way to freedom. Jesus tried to teach the Nation Israel how to come together as black people, to be brothers with one another and to stand against their white oppressors."[20]

There is some speculation that James Forman, who spent considerable time in Detroit, was influenced by Cleage before he penned the Black Manifesto in that city in April 1969. The Manifesto controversy and Forman's cooperation with black church leaders, his willingness to see his ideas translated into theological language, underscored the refusal of many young black men and women to buy into the kind of Marxism-Leninism that dismissed religion as a puerile fantasy. It also pointed to the alienation of African American religious thought from both white liberal theology and black fundamentalism.

Into this vortex of religious and theological confusion walked a practically unknown young scholar from Bearden, Arkansas, an AME minister named James H. Cone. Cone was to make a singular contribution to the developments just reviewed with the publication of his first book, *Black Theology and Black Power,* which appeared during the height of the debate over the Black Manifesto. Even before it hit the bookstores, advance notices in the newspapers had already made the book a sensation. Everyone who was aware of the current situation took note that Cone, the youngest of the new theologians, was the first to suggest the broad outlines of precisely what NCBC's theological commission was looking for, namely, a theology that took the African American experience with utmost seriousness, with special emphasis on the search for black economic and political power, while at the same time not ignoring or degrading the essentially evangelical interpretation of the Christian faith on which almost all black churches were founded.

Cone showed how a radical but sound exegesis of the biblical story can lead to the conclusion that black power can be an expression of the gospel in a particular situation of intolerable oppression. After a careful reading of Scripture, he arrived at his position by a thorough study of Tillich, Camus, and Fanon, finding in their writings correlative data for the assertion that black power is nothing less than the affirmation of black being against the nonbeing attributed to black people by white racism. Therefore, not only must black power be accepted as indispensable for the formulation of a black theology, but it is also necessary for a Christian understanding of freedom and humanization.

> It would seem that Black Power and Christianity have this in common: the liberation of man! If the work of Christ is that of liberating men from alien loyalties, and if racism is, as George Kelsey says,[21] an alien faith, then there must be some correlation between Black Power and Christianity. . . . Black Power is the power to say No; it is the power of Blacks to refuse to cooperate in their own dehumanization. If Blacks can trust the message of Christ, if they can take him at his word, this power to say No to white power and domination is derived from him.[22]

Cone attended the meeting of the NCBC theological commission at the Interdenominational Theological Center in Atlanta on June 13, 1969. What had been demanded by the commission at the Dallas meeting two years earlier came to fruition on that balmy June day—a brief statement of the main tenets of a black theology of liberation. Cone played a key role in the discussion. Out of it came the first public statement on the meaning of black theology, and it reflects his strong influence. The opening paragraph illustrates one of the principal emphases of his early work:

> Black people affirm their being. This affirmation is made in the whole experience of being black in the hostile American society. Black theology is not a gift of the Christian gospel dispensed to slaves, rather it is an *appropriation* which black slaves made of the gospel given by their white oppressors. Black theology has been nurtured, sustained, and passed on in the black churches in their various ways of expression. Black theology has dealt with all the ultimate and violent issues of life and death for a people despised and degraded.[23]

It was Cone's contribution, augmented by substantive abstracts from Preston N. Williams, Henry Mitchell, and J. Deotis Roberts—all seasoned seminary professors—that came through in the statement and was generally endorsed by NCBC as its official theological position. The concept refined in Atlanta became the baseline from which African American clergy developed their posture in relation to that of the white clergy and seminary professors who joined the debate over the Manifesto crisis.

> Black Theology is a theology of black liberation. It seeks to plumb the black condition in the light of God's revelation in Jesus Christ, so that the black community can see that the gospel is commensurate with the achievement of black humanity. . . . The message of liberation is the revelation of God as revealed in the incarnation of Jesus Christ. Freedom IS the gospel. Jesus is the LIBERATOR.[24]

The NCBC interpretation of black theology arose from the existential situation that the organization faced as it attempted to make the white church face up to what African Americans believed to be God's judgment upon the American churches and society as stated in the Manifesto. "Black theology," declared the NCBC theological commission, "must confront the issues which are a part of the reality of Black oppression." That reality was the refusal of white American Christians, after years of tokenism through the private sector and government programs, to make massive funding available for social and economic reconstruction, with the help of the churches themselves, in communities that had been systematically underdeveloped for two centuries. The statement eschewed the abstractions of the debate among disengaged white theologians about whether it was possible for a *race-conscious* theology to be a *Christian* theology. The theologians who met in Atlanta knew that black theology was more of a Christian theology than the thinking of generations of white theologians who had discounted race as a necessary factor in any thinking or talk about God over the past five hundred years.

The issue at Atlanta was not whether a black theology could be authenticated by white churches but whether it could serve the needs of African Americans who were caught up in the oppressive and dehumanizing structures of the United States at the end of the 1960s. Because of the complicity of the Religious Right in those structures, at the heart of the NCBC statement was the issue Forman raised, as Bishop Henry M. Turner of the AME Church had raised it before Forman was born:

justifiable reparations for the years of chattel slavery. A new breed of African American religionists tried to elucidate the meaning of the Black Manifesto by means of a theological analysis of reparations.

> Reparation is a part of the gospel message. Zaccheus knew well the necessity for repayment as an essential ingredient in repentance. "If I have taken anything from any man by false accusation, I restore him fourfold" (Luke 19:8). The church which calls itself the servant church must, like its Lord, be willing to strip itself of possessions in order to build and restore that which has been destroyed by the compromising bureaucrats and conscienceless rich. While reparation cannot remove the guilt created by the despicable deed of slavery, it is, nonetheless, a positive response to the need for power in the black community. . . . As black theologians address themselves to issues of the black revolution, it is incumbent upon them to say that the black community will not be turned from its course. . . . This is the message of black theology. In the words of Eldridge Cleaver: "We shall have our manhood. We shall have it or the earth will be leveled by our efforts to gain it.[25]

Today black liberation theology continues to express both affirmation and negation. It affirms the real possibility of freedom and humanity for Africans and African Americans, and it negates every power that seeks to demean and rob them and other oppressed peoples of responsibility for their own futures. Black theology's contribution to the knowledge of God does not lie in being only the reverse side of traditional Christian theology—a white theology in black clothing, so to speak. At the end of the twentieth century it continued to blaze its own trail in the work of Black womanist theologians.

The informal, unsystematic, and, to a large degree, inarticulate theology of the masses still speaks to their urgent and distinctive concerns. This "folk theology," nourished not only in the African American churches but also in many other indigenous institutions, is still oriented toward an indestructible belief in freedom. The freedom toward which the experience of the people tends is grounded in the ancestral African experience. It is freedom as existential deliverance, as emancipation from every power or force that restrains the full, spontaneous release of the dynamism of body, mind, and spirit to respond to God. It is freedom from every bondage that is not verified as contributing to the elevation of the whole person in the whole community. Here we are not referring exclusively to political and economic liberation but to the liberation of the person as a child of God; to the freedom to be herself or himself most fully; to realize the most creative potential of her or his nature and destiny in the company of many other sisters and brothers—the freedom, in other words, to be a human being.

13

The Role of African America in the Rise of Third-World Theology

A Historical Reappraisal

It was no arbitrary decision of the Ecumenical Association of Third World Theologians (EATWOT) that their second conference, in Accra, Ghana, in 1977, should include an ample representation from the black churches of the United States. This was not the case at the first conference in Dar es Salaam, Tanzania, in 1976. Then only two African Americans were invited, and only one attended. Until the Accra conference doubts were entertained about the appropriateness of African American participation in a meeting designed to stimulate and promote theological dialogue in the Third World. Is it not true that black Christians, no less than their white brothers and sisters in the United States, are citizens of the First World—historically and ideologically identified with Western oppression and neocolonialism? Certainly black American churches and their mission boards cannot be absolved from some of the more lamentable features of the foreign missionary movement.

Granting both these allegations, much more needs to be said. It is too easy to obscure important differences between the historic relationship of African American churches to the struggle of submerged peoples of the Third (more correctly, as mentioned earlier, the Two-Thirds) World, particularly in Africa and the Caribbean, and that of the predominantly white churches of Europe and North America. It is past time to set the record straight.

The shameful neglect of African American church history, and the bland assumption that theological development in black institutions, from slavery to recent times, is indistinguishable from the ethical revivalism and neo-orthodoxy of mainline Protestantism, have falsified the true direction of African American religious thought.[1] The ghettoization of the black minority and its continuing exploitation gives the black underclass the status of a virtual internal colony, including most of the pathologies that Franz Fanon so ably dissected in Francophone Africa and C.L.R. James, from a geopolitical and economic perspective, did for the Caribbean basin.[2] The inclusion of a large segment of African America within the definition of the Third World rests on solid political, economic, and historical reasons and cannot be gainsaid by the bourgeoisification of a few highly visible black elites. Moreover, the precarious middle-class status of some African American churches differs little from that of many black churches founded by missionaries and catering to populations in metropolitan areas throughout Africa, Asia, and Latin America. If the designation "Third World" or "Two-Thirds World" does not exclude the latter, it should also not exclude the former. Third-World liberation theology is vectored from the impoverished mass-based churches of the former colonized areas of the southern hemisphere, and the line of identification runs directly through the black ghettos, the Hispanic barrios, and the Native American reservations of North America.

The purpose of this chapter is to explore the historical connections between African American and African theological developments almost from the beginning of independent black churches, but with special emphasis on events since the end of the 1960s. A more extensive treatment would be necessary to do justice to this trans-Atlantic connection. But even a cursory inquiry into what it has meant for the struggle against white domination should suffice to validate the main contention: that black American religion should be understood in the context of the Third World. Its most exportable product, black Christian theology (after mass choirs and gospel music!), has had, and will continue to have, a critical role to play in the development of indigenous theologies in Asia, Africa, Latin America, and the islands of the Pacific.

Wherever black theology has been heard of overseas, through articles, books, international conferences, and the many lectures abroad by James H. Cone and J. Deotis Roberts, it has occasioned surprise, curiosity, spirited discussion, and appreciation. The crusades of African Americans for freedom and equality have been known and admired by oppressed peoples for many years, but the emergence of a theology of liberation out of the streets and alleys of American ghettos has had a particular attraction for progressive sectors of Third-World Christians—mainly among younger theologians of the 1960s.[3] The seminal black theology of the nineteenth century and the early twentieth century, however, antedates these later influences, and in order to start at the beginning it is necessary to go back to the first stirrings of independence in African American Christianity.

The Trans-Atlantic Connection in Historical Perspective

The sea lanes between Africa, the West Indies, and the North Atlantic mainland carried much more than slaves, sugar, and rum. The ships that plied those lanes also carried free black men and women as colonizers, commercial agents, sailors, and missionaries. For more than 100 years, from the outbreak of the American Revolution to the dawn of the twentieth century, black people moved back and forth across the Atlantic to forge a bond between Africa and the New World, which has been overlooked by most history books. An international experience runs through the history of Africa and African America, and although slavery hindered it for 244 years, it could not totally suppress the triangular relationship that evolved between separated brothers and sisters.

It was the hunger for freedom, progress, and the propagation of the gospel that inspired most of this moving about, and at the center of it was the African American Christian church. We, too, easily overlook that of the four earliest black preachers about whom we know a little—David George and Jesse Peter of Silver Bluff, South Carolina, George Liele, and the man called Brother Amos—three went overseas to establish new churches: David George to Nova Scotia and Sierra Leone, George Liele to Jamaica, and Brother Amos to the Bahamas. Even before the first black denomination was founded, two black Christians, John Kizzel, who was born in West Africa and escaped slavery in Charleston, and Paul Cuffee, who was born in Massachusetts and settled in Westport, Connecticut, led a group of African Americans to West Africa to help lay the foundation for Christian colonies in Sierra Leone and Liberia—Kizzel as early as 1792 and Cuffe, a Quaker sea captain, nineteen years later.

Nine years after Cuffe, the man who almost became the first bishop of the African Methodist Episcopal Church, Rev. Daniel Coker of Baltimore, went to Africa as an unofficial missionary of his church. We may regard Coker, Lott Carey, and Collin Teague (the latter two having been sent by the black Baptists of Richmond, Virginia), and Scipio Beanes, who was commissioned for service in Haiti by the AME bishop Richard Allen, as the first representatives of independent African American churches to go into the foreign field before the end of the first quarter of the nineteenth century. The pioneer Daniel Coker illustrates the zeal of these men, barely out of slavery, to preach the gospel outside the United States. In one of his letters to the American Colonization Society, Coker wrote: "Tell my brethren to come; fear not; this land is good; it only wants men to possess it. . . . Tell the colored people to come up to the help of the Lord."[4]

It would be difficult to exaggerate the importance that the first black Baptists and Methodists attached to the enterprise of foreign missions. For them, it was not only evidence that they now possessed true Christian churches worthy of respect but it was also an emblem of racial pride, and they carried that emblem not only to Africa and the Caribbean but to Asia as well.

Why this enormous interest in leaving families, friends, and the relative security of familiar surroundings to preach in foreign parts? We can better understand it among free white Christians. But here were poverty-stricken black churches, scarcely capable of providing a roof over the heads of their members, fighting off the attempted control of white ministers with one hand while trying to build community institutions out of nothing with the other. They were led by untrained, often illiterate preachers, many of them slaves ministering at the behest of their masters, and more often behind their backs. It was a time when few people knew what it was like to stray more than a few miles from where they were born, and when even affluent white churches found it burdensome to maintain missionaries abroad. Despised and rejected at home, here were a few struggling black Baptist associations and two new Methodist General Conferences trying to launch a missionary program around the world! Certainly this is one of the most astonishing facts of modern church history. What in the world possessed these people?

Somewhere along the way these slaves and former slaves had heard that the essential meaning of the church is the proclamation to the whole world of the Good News about liberation through Jesus Christ. Against tremendous odds they had formed themselves into prayer meetings and churches, and were determined to behave like proper churches—to "go where the Spirit says go"—to the uttermost parts of the world (Matthew

28:18–20) with the gospel of freedom. As the AME bishop Willis Nazery said in 1852:

> It has more plainly and fully set before me the duty of the A.M.E. Church to assist in sending out the Gospel to the heathen, who are out of the limits of civilization and Christianity. We have, as an Episcopal Church, as much right to look after perishing Africa, the West India Island, St. Domingo, as others—and all these who are not Christianized—as any other Christian Church upon the face of the globe.[5]

The presumptuousness and patronizing tone notwithstanding (for that was the way both black and white Christians regarded Africa in those days), this statement by Bishop Nazery at the General Conference of 1852 suggests the peculiar concern and motive behind the missionary activity of those early black denominations. The redemption of Africa and the West Indies was uppermost in their minds and hearts. The major target was Africa, for they were convinced that God wanted them to take the blessings of Western civilization back to their ancestral homeland.

A nascent black theology was already in the making. The passage in Psalms 68:31, "Princes shall come out of Egypt; Ethiopia shall soon stretch out her hands unto God" (which, incidentally, has been emasculated by the translation in the Revised Standard Version) was one of the favorite texts of African American and native African preachers in the nineteenth century. It was considered a prophecy of the coming greatness of the black race, for Ethiopia was the place where the ancients believed all black people originated. And the phrase, "shall stretch out her hands unto God," meant that, in turning to God, the black race would take its rightful place beside the great nations of the world. African American missionaries, and those who zealously commissioned and dispatched them, believed that power and majesty would come out of Egypt, the ancient land of the black children of Ham, and that Ethiopia, the first black Christian nation, would receive from God due recompense for all that black people throughout the world had suffered at the hands of their oppressors.

On the basis of these convictions the African American churches accepted a special vocation to preach the gospel and to take Euro-American learning and technology, such as they had been able to attain, to Africa. Their role was to hasten the day of the fulfillment of the prophecy of

Psalms 68:31. Africa must be redeemed. Indeed, both Africa and the Caribbean, the two geographical centers of black pride and power—symbolized in the former by the kingdom of Ethiopia and in the latter by the Republic of Haiti—had to be restored and liberated through the efforts of the relatively privileged black people of North America. They believed that none other than God Himself had given them this awesome responsibility.

It is not possible to trace here the movement of the black churches from the innocence of the earliest missionary work to the sophistication of twentieth-century Pan-Africanism. Suffice it to say that, after 1900, Pan-Africanism, the movement that sought to bind together in a single family blacks in the United States, Canada, Africa, and the Caribbean basin, could not have come into its own without the influence of African American Christians.[6] Black women and men from all denominations, those of the predominantly white as well as black churches, participated in this movement for an independent Africa that would be blessed by Christian schools, colleges, hospitals, and churches. Alexander Crummell and Bishop James T. Holly were Episcopalians. Lewis G. Jordan and Gregory W. Hayes were ministers of the National Baptist Convention, Inc. Henry M. Turner and R. H. Cain were AME bishops. Edward W. Blyden, William H. Sheppard, and Maria Fearing were Presbyterians, and Alexander Walters was a bishop of the African Methodist Episcopal Zion Church. All these and many more, not cited here, contributed, often in close collaboration, to the development of the spirit of Pan-Africanism issuing from a black ideological and pragmatic orientation, of which W. E. B. Du Bois, a scholar of profound though unorthodox religious persuasion, was the chief architect.[7]

It should be noted here that African American schools and colleges, traditionally imbued with a fervor for human liberation and the elevation of a leadership class, played a crucial role in these developments. The Reconstruction Congress, white philanthropy, and white teachers from the North made a significant contribution to the remarkable flowering of black secondary schools and institutions of higher learning throughout the South after the Civil War. But it should also be remembered that the institutions founded by the black Baptist state conventions and the three major black Methodist churches remained independent of white control and were often the seed beds of pride and enterprise in the heartland of Southern prejudice and discrimination. The main burden for their maintenance fell on the shoulders of struggling black congregations—the penny offerings, chicken dinners, and bake sales.

Wilberforce, Livingstone College, Howard University, Fisk, and Lincoln University in Pennsylvania all helped to educate the first and second generation of African and Caribbean politicians, journalists, novelists, clergymen, and scholars who participated in the social, political, and religious upheavals that inspired the movements for independence from colonial powers in the late nineteenth and the twentieth centuries. Among them were such leaders as Hastings Kamazu Banda, John L. Dube, D. D. Jabavu, James E. E. Aggrey, Orishatukeh Faduma, Nnamdi Azikiwe, Kwame Nkrumah, J. A. Sofala, and others too numerous to mention.[8]

The role of African American churches in the rise of independent religious movements in Africa and the Caribbean has been greatly neglected. The leadership and foreign missionary influence of the two major National Baptist Conventions, the 1897 breakaway Lott Carey Convention, the African Methodist Episcopal Church, the African Methodist Episcopal Zion Church, and the Apostolic Faith movement, sparked by the Asuza Street Revival of 1906, began to propagate, directly but mostly indirectly, black liberation in South, Central, and West Africa, beginning in the last quarter of the nineteenth century to the 1950s. The full story has yet to be told. Black Methodist bishops participated in the first Pan-African Congresses. Most significant among the early influences on Ethiopianism, the anti-racist Christian independence movement that broke out in Southern Africa in the 1880s, was the AME bishop Henry McNeal Turner, who was an implacable foe of racism and an advocate of black nationalism. Turner helped to establish African Methodism in South Africa. St. Clair Drake observes that the planting of revolutionary Christianity in modern Africa was a result of the way the Bible was read in the African American churches during and following the Civil War:

> Black people under slavery turned to the Bible to "prove" that a black people, Ethiopians, were powerful and respected when white men in Europe were barbarians; Ethiopia came to symbolize all of Africa, and throughout the nineteenth century, the "redemption of Africa" became one important focus of meaningful activity for leaders among New World Negroes. . . . "Ethiopianism" left an enduring legacy to the people who fight for Black Power in the twentieth century, and some of its development needs to be understood.[9]

African American Christianity in the United States was no less of an anathema to colonial administrators and trading company owners following Emancipation than it was to governors and plantation owners of the states of the American South prior to the Civil War. A theology of human rights underlay the evangelical piety of black preachers in the United States and the Caribbean from the black Methodist insurrection in Charleston, South Carolina, in 1822, to the Civil Rights movement of 1955 in Montgomery, Alabama. The Universal Negro Improvement Association (UNIA) of Marcus M. Garvey, which was essentially a movement based on a form of religious black nationalism, had an enormous influence in generating pride and a spirit of self-determination throughout colonial Africa and the diaspora in the 1920s. Even though Garvey never visited Africa, his name was legendary all over the continent, and his organization carried on a tradition begun years earlier by black churches, church-related educational institutions, the black press, and Harlem Renaissance writers like Langston Hughes, Claude McKay, and Countee Cullen. In Nigeria, South Africa, Liberia, Sierra Leone, Ghana, and in Kingston, Jamaica, Port of Spain, Trinidad, Georgetown, Guyana, and other areas of the Caribbean, Garvey's UNIA, or organizations based on its general principles, was a part of the religio-political landscape.[10] More research remains to be done in this little-known area of modern church history if we are to grasp the true relationship of African American religion to the emergence of liberation theologies and ideologies that fueled the struggle against racism and imperialism everywhere in the world.[11]

Developments since the 1960s

More recent history of the connection between African American religion and Africa begins in the 1960s with the black revolution in the United States and, more specifically, in the area of religious thought, with the organization of the National Committee of Negro Churchmen (later, the National Conference of Black Christians) in 1967. Two years after its founding, NCBC sent two of its officers as observers to the Second Assembly of the All-Africa Conference of Churches (AACC) in Abidjan, Ivory Coast.[12] In 1950 the white churches of the United States had almost no blacks among the thousands of missionaries they sent to the African continent. Tensions between blacks and whites at home were high in

1969, despite the fact that the predominantly white denominations had played a belated but increasingly active role in the Civil Rights movement after 1963.

The appearance at Abidjan of two uninvited spokespersons of the new movement of black Christian activists was not regarded as propitious by some of the white missionaries present. The state-side interlopers were, for the first few days, studiously ignored by both the Africans and the white patrons of the assembly. The coolness of this resumed encounter between blacks, long separated by distance, the crisis in the United States, and the conspiracies of racist missionaries and sending agencies, must be mentioned here if the whole story of Pan-African developments in the second half of the twentieth century is to be understood. Not until corridor huddles and protocol had been scrupulously played out were the African Americans welcomed and given the floor to state their interests in black solidarity and collaboration to the task force on the new African theology.[13]

The cordiality of the discussions that ensued after the initial embarrassment completely nullified the coolness of the first few days of the conference. For many, this was the first acquaintance with African American church leaders who spoke positively about black power and the new black theology that was just beginning to be discussed. Most of the Africans warmly endorsed the appeal for fraternal bonds in theological work, and formal action was taken to commence joint projects. At this assembly, Canon Burgess Carr of Liberia was elected general secretary of the AACC and, with his familiarity with what was going on in the black church in America, he promptly moved to implement a "Round Table Discussion on African Theology and Black Theology" with a budget request of $40,000.[14]

At least four other important meetings between African and African American theologians have taken place since that almost frustrated effort at Abidjan to overcome the estrangement of many years. A consultation in Dar es Salaam, Tanzania, in 1971, involved a large delegation from the United States, including theologian James H. Cone, of Union Theological Seminary in New York, and L. Maynard Catchings, chairman of the NCBC Africa Commission. The Makerere University (Kampala, Uganda) consultation on "African Theology and Church Life" met in January 1972. Ndugu T'Ofori-Atta, a professor at the Interdenominational Theological Center in Atlanta and a minister of the AME Zion Church, presented a paper on black theology and its relationship to African religion at the meeting.[15]

In 1973, at Union Theological Seminary in New York City, an exploratory consultation was held between African theologians, led by John S. Mbiti, and the Society for the Study of Black Religion (SSBR), led by the late C. Shelby Rooks, a black UCC minister and former director of the Fund for Theological Education. That meeting was preliminary to a longer gathering of theologians that was convened at the Ghana Institute for Management and Public Administration (GIMPA) in December 1974. On this occasion the African delegation represented the official theological commission of the AACC.[16] Most recently, since 2000, Professor Peter J. Paris, of Princeton Theological Seminary and president of the SSBR, has initiated new annual consultations between younger African American scholars in religion whom he has taken abroad to meet with counterpart groups in Africa and the Caribbean. A new book about these latest encounters is forthcoming. Also the SSBR has had two meetings in Kingston, Jamaica.

All these dialogues have been increasingly amicable as individuals have become personally acquainted with one another and as points of view have become better understood through many books and articles published on both sides of the Atlantic. These have appeared in greater numbers since the publication, in 1969, of John S. Mbiti's remarkably influential *African Religions and Philosophy.* Interestingly, in that same year James H. Cone's *Black Theology and Black Power* set forth the normative position of black theology in the United States. Cone's book was followed by several new publications by African American scholars in religion.

In this atmosphere of growing excitement and theological maturity, agreements and disagreements began to be clarified. Neither side made a deliberate effort to overwhelm the other in a bid for intellectual ascendancy, nor has there been any haste to arrive at what many would consider a premature consensus. At least that has been the position of the African Americans. While there have been certain convergences on the issue of racism in Western theology, the desirability of bringing an end to domination by white theology, and indigenizing the gospel in thought-forms and cultures other than European and North American, there has also been dissent about how this is to be done—with what risk of "throwing out the baby with the bath water"—and about the ineluctable consequences for churches, financial and otherwise, that attempt to address social and political questions.

It is probably true that the African Americans have been the more aggressive partners in this Pan-African dialogue. No subject people have been more thoroughly attracted to the Christian faith, more thoroughly indoctrinated in it, and then have gone on to develop their own interpretation of that faith in order to survive. And no group better understands their white brothers and sisters, and their capacity for good and evil, than black Americans. They have, as the old folks used to say, "wintered them and summered them."

This peculiar situation of being Christian and black, rooted in the cultures of the West, and yet possessed of a sober apprehension of the foibles and pretensions by which that culture and society oppressed them for more than 350 years, has made African Americans impatient with certain evidences of ingenuousness on the part of their African brothers and sisters. Although it is true that Martin Luther King Jr. taught unconditional love and that black Christians should take seriously the "hard sayings" of Scripture, African Americans are anything but naive. They are acquainted with racism in all its forms and features, and look with some curiosity and disbelief on other people of color who seem to have persuaded themselves that Christianity is color-blind and that the greed of a people totally committed to unbridled capitalism can be sated by showing them unguarded hospitality and obsequious good-will.

Africentric black theology is hard-headed about the realities of power in the world and the obduracy of sin, black no less than white. It expresses the need for all believers to have "the wisdom of serpents and the harmlessness of doves" (Matt. 10:16), and it seems to some black theologians that the African brothers and sisters may sometimes be a trifle more dove-like than they have reason to be.

The Significance of the 1977 Accra Conference

At the second conference of the Ecumenical Association of Third World Theologians, in Accra, Ghana, from December 17 to December 23, 1977, it was apparent that the courtship between African and African American theologians would no longer preclude an open confrontation over the issue of whether blackness, as a symbol of radical alienation and of a hard-fought for liberation, could serve for both groups as a defining concept of biblical faith. Although a certain deference was paid to the African hosts, who outnumbered the other delegates and had written most of the more than twenty scholarly papers, there was an undercurrent of latent controversy at this conference. It broke out most decisively between the African and the African Americans on the significance and meaning of black theology as it is understood in the United States. What had happened at other consultations also happened at this one: the South Africans, represented conspicuously by Allan A. Boesak, of the University of the Western Cape, stood squarely with the black Americans, whose experience of extreme racism they shared. One exception among Boesak's South African comrades was Gabriel M. Setiloane, a black theological lecturer from Botswana, who accused the Americans of trying to tell Africans how to do theology in Africa. This issue had been just below the surface since the initial encounter in Abidjan. What brought it out on this particular occasion?

In 1974 an article by John S. Mbiti appeared in which he sought not only to differentiate between African and African American religious thought but also to separate them once and for all.[17] Mbiti found black theology "full of sorrow, bitterness, anger, and hatred," preoccupied with ideas of political liberation, and having little meaning for African Christians. He wrote:

> As an African one has an academic interest in Black Theology, just as one is interested in the "water buffalo theology" of Southeast Asia or the theology of hope advocated by Jurgen Moltmann. But to try and push much more than the academic relevance of Black Theology for the African scene is to do injustice to both sides. . . . There is an obvious temptation to make a connection that should not be made.[18]

Many African Americans took this as a subversion of the incomplete rapprochement that had begun so hopefully at Abidjan and, indeed, a repudiation of the whole history of Pan-Africanism in which black Americans, from W. E. B. Du Bois to Stokely Carmichael, had played a leading role. James Cone's response to Mbiti occurred at the same conference, when he had an opportunity to speak:

> In order to appreciate the seriousness and depth of Mbiti's concern, it is necessary to point out that his perspective is not based upon a superficial encounter with Black Theology. On the contrary, Mbiti made these remarks *after* he and I had had many conversations on the subject in the

> context of our jointly taught year-long course on African and Black theologies at Union Theological Seminary. Nevertheless, it seems to me that he misrepresented Black Theology. More important, however, was Mbiti's contention that African and Black American theologians should have no more than an indirect or accidental interest in each other. This perspective on African Theology not only makes substantive dialogue difficult, but also excludes Black American theologians from a creative participation in the future development of African Theology.[19]

Not all Africans agreed with the position taken by Mbiti, their premier theologian. The South Africans were particularly unhappy, as were some blacks from Angola and Zimbabwe. Polarization over the Mbiti article was circumvented by a paper read at the Ghana consultation in December of the same year by Desmond Tutu of South Africa.[20] Tutu acknowledged that the two theologies arise out of different contexts but concluded that they were "soulmates." He observed that African theology had something to learn from the more abrasive black theology of the African Americans. He feared that "African theology has failed to produce a sufficiently sharp cutting edge," and in a direct response to Mbiti's allegation that the people of Southern Africa "do not need a theology of liberation—they *want* liberation," Tutu rejoined, "Could we not say the same thing about a theology of hope, that what people want is hope—not a theology of hope?"[21]

The issue was taken up at the Accra meeting when James Cone's paper occasioned a clash with Setiloane and, to a lesser degree, with Mbiti. Cone attacked what he considered to be the latent conservatism of an African theology that rejects black theology for Africa because it emphasizes blackness and political liberation. In his paper Cone cited several African theologians whose perspectives differ from Mbiti's and who recognized that only a theology that deals directly with social, economic, and political oppression can meet the needs of Christians on the continent.

> No African theologians . . . have expressed the theme of liberation more dramatically than South African theologians. Desmond Tutu and Manas Buthelezi are prominent examples of this new theological perspective emerging from behind the apartheid walls of the Republic of South Africa. . . . The central theme among these new theological voices from South Africa [after also mentioning the work of Allan Boesak] is their

> focus on liberation in relation to politics and blackness. They insist that blackness is an important ingredient in their view of African Theology.[22]

Cone cheerfully conceded the need for Africans to do theology for themselves and spoke appreciatively of the reciprocal influences that need to be actualized across the Atlantic. But, he said, "indigenization without liberation limits a given theological expression to the particularity of its cultural context. . . . It fails to recognize the universal dimensions of the Gospel and the global context of theology." It was clear that Africentric liberation theologians in the United States intended to play a role in the development of an African theology that includes the black diaspora.

The obsession of some African theologians with indigenization had already been criticized in an essay by Manas Buthelezi, who thought it to be a "pet project" of white missionaries looking for a way to make their continued presence in Africa acceptable. He quoted John V. Taylor to the effect that those white missionaries were trading on the conservatism of the African clergy.[23]

Buthelezi distinguished between ethnographic and anthropological approaches to the theological task in Africa. It is in the latter that he saw an opening to a "first person," situationally oriented African theology—a black theology that is truly indigenous to the post colonial reality and faithful to the redeeming work of Jesus Christ in the context of the black experience.

Conclusion

The purpose of this excursion into one fascinating aspect of the dialogue between African and African American Christians over the last century and a half was to recount the high and low points, the intensity and diminution of the interaction which will probably continue that way into the future. It actually began more than two hundred years ago when George Liele and David George set sail for Jamaica, Canada, and West Africa. The conflict, as in the case of Lott Carey who actually took up arms against Africans to defend black settlers from America, was sometimes occasioned by the intrusion of African Americans and the founding of expatriate African American congregations on African soil. At a later time conflict arose over the dissemination of what seemed to some African intellectuals to be an inflammatory black theology. There have been hints at church gatherings about a delicate situation where the value of African American thought had to be measured against the support and friendship of white mission boards with money, but on the whole discussions have been positive and creative. Although tempers have been heated and nerves frayed, the dialogue has been clarifying. It has had the effect of breaking through a silent and alienated consciousness on both sides to bring the powerless together in a search for a common dignity and identity that stands in contrast to the smiling paternalism and subversive oppression of those who would be masters of the world. The African Americans have usually taken the initiative. Their long sojourn in "the belly of the whale" has given them, for all the suffering and struggle, the equipment, both intellectual and spiritual, to "come over into Macedonia" to help their separated sisters and brethren to resist subtle domination.

Similar influences of African American religious thought, from Prince Hall and David Walker to Malcolm X and Martin Luther King Jr., will doubtlessly be demonstrated by future research on liberation movements in Latin America and Asia. In addition to the almost universal impact of the black revolution worldwide—a revolution fueled by the religious sensibilities of the grandsons and granddaughters of slaves—the Black Theology movement of the 1960s triggered theological speculation from South America to the Islands of the Pacific.[24] The reigning theologies of the North Atlantic community, and the systems of economic and cultural domination that they have undergirded, can no longer be expected to receive the hat-in-hand deference that was shown them by the so-called younger churches since the beginning of European expansionism. Black theology, explicating the faith that Jesus Christ came to liberate the captive masses of the world, has played a critical role in unmasking the root sin of Western Christianity—white supremacy.

African Americans, of course, have not been alone in this dethroning of the gods of racism and imperialism. Progressive white theologians and churches have not only supported but at times have been in the vanguard of African American thinkers and movements in engaging the faiths and ideologies that justify oppression. Color aside, the resistance has often been spontaneous. People can never be totally oppressed as long as a spark of humanity remains in them. What Manas Buthelezi calls "a theology of restlessness" has existed everywhere the gospel has been preached, notwithstanding its most malevolent distortions.

At a time when American capitalism wants to persuade black Americans that they now have a seat at the banquet table and thereby should disassociate themselves from those who are banging at the back door, at a time when there are enough crumbs falling from the table to satisfy some of the uninvited who managed to crawl in out of the cellar, at a time when others of those wretched are mounting an assault on power and privilege, Christians of the Third, or Two-Thirds World, need to strengthen their bonds with black churches in the United States. They need to understand the contributions those churches have made to whatever freedom exists today in parts of Africa, Asia, Latin America, and the islands of the Pacific. Much more needs to be done by black people in the twenty-first century, but it will, of necessity, be built on the foundations laid by those intrepid women and men, on both sides of the pond, who led the way.

PART IV

Africentric Pastoral Ministry

14

What Is the Relevance of Black Theology for Pastoral Ministry?

The question is sometimes asked in the theological academy, why did it seem so urgent and necessary for African American Christian activist theologians to develop a black theology at the very time that Dr. Martin Luther King Jr. was leading a successful movement that had large numbers of Americans—black and white, Protestants, Catholics, Jews, and secular humanists—working together for racial integration, the repudiation of war and all forms of violence, and the love of one's neighbor as a universal law for ending all forms of oppression?

A closely related series of questions, which pastors often ask, is the following: Is it not true that black theology is essentially a political ideology rather than a sacred theology? What possible relevance can it have to the normal ministry of the church, the responsibility of pastors to lead their people into the kind of spiritual maturity and ethical behavior that will help them deal with the daily problems of life and death? Does this particular brand of theology not seem alien to the pastoral ministry of the church?

Another question one hears, particularly in discussions of interchurch and ecumenical concerns between white and black Christians, is this: What can a theology designated by reference to skin color, ethnicity, or human culture have to do with what might be called "basic *Christian* theology?" And further: Is it not true that black theology is so focused on African American culture and ethnic experience as to be devoid of any real significance for Christians who are not of African descent or members of African American churches?

These are challenging questions. And, of course, one cannot expect that any simplistic or definitive answers can solve all the difficult problems of ontology, epistemology, sociology, value theory, ethnology, and ethics (to mention only some of the disciplines involved), all of which resist any superficial analysis or casual interest.

Such questions, however, are fair and appropriate, and anyone who purports to think theologically about the African American Christian experience must face them honestly. We may insist, nonetheless, that white theologians and others who ask such questions must ask them sincerely and be prepared for equally difficult and demanding rejoinders that may challenge their most serious and thoughtful consideration.

All theologies are human ways of thinking and speaking about God out of a particular context. All theologies are qualified by time, geography, culture, and the material conditions of existence. It is not possible to understand the theologies of a people, or to have deep fellowship and bonding with them across lines of demarcation such as race, ethnicity, class, gender, sexual preference, or denominational affiliation, without approaching their thought-life with humility, sensitivity, and an openness to differences from one's own strenuously held convictions. The time is past when white theologians and ethicists can expect to understand black liberation theology, or to contribute to interracial unity, without knowing the history, studying the texts, and appropriating for themselves the subtlety and complexity of the African American religious experience in the United States.

Nor can white pastors and scholars in religion assume any longer that all God-talk must be in the form of the abstract, literary language characteristic of discourse contingent on mastery of the philosophical heritage derived from ancient Greek and Roman civilizations. The Bible may have been written originally in Hebrew and Greek, but its content transcends the limitations of those languages and thought-forms. The Eurocentric mode of thinking and talking about God is only one model. We African Americans, after all, continue to be an oral people. Most of us prefer to paint pictures with words that convey our feelings, moods, and motivations rather than deal with abstract ideas and concepts. We have always preferred to sing our philosophies, to tell our stories, and to write and recite poetry that expresses our thoughts better than systematic theologies in the Euro-American academic tradition.

In this discussion of the thought-world and pastoral implications of black theology it would be most appropriate to create a mood, a context of empathetic understanding, a universe of intimate discourse within which experimental and tentative answers to those opening questions could be explored. That is not possible in a brief statement in a book, nor can it be done without an intensive, face-to-face encounter when black and white learner/teachers and teacher/learners can take the time, consult the sources, and experience the dialogical interaction necessary for probing the deep-seated emotions and the intellectual beliefs and misunderstandings that have separated us for so many years. Still, we must do the best we can with the medium we have in hand. In the following pages, I will not so much answer all the questions that black theology raises for pastors as to point toward answers that are still largely inarticulate, or are imperfectly construed, in the discursive, analytical language of academic theology. Indeed, this is precisely why some black theologians have chosen to speak of black theology as a "pastoral theology" but with broad implications regarding our continuing struggle for liberation on a wide front.[1]

In the following I address the questions raised above consecutively. In doing so I explore black theology as a particular way of practicing Christian theology in the United States, how it came to be what it is today with regard to both its relatively distant and more recent history, and, most important for my purposes, the function it serves in pastoral ministry in African American churches. I will argue that appreciation and understanding of this way of doing theology out of both the pastor's study and the streets, out of both prayer and political action, can help to close the widening gap between black and white Christians and enhance the whole ecumenical movement in terms of relations between the developed and the developing churches.

Theology and the Color Line

W. E. B. Du Bois made the now famous statement that the problem of the twentieth century would be the problem of the color line.[2] What did he mean? He was making the point that race and color have ontological significance in Western societies, that the mystique of race, symbolized in the United States by blackness and whiteness, would present an inescapable problem to our thinking, our feelings, our politics, our economics, our religion, and our culture, for at least one hundred years. Du Bois would agree that it makes little sense to talk about a Christian theology that is somehow unaffected by the problems of race and ethnicity.

The race problem is ubiquitous in this nation of European, Latin American, and Asian immigrants and former African slaves. It is almost impossible to escape it.

So it should come as no surprise that, for millions of black believers, African American ethnicity is inseparable from the practice of Christian theology, or that there are legitimate ways of doing theology that evolve from reflection on African American ethnicity in the light of the gospel and in the context of the history of Western civilization. This theology, therefore, is not some *other* theology that stands in opposition to the Christian theology that is primarily the reflection of the white church. Black theology *is* Christian theology, without qualification. Jesus Christ authenticates our will to *be*—to exist and flourish as a black people in a majority white environment that has barely tolerated us. Jesus Christ *must* have to do with our affirmation of black being and the requisite power without which *being* is not possible, or he was not involved in our creation, does not know who we are, and therefore cannot be our Savior.

When young black people accuse Christianity of being the "white man's religion," they are saying, consciously and unconsciously, that they have not been introduced to the rudiments of this kind of theology. They are expressing distress and dismay at the failure of the African American churches to portray Jesus as the Black Messiah who satisfies their yearning for acceptance as negated human beings by taking on himself their blackness and feeling of forsakeness in a world unduly dominated by white people.

Dr. King believed in love, nonviolence, and racial integration, but he also began to appreciate the agony and aspirations of our young people after they confronted him on the march between Memphis and Jackson, Mississippi, and again toward the end of his life. Although he did not outwardly affirm black power and black theology as such, one sees in his sermons and writings a late turn toward blackness as providential, vocational, and destined for a special role in the economy of God. In his last book he spoke of black people being called "to imbue our nation with the ideals of a higher and nobler order." Many black ministers before him had made a similar messianic claim for black faith. They spoke out of a tradition that began as early as the eighteenth century. King finally recognized that African American Christians have an all-inclusive cultural and spiritual vocation to speak truth to white power in the United States.[3]

This sense of what I have elsewhere referred to as the "comprehensive cultural vocation" of the black church imposes an enormous burden on sensitive pastors, church executives, and academics.[4] For many pastors it means, first of all, finding a way to respond to the challenges of the Black Power movement of the 1960s through which God was awakening the black church and community to certain truths about America which they had sought to ignore or evade.

During that period, nationwide but particularly in such cities as New York, Philadelphia, Detroit, Cleveland, Chicago, Los Angeles, and the San Francisco Bay area, where young freedom fighters of the Civil Rights and Black Power movements were concentrated, black preachers faced a formidable competitor for "the souls of black folk." This was not the first time they had been challenged by rebellious forces that vied with the churches for a definitive interpretation of the signs of the times. That had happened in the early decades of this century when benevolent and fraternal organizations, social and business clubs, trade unions, the National Association for the Advancement of Colored People, and the National Urban League had helped to unseat the clergy from the pinnacle of the black community's power structure. The difference was that most of those groups were either spawned by the churches or loosely affiliated with them. In those earlier days they shared, in a general way, the same philosophy of peaceful progress toward racial integration that the churches more or less espoused, but they and the artists and novelists of the Harlem Renaissance challenged the churches for community leadership.

The new urban organizations of the mid-1960s were different. A more radical separation existed between them and the churches. The small, disciplined cadres of street people that helped to foment (though were by no means solely responsible for) the northern city rebellions were neither in tune with the southern wing of King's movement nor with the official leadership of the national black denominations. Perhaps the most we can say about the ideological stance of those new grass-roots organizations in Newark, Detroit, and Los Angeles is that they were aggressively black nationalist in terms of domestic policy, Pan-Africanist in their cultural leanings, and oriented to Fidelism and Latin American–styled radicalism in international affairs. By 1965 most of the individuals in such groups were sharply critical of King's go-slow politics and pacifism. This does not mean they had no respect for him or were opposed to the movement he was leading among southern clergy; rather, they were no longer on the same wave length with regard to social change.

Influenced by the rhetoric of Malcolm X, the black power philosophy of Stokely Carmichael and H. Rap Brown, the political nationalism of the

Henry brothers and the Republic of New Africa, and the cultural nationalism of Maulana Karenga and Amiri Baraka, these young revolutionaries changed the vocabulary of the northern struggle from what the newspapers called "random rioting and looting" to something closer to strategic civil rebellion. And drawn into their ranks as sympathetic observers, if not active participants, were a number of African American Christians, seminary professors, and assorted artists, intellectuals, and ghetto activists.

I remember the number of "respectable" Methodist, Baptist, Presbyterian, and Episcopalian ministers and lay leaders who participated in the first national Black Power conference held in Newark, New Jersey, where many of the ideas and commitments voiced were contrary to everything familiar to most of us. Perhaps an experience from those days will more clearly illustrate the pressures we clergy were under from 1964 to roughly 1972, and the direction our thinking was taking as we mounted our pulpits and preached to those entering our churches who came to hear "what thus saith the Lord."

In the midst of the Brooklyn uprising in the summer of 1964 one black pastor, whom I shall call Reverend Black, came to a reluctant conclusion that had the force of a Damascus Road experience shared by many of his brother and sister pastors and church leaders who were trying to give faithful and intelligent leadership during that strange twilight time for black moderation in the United States.[5]

One night Reverend Black was informed that some of the young people of his congregation were under siege in a riot-torn area, which the police had cordoned off and were preparing to invade with tear gas and shotguns. Black instinctively knew what had to be done. He drove his car to the roadblock, and, pretending to be on a pastoral errand of mercy that had nothing to do with the riot, he deceived the police in order to pass through the barricade of squad cars. Once inside, in the midst of the noise and confusion, Reverend Black rounded up his youngsters, threw their gasoline cans and homemade weapons into his trunk, and then drove those young guerrillas to safety by telling the police another lie to keep them from searching his automobile. It was, he later told me, the strangest night of his life. Most important, it completely changed his way of doing Christian theology.

Reverend Black and many other young African American clergy were brought face to face, for the first time in their lives, with the disquieting fact that some of the people of their congregations and their neighborhoods, people whom they often greeted with a smile and a wave as they walked or drove through their parishes, people to whom they had been preaching Sunday after Sunday about justice and the meaning of the world struggle for freedom from oppression, these very people were out there in the streets or on the rooftops with bricks and Molotov cocktails. The people themselves had chosen the white police, the ones who patrolled their neighborhoods like an army of occupation, as the most immediate and offensive symbol of the racist society they were living in, and they were convinced that they had to resist by any means necessary.

After that dramatic night, Reverend Black realized that he could no longer rely on the resources of his seminary courses or the mild-mannered materials he had been using in his Sunday School and adult Bible study classes to provide the theological and ethical guidance that was needed in the volatile situation in Bedford-Stuyvesant. Reinhold Niebuhr, John Bennett, the social Christianity and political liberalism of Union Theological Seminary, and *Christianity and Crisis* may have taught these pastors a hermeneutic for understanding what King's movement was all about, but they were practically useless in this urban warfare context of the northern cities. As the crisis deepened and the assassination of King in May 1968 seemed inevitable, Reverend Black realized that white theologians, as helpful as they had been in other situations, could not supply the answers he and his congregation needed for the new questions that were rising with increasing vehemence from the young people, questions about black history, black belief, black consciousness, and violent resistance to unrelenting subjugation.

Reverend Black and a few other pastors, together with a group of academics and church bureaucrats, began to reflect theologically about the liberation struggle, not prior to but literally in the midst of trying to minister to people who themselves had sensed that a new understanding was necessary. People who had accepted the gospel from our lips and writings now insisted on a demonstration of its realism and practicality in the fight against institutional racism and grinding poverty. It was nothing less than a crisis of the credibility of the gospel, the Bible, and the church for many African American Christians.

So black theology is not something strange for thinking people to be attracted to as they tried to make sense of the Christian life. Martin Luther King Jr. is misrepresented when he is interpreted as having repudiated the implications of black theology. He repudiated the violence some people associated with it, but toward the end of his life he accepted its basic presuppositions about the comprehensive cultural and political vocation of the church. He would have welcomed the fact that black theology was created by pastors and ordinary church folk in the trenches of the northern cities—in Newark, New Jersey, in the Watts section of Los Angeles, and in many places in between—in dialogue between African American Christians from inner-city churches and members of the same communities who rarely darkened the doors of the churches. That is why black theology can be regarded as partly a *pastoral* theology, because it originated among preachers and their lay workers, fathers and mothers of the congregations, who were "sick and tired" of crying "peace, peace, where there was no peace," who were trying to find a meaningful and faithful way to minister to their neighbors in a time of great social and political change.

Pastoral Theology in a Time of Social Change

Another question at the start of this chapter asked what possible relevance can this way of thinking have for pastoral ministry. This question reminds me of the unforgettable day that James Forman, the drafter of the Black Manifesto, came to San Antonio, Texas, to speak to the General Assembly of the United Presbyterian Church in May of 1969.

On the night before his scheduled speech I found myself engaged in a long and heated discussion with a group of young urban guerrillas whom I had, probably unwisely, permitted to occupy my hotel suite because they could not afford to buy a cup of coffee much less to rent a hotel room for the night. At the time, I was on an expense account as the executive director of the United Presbyterian Council on Church and Race (COCAR), headquartered at the Interchurch Center on the Upper West Side of New York City.

Our conversation that night wove in and around the ideas of reparations and the Bible, the complicity and guilt of the white churches, the relevance or irrelevance of belief in Jesus Christ, and the sexual cravings of black preachers. At the climax of our disagreements about almost everything that came up for discussion, the three or four young men stopped arguing and decided to show me how serious they were about being willing to sacrifice themselves for the black revolution. To my utter amazement, they pulled out from under my bed two long wooden boxes that, as a veteran of the Second World War, I immediately recognized. Each was packed tightly with brand new automatic weapons. I learned later that this ordnance had been shipped by Greyhound bus from Miami, although I cannot say that Jim Forman knew anything about what must have been a plan to intimidate the Presbyterians, forcing a decision at gunpoint to pay reparations after his speech to the General Assembly the next morning, a speech I had helped to arrange. It was the Riverside Church confrontation all over again, except this time potentially more deadly.

To say I was shocked would be the greatest understatement of my life. I had to assume that my young guests were not bluffing this time. Verging on panic, I tried as hard as I could to disguise my anxiety by continuing to discuss with them the question of reparations and whether a violent ultimatum could be ethically and strategically justified. All the time, as we argued, I had an image in my head of a ludicrous stickup on the stage of the San Antonio convention hall, a televised shoot-out with the police and the FBI that would set the racial justice cause back one hundred years, and put me in jail for almost as long.

We talked all through the night. Young guerrillas, male and female, seemed to be taking turns debating with me. The discussion ranged from what it means to be black and Christian, to the Black Muslims and the Black Jews, to holy wars, and to Jesus as the Black Messiah, the liberator of the downtrodden. We ruminated about God's judgment and grace in political and cultural struggle; the apostasy of the white church and the cravenness of the black; and what kind of theology and behavior would do justice to the legitimate grievances of college-educated but unemployed and disillusioned young African Americans while at the same time remaining faithful to the demands of the gospel.

When the sun finally lit the skies over San Antonio, I emerged from that smoke-polluted hotel room dry-mouthed and bone weary, drugged with fear. I did not know what the young people would do that day. But I knew that I had to get the weapons out of my room and that I had been these young people's pastor during the night—probably the only one any of them had ever talked to about something other than why they didn't attend Sunday school. I also know that what was troubling their souls had an external source in our racist and unfeeling society. And I know now, looking back these many years later, one other possibility: that during that long night I, as their ad hoc minister, and they, as my young, unintended congregation, had in fact been trying to create out of whole cloth a black theology of liberation.

One of the most articulate of the young men was an irrepressible Pan-Africanist and former SNCC freedom fighter named Irving Davis, of Teaneck, New Jersey. He had been in charge of the BEDC sit-in at my office in the Interchurch Center and later became a close friend with whom I and J. Metz Rollins, executive director of the National Committee of Black Churchmen, worked hard to keep up contact between our clergy group and the followers of James Forman. Irving also, during the next four or five years, became something of a black lay theologian. When he died on April 22, 1981, as a result of injuries suffered in an "accident" in Dar-es-Salaam, an "accident" that he and some of us believed was arranged by the CIA, I wrote a piece for *Presbyterian Outlook* entitled "A Prophet without Portfolio." I wanted other Christians to know that Irving Davis was a member of that "invisible church" to which I and Reverend Black, Albert Cleage, J. Metz Rollins, Calvin Morris, and many other preachers had ministered to in our fumbling ways during the 1960s. But what is most interesting about pastoral ministry under those conditions is that we, clergy and non-clergy alike, became pastors to one another. The truth is that it was people like Irving Davis and Jim Forman who ministered to public Christians like me and taught those of us from the churches how to lay down our reputations, fortunes, and lives for our brothers and sisters. So I wrote, in part, in the *Presbyterian Outlook:*

> I will remember Irving Davis most for what he did for me and several other clergy who were drawn, sometimes kicking and screaming, into the magnetic field of his vision of what the churches should be about in Africa and the Caribbean. Some of us used to say that we evangelized this hard-nosed black revolutionary who came to throw a monkey wrench into the ecclesiastical machinery which he believed was grinding the faces of the oppressed, and stayed to become a partner in mission and a brother. We now know that *he* evangelized *us.*[6]

My intention here is not to glorify young black revolutionaries of the 1960s or to present black theology as a new situation ethics or black antinomianism that justifies anything we do and calls it Christian by convincing ourselves that it serves the cause of black liberation. Rather, I simply want to make two points: first, that many African American pastors were forced to face the problem of having to minister to disappointed and dispirited young people during the Black Power period, and it was out of the struggle to find meaning and redemption in the cause of black dignity and liberation that a contemporary black theology came into existence; second, that this new black theology we were developing was partly, at least, a *pastoral* theology. Rooted in the daily experience of black ministers, it sought to bring the gospel of Jesus Christ to bear on the most exasperating problems of marginalized and cynical people—primarily young, black, and embittered—in the frustrated and alienated African American community that was becoming more and more restive in the belly of the great white whale.

Reverend Black's dramatic night in that riot-torn area and and my own memorable night in San Antonio are good illustrations of what I call the "pastoral dilemma" that some clergy found themselves in as they attempted to interpret the events of the 1960s and 1970s in the light of the gospel and to combat the allegation that "Christianity ain't nothin' but the white man's religion." We were sure that although no one could entirely dispute the fact that "the white man" acted as if he owned Christianity, lock, stock, and barrel, it was a great deal more than that, and, to our understanding, it had everything to do with black liberation.

Whatever one can say about the truth or error of our attempt to do theology at the street level, it did not emerge primarily from libraries, doctoral dissertations, and lectures in seminary classrooms but, rather, from the hurly burly of the real world, from the physical strain and emotional distress of interracial conflict in the inner city. But it also came from a new enthusiasm, a bounding sense of hope, an experience that can be best described by the Greek term *kairos,* a moment of blinding revelation that the times are suddenly full of transcendent meaning and an ultimate decision must be made whether to be faithful to the God who creates, judges, and redeems or to cut and run. Such a moment of unprecedented illumination and urgent decision making came to us more than once between 1955 and 1975, and only many years later, at a time of diminished commitment to revolutionary change in the United States, can we appreciate what God was doing with us during that period. The new theological reflection and social activism that came out of those appointments with what Dr. King called the *Zeitgeist,* the spirit of the age, or "the forces of history and the forces of destiny,"[7] were basically pragmatic and pastoral.

In spite of the legitimate ethical questions begged by the two stories I have related, it is important to remember that black theology did not present itself as a philosophy of the ends justifying the means. Although it is unlikely that most black pastors agreed with the recklessness that some street people displayed, many felt the sting of racism and oppression and the urgency of resisting in order to identify with the young people; to have an "understanding and compassion" for kids who were, after all, our sons and daughters. It was indeed a time to give counsel and pastoral guidance to a radical sector of the black community, but what kind of counseling and to what end?

If we ministers are to be accused of a certain naivete about ideological corruption and of having too easily absolutized the cause of the oppressed as if it were God's unconditional proclivity, I, for one, am prepared to concede the point. If anything authenticated Reverend Black's response to his young church school students in Brooklyn and my response to the would-be guerrillas in my hotel suite—whom I might have, on more careful consideration, immediately turned over to the police—it was the profound feeling, which I am so bold to call the internal testimony of the Holy Spirit—that we did the right thing. Or put another, and perhaps better, way: we were more right than wrong.

In retrospect I can only testify, with the apostle Paul, that it was "the Spirit himself bearing witness with our spirit" that we were children, heirs, and fellow sufferers with Christ (Romans 8:15–17)—or so it seemed to us. Nothing struck us as being more truly God's will than to take the side of the black and poor in the fight for justice, calling them in the name of Jesus Christ, who himself was poor and marginalized, to the vision of a liberated existence, free from the racism and hedonism of a greed-motivated, materialistic culture. Some will call it hopeless idealism, but a pneumatological basis supported our conviction that, even if mistakes were made, we were on the right track. The Holy Spirit in the African American church sanctified our praxis and gave us an assurance that the old wineskins could no longer bear the new wine we were imbibing.[8]

Although King did not live long enough to lend his enormous prestige to the new movement that broke out all around his last years, black theology was a further extension of the militant reorientation that he gave to the black church and community. James H. Cone, and all the theologians who rallied around him after the publication of *Black Power and Black Theology* in 1969, did not so much change the direction of the movement as they deepened its analysis, relating it to history and culture and making it more responsive to the growing impatience of the masses in the North.[9] Because Cone himself was one of those young radicals of the period, he, more than any of us who had already marched with King, understood what that younger generation was demanding of us. Cone had the youthful audacity, the intellectual aptitude, and the education to criticize our obsequious dependence on white theology and to lead us to a new time when black people were asking their religious leaders for a different and more relevant "Word from the Lord," a word full of power, courage, and hope.

That word, strangely enough, often came from the people themselves. Although it is closer to them than to us, they may be completely unaware of that characteristic of divine revelation until it is made known to them in Bible study or theological dialogue. The pastor's role becomes that of a theological midwife. In any case, it may first be necessary to help the people divest themselves of total dependence on the conventional theology one finds in the rotating wire racks of the Christian bookstores. Most of the people writing those paperbacks have been too insensitive to the black experience to have much to teach African Americans about the God who liberates. They have too often assumed that black faith was little more than a poor carbon copy of what they have been saying more faithfully and eloquently than anybody else for years.

It is not surprising that the black church's grounding in African spirituality, its political salience, and its sense of comprehensive cultural vocation almost completely escaped the attention of most white religious writers and seminary professors. They may have understood Dr. King, but Dr. King did not talk about such things. The late Bishop Joseph Johnson Jr. of the Christian Methodist Episcopal Church, one of the most insightful of the African American theologians of the period who remained close to the church, explained his own and Cone's restiveness.

> For more than one hundred years, Black students have studied in predominantly white seminaries, and have been served a theological diet created, mixed, and dosed out by white theological technicians. The Black seminarians took both the theological milk and meat, and even when they consumed these, their souls were still empty. Those of us who attended white seminaries passed our courses in the four major fields of study; we knew our Barth and Brunner, and we entered deeply into the serious study of Bonhoeffer and Tillich. But now we have discovered that while these white theologians have elucidated a contemporary faith for white men, they know nothing about the Black experience. To many of the white scholars, the Black experience was (and is) illegitimate and inauthentic.[10]

A Pastoral Critique of the Liberation Emphasis

One of the most consistent criticisms of black theology is that it does not include a vertical dimension, that the profound "God-ward" aspect of traditional black faith is missing. How justified is such a critique? Early on, at least two black theologians—Cecil Cone (the brother of James H. Cone) and Henry Mitchell—seemed to support this criticism by accusing black theology of being excessively action-oriented and political. Mitchell, a seasoned homiletician, continued to argue that, unless it found a voice to express greater inwardness and began to address the felt needs and hurts of individuals, black theology would never become a viable option for the masses.[11] Such criticism is difficult to deny. There is little doubt that black theology stands in danger of becoming too impersonal and theoretical, just another political ideology with a thin veneer of religiosity. As such, say its critics, it will be ignored by the majority of both the clergy and the people.

In their book entitled *Soul Theology: The Heart of American Black Culture,* Henry H. Mitchell, a professor at the Interdenominational Theological Center in Atlanta, and Nicholas C. Lewter, a Baptist pastor and psychotherapist in private practice, uncover the core belief system of the black church with the intention of reconstructing what they call "our soul theology." It was their purpose to demonstrate how it is possible to lead people to greater emotional stability, physical well-being, and spiritual wholeness by raising latent folk affirmations to the level of consciousness and encouraging clients to reappropriate the therapeutic power of black belief. Their contention is close to the observation that the truth of God is frequently buried in the subconsciousness of the ordinary folk in the pews. Mitchell and Lewter contend that soul theology, "unlike the widespread classification of Black theology with the theologies of liberation" (which they evidently rejected) preserves the "nourishing spirituality" of the African American folk belief system.[12]

Here is an important corrective to the black theology movement that has sometimes been almost exclusively committed to polemics and politics. It rightly brings us back to the pastoral function of theology that King understood so well but that was neglected after his assassination. But these authors fail to make clear that what they are proposing cannot be an either-or proposition but must, instead, be a both-and statement. It is precisely the nature of black spirituality that ensures that *both* the personal *and* the social aspects of our experience must be included in the mission of the church. And because the personal and social realms are also inseparable in real life, black or soul theology, properly understood, cannot make pastoral ministry a personal and spiritual service that can be separated from Christian social and political action. C. Wright Mills was fond of saying that personal ills ineluctably bisect social problems. That bisection is simply taken for granted by many mental health practitioners who work in the African American community.

During the 1960s two black psychiatrists, William H. Grier and Price M. Cobbs, published a study based on their clinical work with black patients. They examined scores of cases of psychological suffering that required professional counseling. They found that in many instances mental illness was directly traceable to internalized frustration and rage induced by the effects of racism and oppression in the environment.

> One of the problems in understanding the discontent of black people in America is highlighted in this material. The relationship between intrapsychic functioning and the larger social environment is exceedingly complex. Among other things, Negroes want to change inside but find it difficult to do so unless things outside are changed as well.[13]

Price and Cobb present an even more sobering thought. They concluded that the role of the Christian religion, as shaped by white norms and values, had more frequently served to depreciate and debase black people than to make them more self-esteeming and psychologically healthy.[14] Their data seem to argue for the necessity of African American Christian theologies to counteract the negative, guilt-producing effects of the religion that was preached to blacks during slavery, a form of Christianity that regarded blackness as symbolizing that which is innately evil and inferior.

Perhaps both Grier and Cobbs, and Mitchell and Lewter, have overstated their cases in opposite directions. A more correct view is that authentic black religion has refused to disengage the spiritual from the secular. The best of black preaching down through the centuries has made it clear that piety and practical action go together, that neither personal counseling nor political activism is sufficient to ensure peace of mind and happiness. My childhood pastor, Rev. Aurthur E. Rankin, always reminded us that "you ought to pray about it, but soon you have to get off your knees and *do* something." Another familiar saying among some black preachers in the Philadelphia area was, "if you don't do the devil, the devil will surely do you." These choice examples of folk wisdom tell us that continuous engagement in struggle is one way of keeping Satan off-balance and defending oneself against the ever present machinations of internal and external evil.

Mitchell and Lewter are to be commended for trying to make black theology more of a pastoral theology. But that does not require that it be divested of its theory and praxis as a theology of liberation. Because it cannot speak of *Shalom,* of wholeness and healing without, while at the same time speaking of health delivery systems, government bureaucracies, social security, affordable housing, and gainful employment, black theology will not offer people a spiritual bromide for a slashed throat. Instead, it seeks to motivate us to work for the economic and political changes that abolish misery and promote permanent health care for the masses. The Mitchell-Lewter emphasis on pastoral ministry is therefore a welcome improvement, but it must delve more deeply into the historic black response to the climax of the Lord's description of his own ministry—"to set at liberty those who are oppressed" (Luke 4:18).

Black theology must have a pastoral focus but in a different sense than what is usually meant. It has been mistakenly assumed that what is called pastoral theology is an academic field considerably less demanding than systematic theology or biblical studies. At some seminaries pastoral theology has to do with the "nuts and bolts" of ministry, understood as pastoral care and counseling and such areas as preaching, celebrating the eucharist, hymnody, Christian education, church administration, and other matters that pastors do daily. But in the African American church it is precisely what pastors do each day that connects the gospel message about personal salvation to the realities of structural unemployment, inadequate welfare reform, teenage pregnancy, personal illness, and public misery. In other words, mobilizing, motivating, and instructing the saints to take charge of their lives by using the church as an enabler of social change has been a key aspect of pastoralia in the African American church.

Thomas C. Oden, a white pastoral theologian, recognizes this sense of what we mean by pastoral theology when he writes that it "seeks to join the theoretical with the practical."[15] He suggests the action-reflection model as a paradigm for pastoral theology. African American pastoral theologians would, however, put greater emphasis on leading worship, preaching, and praying as *setting the spiritual or pneumatological context* for the practical, external responses of the congregation on behalf of all who suffer from depersonalization and oppression.

This means that black theology is a form of pastoral theology in a very specific sense. Not merely because it "deals with those consequences [of God's self-disclosure in history] as they pertain to the roles, tasks, duties, and work of the pastor" (Oden) but also because it draws from Scripture, tradition, culture, and experience that power in congregational worship that unites sanctification and liberation. It enables the pastor and others who have shepherding responsibilities to bring together personal ills and social problems for the purposes of survival, elevation, and liberation.

Although James H. Cone, the leading exponent of contemporary black theology, does not define what he does explicitly as a pastoral theology, his writings have consistently recognized the need for coherence between spirituality in the sanctuary and the struggle in the streets. For Cone, any study of the pilgrimage of blacks from slavery will confirm the inseparability of the basic disciplines of pastoral theology for nurturing the souls of black folk and helping their churches to be agents of God's liberation.

> The contradiction between the experience of sanctification and human slavery has always been a dominant theme in black religion. It is found not only in the rise of independent black churches but also in our songs, stories, and sermons. When the meaning of sanctification is formed in the social context of an oppressed community in struggle for liberation, it is difficult to separate the experience of holiness from the spiritual empowerment to change the existing societal arrangements. If "I'm a chile of God wid soul set free" because "Christ hab bought my liberty," then I will find it impossible to tolerate slavery and oppression.[16]

The Challenge to the White Churches

I come now to the final question being asked of black theologians. Is black theology so narrowly focused on the black condition in the United States that it loses any relevance for people who are not black?

Sydney E. Ahlstrom, the celebrated American church historian at Yale Divinity School, made a remark about black religious history that might well be applied to the fields of systematic and pastoral theology. Ahlstrom observed the necessity of a "thorough renovation" of American church history in the course of recommending that the paradigm for such a renovation is the black religious experience that had been excluded from all previous synoptic histories of Christianity in the West. With the same concern for recovering hitherto discarded traditions that radically challenge the norms of majority scholarship, I would argue that black theology provides a paradigm for the renovation of American theology. Indeed, in view of the fact that black theology has already opened itself to criticism and reform from other Third-World theologies, it has made a constructive contribution to an emerging consensus among Third-World Christians. What challenge does this development present to the predominantly white mainline churches of the United States?

Throughout the so-called Third World a flood of evangelical conservatism is bursting forth from the masses of people who had not been closely bound to conservative Roman Catholicism or to the old-line Protestantism of Europe and the United States. Not the least responsible for the revival of "old-time religion" in the heartland of North America and its satellite countries south of the border has been the skillful utilization of the mass media, particularly television, by evangelistic preachers whose knowledge of the Bible is no less developed than their knowledge of modern communications and sharp business practices. On the other hand, the upsurge of born-again religiosity, which has the strong odor of the bourgeoisification of previously impoverished populations, tells us that there is little inclination on the part of some overseas churches to defend the human rights their people have been denied or to oppose the obvious excesses and injustices of globalized capitalism. Indeed, this new fundamentalism emerging in Africa, Asia, and Latin America is politically reactionary, is so moralistic as to be ready when it comes into power to suppress any dissent, is opposed to cultural pluralism and secular humanism, and is hysterically anticommunist. Is this what was heralded one hundred years ago as the "Christian century?" Is this what is called the triumph of the gospel in the post-modern world?

Although the black churches have not been invulnerable to enticements from the Christian Right, they have not suffered a large defection of members to conservative churches comparable to the older white denominations. Nor have they been inclined to pull in their horns and become theologically fainthearted in order to deflect criticism coming from the new born-again movements. The theological tradition of black Christianity in the United States has been both pragmatic and spiritual. It has been generally ready to do battle with any interpretation of the faith that either removes it from politics altogether or strikes an unholy alliance with political and economic conservatism. That is changing slowly but has not yet become a new status quo in the African American community. Therefore black theology, which represents this tough but resilient tradition, is a prime candidate for the renovation of the embattled ecumenical theology of the mainstream at this point in history.

Nothing is more urgently needed than such a renovation when the Sunday morning televangelists, the Jerry Falwells and Pat Robertsons, are successfully calling the white middle class to retrench from social legislation at home and to help fight against liberation movements abroad. One popular Pentecostal minister in Atlanta, whose congregation of almost ten thousand members includes many middle-class Negroes, offers what he calls a "kingdom theology." In an interview with an *Atlanta Constitution* reporter he is alleged to have said: "It is a whole new theology. . . . What we're doing is setting up a network by which we can spread propaganda. . . . We will accomplish enough [so] that the systems of the world will collapse because of their inability to survive, and what will be left will be a system the church has built."[17]

The kingdom theology of the conservative evangelicals intends to impose infallible Christian politics, Christian economics, Christian public education, and a federal government–supported Christian culture that "will take dominion over the world." It would snatch us all from the jaws of the secular humanists, the gay community, and Godless socialism. It need not be concerned with poverty and degradation, because it teaches that the poor and oppressed are God-forsaken because of their sins. It has no use for the World Council or the National Council of Churches because they are both agents of Satan championing contextual theologies and cultural pluralism.

Black theology, both systematic and pastoral, has long grappled with religious people who make such claims. We suspect that the evangelical revolution of today frequently masks an old-fashioned white supremacy. Therein lies one answer to the question regarding the broader implications of a black pastoral theology. Such a theology has to do with more than the black church because it contributes to the enlightenment of white Christians by unmasking the racism and cultural imperialism that lurks under the outer garments of this new Christian fundamentalism. In its best form, therefore, black theology presents a pastoral and political option for the poor and oppressed that can help American churches recover a compassionate and holistic ministry that recognizes a coherence between authentic spirituality and liberal politics.

The Dutch theologian Theo Witvliet writes about black theology as representative of the underside of history where Christ is and where the church must also be.

> The confrontation with black theology here represents an enormous positive challenge. Its polemic has a positive side, "Polemic is love." In its unmasking of the contradiction of Christianity there is a plea for conversion, *metanoia,* for a radical transformation of perspective, which leads to the domain of the hidden history, the history which, judged by the usual church norms, belongs rather in the history of heresy. Black theology wants to argue from this specific history, extending from the invisible church of the time of slavery [that in this history] there is a glimpse of liberation, of the great light that shines over those who live in a land of deep darkness. (Isaiah 9:1; John 1:5)[18]

It may not be necessary for white Christians to become as explicit about "the blackness of God" as Witvliet recommends,[19] but the point ought not to be missed that a thoughtful appropriation of black theological concepts could help white pastors and church leaders to identify with "the wretched of the earth" and be able to de-program middle-class white Christians who have become accustomed to picturing Jesus as a long-haired, blond suburbanite with a beautiful tan who vindicates their most pious pretensions of white power over "lesser breeds without the law."

White American Christians can also learn from black theology that pastoral care and counseling is able not only to bring "the peace that passeth understanding" but must also redirect congregants to the *missio Dei,* to God's work of liberation and reconciliation in the world. Black people are certainly not the only people in bondage. The white churches need to help their people experience the power of the Holy Spirit in black worship that not only renders a psychosomatic liberty more freeing than what some patients experience on the psychiatrist's couch but, as Dr. King's movement demonstrated, can also march them down the aisle singing the songs of Zion and out into the highways and byways to unbind the world from the tentacles of injustice and despotism.

Finally, the world mission of the church, which was so notably influenced in the United States by the religiously motivated and nonviolent Civil Rights movement, can be reinvigorated by drawing certain insights about spirituality and struggle from the Black Theology movement. James H. Cone contends that black theology is modest in its claim to have the whole truth and, by respecting the "pre-reflective visions of the poor as defined by their political struggles," opens itself to revelations of God's will from religions other than Christianity.[20] In a world that has almost become a single neighborhood, the ecumenical movement needs to be instructed by such a recommendation regarding truth. Theological absolutism is not only counterproductive for world peace, but it is also contrary to the most universal meaning of the religion of Jesus. Black Christians have usually been wary of people who rush to judgment about what is right or wrong, or of dogmatic statements of faith and churches that are so proud of their doctrinal purity that they cannot imagine any imperfections in their social policies and practices. Only when one has been lowered into the depths of suffering and sacrifice does one give up illusions about infallibility and perfectibility. Only when we cry out with Jesus, "My God, why hast thou forsaken me?" does it seem right, good, and grace-filled to be able to welcome the truth that consoles and frees wherever it may be found.

Today the world mission of the church is challenged to openness, dialogue, and collaboration with other faiths and ideologies, particularly in the Third World where the gifts that God has given to other races, nationalities, and religions have been deprecated and submerged by a triumphant Christian civilizing missiology. Black theology has much to learn about other people, but because most of the excluded races, ethnic groups, and religionists are people of color, it has been more empathetic with pilgrims on other paths to God, and therefore has something valuable to say to the ecumenical movement about tolerance and the love of one's neighbor. This teaching should take place in the world of politics and religions, but it must begin at home in the sanctuary and the study where the pastoral office opens the way for the Holy Spirit to come to the people in the midst of their personal suffering and communal struggle.

15

Black Christians, Church Unity, and One Common Expression of Apostolic Faith

Something like 95 percent of the more than 25 million black Christians in the United States are now concentrated in seven historic African American churches and nine of the largest predominantly white churches, including the Roman Catholic Church. African American Christians who hold membership in the white churches worship mainly in all-black congregations and comprise less than a quarter of the total number of black church members in the nation. They experience what can be called a relative separateness and insulation from the majority of white Christians that is little different from what is experienced by the millions of their family members and friends who never left the all-black or predominantly black denominations that were founded in the eighteenth and nineteenth centuries. For all these reasons some observers have described eleven o'clock Sunday morning in the United States of America as the most racially segregated hour of the week.[1]

An attenuated but continuing nexus to an African past has stamped a distinctive mode and mood of being Christian on the African American community. This distinction is reflected primarily in the spirituality, theology, music, and styles of worship of this ethnic sector of North American Christianity. A common participation in what was originally a blend of diasporic African culture with a culture of domination and poverty in depressed rural areas and urban ghettos has given these black Christians an awareness of shared life-styles and group identity that up to the middle of the last century has been difficult to erase. The mutual experience of racial prejudice and discrimination has bequeathed to these dark-skinned American Christians a sense of solidarity in suffering and struggle for more than 375 years.

These characteristics have convinced many scholars that it is not inaccurate to speak of an African American or black church in the Western hemisphere, even though there may be considerable diversity among its constituent parts. The trend toward racial integration in American society in the second half of the twentieth century has only slightly dissolved this apparently unmeltable ethnic institution. It continues to grow, particularly among Pentecostals, Baptists, Methodists, and Roman Catholics, and it continues to wield a disproportionate influence (in terms of its numerical size compared to the white majority) in the social, political, and economic life of the nation. With regard to Protestantism, the African American churches, considering numbers, size, real estate ownership, and the conspicuous public activities of their congregations, are now American Protestantism's principal representative in more than a score of the largest central cities in the United States.

Not surprisingly, therefore, the National Council of Churches (NCC), the World Council of Churches (WCC), and other world confessional and ecumenical bodies have been interested in what the African American churches believe and are prepared to commit to the movement toward visible unity among all Christians. Accordingly, the Commission on Faith and Order of the NCC, in response to initiatives from the Geneva headquarters of the WCC, undertook some years ago to encourage black theologians and church leaders to articulate the ideas and beliefs that seem generally to be shared by black churches, including those continuing to exist as separate entities within predominantly white communions.

Interesting and critical questions immediately come to mind. To what extent do black Christians today hold the same faith professed by other Christians in the United States and other parts of the world? To what extent do they believe and practice a variant faith which is, nevertheless, rooted and grounded in the Apostolic tradition of the early Christian churches, as far as it is possible to accurately reconstruct that tradition today? What distinctive contributions do the African American churches and individual congregants have to make to the quest, accelerated since the founding of the World Council in 1948, for the visible unity of the one, holy, catholic, and apostolic church and the one common expression of faith that was handed down to contemporary believers from Jesus and his disciples? These questions not only concern the official bureaucracies of the black denominations that claim membership in both confessional and ecumenical bodies on a national and world level, but, more important, they also concern the pastors, the Christian educators, and the lay leadership of local congregations where the real work of the church is carried out daily and where the true oneness of the Christian family must be made manifest in order that the world might believe and turn to its Creator (John 17:21).

The purpose of this chapter, originally prepared as a working paper for an ecumenical conference, is to discuss briefly some of the factors that may determine an agreeable context for addressing such questions as those above. What follows below has no official status except as a stimulus for an exploratory conversation that took place at the Interchurch Center in New York City on May 30, 1984, and further at a national consultation in December of the same year. Its significance lies in the fact that it helped to inform discussions following those events when African American seminary professors, pastors, and ordinary church members began to talk to one another about Christian ecumenism with greater interest and on a broader front than has been possible to replicate during all the years since the 1980s. The content of this chapter represents, therefore, a high point in ecumenical discussions among African Americans. At that time it was hoped that some of the problems and issues explored in this and other published documents would be examined at a historic consultation that was held at Virginia Union University in Richmond, Virginia, among African American academics and denominational representatives on December 14–15, 1984. Those problems and issues were explored in Richmond, but that much neglected work needs to be renewed in the twenty-first century if African American Christians, beginning with local pastors and lay people, are to bring the full resources and influence of their churches behind the perennial effort to bring about unity and renewal in the church of Jesus Christ in the United States and throughout the world.

Christianity and Racism

The effort to enlist African and African American denominations and congregations in the quest for unity and renewal may have been frustrated to some extent by the slowness of ecumenical bodies to face and deal forthrightly with the problem of racism in the historic churches of Europe and North America in the ways, and with the same determination, with which they dealt with it in South Africa before the turn of the century. In 1975 this author moderated a WCC consultation in Europe entitled "Racism in Theology and Theology against Racism." The second chapter of the official consultation report was published in a compendium of World Council of Churches "Statements and Actions on Racism, 1948–1979," edited by Ans J. van der Bent (Geneva: WCC Document, 1980). Why was the first chapter on "Racism in Theology" eliminated from the collection of church and ecumenical policy statements?

Could it have been because that section contained one of the most devastating criticisms of Euro-American Christianity ever issued by an international conference of Christian theologians, church officials, and social scientists? That part of the document that the WCC has neglected to publish analyzes Christian history and declares outrightly that theology has been infected by the ideology of white racism almost from its beginning. From the infiltration into the medieval church of the disparaging accounts of the origin of the color and physiognomy of African people—first promulgated by the Babylonian Talmud of the sixth century A.D.—to the modern defense of the subjugation and enslavement of black people by some of the most prominent leaders of the American churches prior to 1861, Western Christendom, with few exceptions, has been corrupted by a more vicious form of racism than was ever known in the pagan world.

If racism, as the late George Kelsey has so powerfully argued, is diametrically opposed to a Christian understanding of creation and redemption, one might ask if European and American Christianity was not totally corrupted—particularly in its Anglo-Saxon versions—by a deep-seated antipathy toward black skin color.[2] Certainly many African American Christians have thought so. For years some of our best thinkers and writers have expressed the opinion that what most white people believed and practiced as their *operative* religion could never be properly called the religion of Jesus Christ. Thus the Reverend W. Paul Quinn, later to become a bishop of the African Methodist Episcopal Church, wrote, in 1834, words that have resounded from African American pulpits for more than two hundred years.

> Can anything be a greater mockery of religion than the way in which it is conducted by the Americans? It appears as though they are bent only on daring God Almighty to do his best—they chain and handcuff us and go into the house of the God of justice to return Him thanks for having

aided them in the infernal cruelties inflicted upon us. . . . Will He not stop them, preachers and all?[3]

Some have held that the faith once delivered to the Apostles could only be found in the church that formerly practiced and defended slavery if and when those churches experienced true repentance and total reformation. To the extent that the churches of Europe were participants or silent partners in the enslavement and subsequent oppression of blacks and other non-white peoples, it was argued that they needed to demonstrate genuine repentance and love of subjugated peoples through the *koinonia* of the gospel before their professions of the faith could be taken seriously.

This is only to say that African American Christians, for the most part, have never taken for granted that the Apostolic Faith, being invoked by the World Council of Churches, is resident in the white churches of Europe and North America—Protestant or Roman Catholic. This is *not* to say that the black churches themselves have been without fault with respect to slavery and its accompanying sins but, rather, to make a simple statement of fact about the glaring complicity in this infamy on the part of most white churches claiming the legacy of the Apostles. It does appear, and this is the main point of the rejoinder by African American Christians to the initiatives of the NCC and WCC, that mere assent to the Nicene Creed and adherence to the great confessions of the Reformation do not, by themselves, add up to apostolicity.

As the church leaders that supported the Black Manifesto of 1969 contended, many white churches in the United States and abroad are still enjoying prosperity and wealth accumulated from the ill-gotten gain of the Atlantic slave trade. Until there is among such churches "fruit meet for repentance," as the old preachers used to say, African and African American Christians may feel justified in looking elsewhere for signs of the unbroken continuity of pure religion from the Apostles to the present. It is not unfair to ask whether at some time during the last millennium the message of Jesus Christ and the New Testament all but evaporated from the Euro-American churches and societies because of the gross incompatibility between faith and practice in race relations among those who called themselves Christians.

Black Theology as Apologia and Critique

Black theology, from George Liele and David George to James Cone and J. Deotis Roberts, has had a double edge.[4] It has been a reasoned defense of the conviction of most black believers that the justice and righteousness of God with regard to race relations is the essence of the gospel, and a sharp and continuing critique of what many regard as an apostate white church. This does not mean that black Christians never appreciated the theological symbols of white Christendom such as the two historic creeds, the Nicene and the Apostles Creed. Indeed, the African American churches used them and extrapolated their affirmations for our own African Methodist Episcopal Disciplines and other official statements of faith. Most of the blackness or "ethnic-specific" content in our theology at the level of the local church has been in defense of the way we perceived and worshiped God. This concern is evidenced in exhortations to blacks to be more faithful to the gospel than to their masters and mistresses, and in protests against the abuses and injustices of the white church, the white state, and the economic, social, and cultural institutions of the nation from the American Revolution until now. That most of this African American content of theological thinking has never been written down in books or ensconced in creeds and confessions does not make it any less theological and authentic.

Nevertheless, any study project declaring that it seeks, as does the leadership of the WCC, to know what perceptions of black Christians might be called on for developing a contemporary ecumenical statement of the Christian faith for WCC member churches should, first of all, consider the writings, addresses, and sermons of black preachers, church leaders, theologians, and philosophers—from Prince Hall, who founded the first order of African American Masons in the late eighteenth century, and Henry M. Turner, an AME editor and bishop in the nineteenth century, to W. E. B. Du Bois and Cornel West in the twentieth.

Second, the folklore, proverbs, spirituals, hymns, and gospel songs are indispensable resources for understanding the belief structures of poor black Christians who consider themselves just as much in succession to the Apostles and Fathers of the early church as do white Christians. In fact, some African American preachers assumed that the mantle of authority had actually fallen from the shoulders of the white churches to land on those of black believers in America, most of whom were slaves and illiterate. It was they, these spokespersons for African American

Christian thought, who reconstructed an authentic Christian faith from the failed and compromised religion of the white churches.

The themes and motifs of this black folk religion still reverberate in our churches, particularly those of the Baptist, Methodist, and Holiness-Pentecostal traditions. Therefore any consideration of black theology that fails to consider these data will be incapable of identifying the strands of the popular religion that may not have been woven into the official theologies of the churches but are, nonetheless, essential for understanding the operative belief systems of the people.

The purpose of these remarks about black theology is to suggest that although black and white Christians received what is basically the same gospel, they have differed from each other in the thematic emphases and nuances of interpretation given by their preachers and theologians to both Scripture and tradition. The importance of this fact for doing theology today, which some of us have almost taken for granted, seems difficult for Christians outside the United States to appreciate. Some of us have noticed, while participating in WCC consultations and international conferences, that many white conferees want to brush it aside as of no consequence. During the Civil Rights movement European church leaders were more intrigued by unfamiliar theological ideas that exploded like errant firecrackers out of the black communities of the United States, but today they seem to dismiss both the seriousness and significance of what African Americans think about the mission and unity of the worldwide church.

In any international study of one common expression of the Apostolic Faith there is a need for African Americans to restate and clarify what we mean by black theology. African American churches need to bestir themselves to explain how the spiritual and material conditions of survival and liberation for people of African descent living in racist societies have, by the grace of God and the inspiration of the Holy Spirit, given the same faith presumed to be the property of white people different emphases and interpretations among African American believers. The relevant question is, what *is* this African American interpretation today and to what extent does it remain faithful or unfaithful to what the ecumenical church recognizes as the Apostolic residuum?

The Black Perspective and Church Priorities

What we call a black or Africentric theological perspective on the Christian faith can also be discerned by a careful study of the polity and programmatic priorities of the African American denominations and congregations down through the years. The theology that thundered from the pulpits on Sunday morning was less concerned about how to understand the first three articles of the Nicene Creed than about the relevance of faith, hope, and love for obtaining the next three meals, a roof over one's head, a job and an equal education for one's children. Our churches were missionary outposts on the frontier of abject poverty and on the borders of a hostile white world. As such, they sent out deacons and deaconesses, teachers, Boy Scout and Girl Scout leaders, social workers, nurses, and community organizers to encourage a dispirited people. They advocated for the poor and dispossessed, and led religious and secular movements for freedom and social betterment. By examining these priorities of the black churches of America, we can begin to understand the special angle from which the leadership viewed the gospel and the actual significance they attributed to various aspects of faith and order.

What was important to the white churches and theological seminaries was not necessarily important to their black counterparts. White churches became embroiled in many disputes between fundamentalists and theological modernists or liberals. African American churches almost never did. White churches emphasized peace, purity, and organic unity in the body and tried assiduously to avoid schism. African American churches, despite the pain associated with wrenching disaffiliations in the body, seemed somewhat better able to tolerate splits and splinter groups, and to override the resultant animosity. In fact, black religious institutions enjoyed luxuriant growth through a pluralism and proliferation that was frowned on by white mainstream churches. The white laity exercised almost rigid control over most white ministers, and charismatic and autocratic preachers in the mainstream churches were often regarded with suspicion and relegated to backwater appointments. Black churches preferred strong, charismatic leaders, and black preachers, sometimes to a fault, brooked no interference with the freedom of the pulpit. For many years white churches generally felt that "religion and politics don't mix." Their frequent excuse for not taking an aggressive position against slavery in the nineteenth century was the impropriety of encroaching on the civil domain. Black churches usually had no such squeamishness. After some initial hesitation over whether it was a war only among racist white Americans, they eagerly promoted the Civil War as a holy crusade for total abolition and were rarely boosters of pacifism or nonviolence until the era of Dr. King. White Christians drew a sharp line between the secular and the sacred. They assigned their churches to an increasingly narrow sector of daily life and were satisfied that they were doing their Christian duty. Black Christians, on the other hand, recognized no sharp division between what belongs to Satan and what belongs to God, and their churches were cultural centers that embraced and coordinated many aspects of culture and community life. White churches, particularly those of the Protestant establishment in the urban Northeast, adopted the Social Gospel, a historical-critical approach to Scripture and the work of social welfare, and sought to accommodate the faith to the Enlightenment and the Industrial Revolution. Their African American denominational counterparts, while they, too, came to stress the importance of an educated ministry, were never so sanguine as the white brethren about theological seminaries, demythologizing the Bible, or making systematic and moral theology subservient to secular philosophies and ethics.

These are only a few contrasts and comparisons that illustrate the divergent life-styles of the two churches during most of the nineteenth and twentieth centuries. Although many of them refer to sociological differences, they all point to important theological causes and effects that the ecumenical movement should not ignore. The trajectory of traditional black Christian faith can be discerned by focusing on these and other priorities of the churches that tell us what they have regarded as critical for faith and order, life and work. Whether it is correct to speak of one theological perspective or of many remains, of course, an open question that black theological academics must determine by the degree of commonality and integrity they discover in the beliefs and practices of African American church members.

As an example of some issues of faith and order that may be clarified by examining black church priorities, and that may help us to formulate an African American perspective on the Apostolic faith as contained in the Creed of Nicea, I list below some questions, which are adaptations of similar questions contained in a WCC Faith and Order document entitled "Toward the Common Expression of the Apostolic Faith Today" (Geneva: FO/81:9, August 1981). Are African American Christians willing to measure their agreement or disagreement with the Apostles and the

Nicene Creeds by using these questions to establish some criteria for ecumenical solidarity today?

> 1. The creed confesses faith in one God. How do we explicate "one God" against our ancestral background in African Traditional Religions, our historic valorization of many aspects of Islam, and the modern tendency to absolutize finite "secular" realities such as freedom, economic prosperity, and social security?
> 2. The creed confesses Jesus Christ, God's only begotten Son, to be "of one essence" with the Father. In view of the openness of many African American Christians to a kind of practical mysticism and the transcendence motifs of Eastern religions, how should we understand this claim that human salvation cannot be real without our human participation in that which is divine and eternal?
> 3. The creed confesses that God's only Son has become human. How does this faith in the incarnation illumine our understanding of the Black Messiah, our incorporation into him, and the significance of such symbolic representations for the rest of the human family?
> 4. The creed confesses faith in the Holy Spirit of the Triune God. To what extent have our African and slave religions enriched our understanding of the Spirit? How do we discern the Spirit in the Church and in the world of politics, economics, and social systems?
> 5. The creed confesses One, Holy, Catholic, and Apostolic Church. How much are the African American denominations willing to sacrifice in order to make this ecumenical church manifest in North America? What sacrifices must we make and demand from others in order for all of us to experience this undivided, holy, and universal church of the Apostles?
> 6. The creed confesses one baptism for the forgiveness of sins. What is the significance of baptism by water and the Holy Spirit in African American churches? What implication does this article have for our acceptance of persons of other races, classes, and creeds whom God has already called in Jesus Christ?
> 7. The creed confesses life in the age to come. How have our Spirituals and gospel songs helped us to lay claim to a life that transcends death and yet can be experienced in the here and now?

What do the black churches believe about heaven, hell, human utopias, and the end of the world?

The Need for Further Investigation

Clearly this brief chapter barely scratches the surface of the problems that need to be addressed in responding to the question, "What are the distinctive perspectives of African American Christians who want to be engaged in the search for one common expression of the Apostolic Faith?"

That question cannot be answered by conferences and consultations that only involve theologians and other academics. The discussion must take place at the level of the local congregation and include participation by ordinary lay people, equal numbers of men, women, and the younger baptized members of congregations, before we can be assured that the considered judgment of the black churches of the United States have been fairly represented.

A longer and carefully prepared consultation involving both lay and clergy discussants took place at Virginia Union University on December 14–15, 1984, sponsored by the Commission on Faith and Order of the National Council of Churches, but was not followed up with the educational materials and guidance for local congregations that were required for an extended study of the issues at the grass-roots level. The major papers that were written for the Virginia Union consultation and other working papers recommended for study and discussion, together with the report entitled "Toward a Common Expression of Faith: A Black North American Perspective," were published in 1985 by the Council on Christian Unity and stand today as a mute though quasi-authoritative witness to the yet unfinished task of discovering whether the African American churches, though different in important respects from First World members of the WCC, still fall within the circle of Christian communions worldwide that confess the Nicene Creed.[5]

It is no secret that African American Christians, both those who are members of black denominations and those within predominantly white denominations, have not been conspicuous in the World Council of Churches' studies of "Faith and Order" questions before the Christian churches of the world. Considering the current trends at home and overseas, the numbers of African American delegates to WCC Assemblies and regional conferences are likely to be even fewer in years to come because of the necessity for the WCC to give greater voice to Third-World churches. As African and other Third-World churches join the WCC they will reduce the proportional representation, and hence the visibility, of black American Christians. African Americans do care about the visible unity of the one church of Christ across all barriers of race, class, gender, and nationality. But although a few black bishops and other spokespersons have been active in the world confessional bodies and at various international conferences, on the whole African American churches and theologians have not received the attention and welcome accorded other groups by the secretariat of the WCC.

African American Christians must accept some responsibility for their marginality in the ecumenical movement, but not all of it. In any case, the present situation is woefully deficient and needs to be remedied by whatever means are possible. Our churches have played too great a role and have paid too heavy a price in Christianity in the West to be absent from theological discussion and decision making regarding the unity and mission of the world Christian family.

At the Fifth Assembly of the WCC, which met in Nairobi, Kenya, in December 1975, the following recommendation was adopted with great hope and prayers for the future of faith and order studies.

> We ask the churches to undertake a common effort to receive, reappropriate and confess together, as contemporary occasion requires, the Christian truth and the faith, delivered through the Apostles and handed down through the centuries. Such common action, arising from free and inclusive discussion under the commonly acknowledged authority of God's Word, must aim both to clarify and to embody the unity and the diversity which are proper to the church's life and mission.[6]

The time is late but still available for African American Christians in the United States to make their concerns known and contributions accessible to Christians around the world. The attempt of our sister churches to express together a common understanding of the Apostolic Faith gives the black churches and blacks in predominantly white denominations an opportunity, even a responsibility, to share with others the wealth of the hard-earned wisdom and experience with which God has blessed us. These "gifts of blackness"[7] come from many years of intense wrestling with the Spirit, like Jacob at Bethel, and many long years of a sometimes successful but more often frustrating effort to participate equally with others in the ministry and mission of Jesus Christ, a ministry and mission which we have always recognized as being not only for black people in the United States but also for the salvation of humankind around the globe.

16

Lessons from My Father's World

A Sermon

African American scholars in religion generally agree that, no matter how intellectually adequate, if an idea "doesn't preach" it will not edify the black church. That may be a slight exaggeration, but no movement prospers in the black church and community that fails to heed it.

This chapter comes in the form of a sermon. It is a modest example of how the author attempts to put into a homiletical mode some of the enduring themes of Africentric ministry that have been presented in the preceding chapters: the church, cultural and political liberation, black pride, faith, and solidarity, namely, the mission of humanization.

The Africentric sermon, admittedly, comes through most clearly when it is preached, not read. Nevertheless, a sermon may be the best vehicle by which we can help the laity to critique unsparingly and build on the claims of their own pragmatic spirituality in an era of "dumbing down" the Gospel with mushiness and mystification.

I am not taking a text this morning and this will not be a traditional sermon. I merely want to rap for a few minutes with the men and boys who are here today about the world that my father lived in. I want to tell you how becoming conscious of my father's world helped me to take my place and play my part in God's world.

So this is a very personal message that I have for you on this Father's Day. There is no better way I can say what I want to say. So I want you

The sermon presented in this chapter was preached by the author on June 17, 2001, at the Sargent Memorial Presbyterian Church, Washington, D.C., where Rev. Dr. James L. Allen was pastor at the time of its presentation.

to excuse the many personal references and try to focus on the lessons behind them that this sermon seeks to teach. I truly believe that what I learned from the world of Gayraud S. Wilmore Sr. will be useful to you as you try to understand and live out what it means to be a black man and, more than just a man, a black Christian father in this time of our lives.

Before I begin let me be clear about one thing. Everyone here should know that although we customarily refer to God as He, God is a Spirit and is without gender. In talking about God and fatherhood today I am by no means forgetting for one moment that without the women, and especially the mothers, there would be no knowledge of God, no church, and indeed no world.

My brothers, let us never forget that you must always give the women their due or, to quote the Clerk of Session in my first church in West Chester, Pennsylvania, "the women will do you." I'm not sure of all that old Clerk of Session had in mind when he made that sly quip about the female of the species, but I know that in the church and even out of it, without the women, our mothers and sisters, our grandmothers and aunts, we men would be nothing.

But having conceded that, this *is* Father's Day, isn't it? On this one day of the church year we might ask the women if they would be so gracious as to permit us to say some idealistic and perhaps somewhat exaggerated things about manhood and fatherhood without being considered hopelessly sexist.

Fatherhood has always been important to me, though I fear I have never quite lived up to its ideals. But before I understood the meaning of the Fatherhood of God, I experienced the fatherhood of a small black man, five foot, five inches, tall and about 120 pounds, who was my earthly father. He was born in Philadelphia, Pennsylvania, in 1896 and died in that same city in 1973. He was my first teacher of religion. I'm not saying, mind you, that I did not learn anything about God from my mother, but my father's world was mainly outside the home, in the church and in the neighborhood, and it was in those venues that I discovered my own place and my own life's passion.

I mean to say that it was my biological father who first gave me my first intimation of the existence of a heavenly Father. It was by observing and experiencing something of my father's world that I first began to wonder about, realize, and appreciate the privileges and responsibilities of living in God's world. My manhood began with this enlightenment.

If I haven't lost all the sisters in the congregation by now, and you brothers are still with me, let's go on!

My father's world was anchored in four clusters of basic institutions—the institutions of the family and the school; the political and civic institutions; the fraternal and social institutions; and, finally, the black church. He found a place to stand in each of these fundamental human institutions, and he himself was an indefatigable institution builder. In his way of thinking, joining and participating in some kind of community organization that served the common weal was the highest of callings. Hence he had a high regard for politics. Nonetheless, it seemed to me that, for him, the most important of all human institutions was the church, because it was, at one and the same time, the teacher and the servant of them all.

I have no doubt that in my father's mind the church, in some sense, came before the family in importance. Or perhaps it would be more accurate to say that without the church and the other institutions, the family itself would be unthinkable. The family could not survive. When he came home from the First World War in 1918 my father founded the first American Legion Post in the nation for black men: the Crispus Attucks Post 151, of Philadelphia. In the early 1930s Gayraud S. Wilmore Sr. and John K. Rice, a local dentist, organized the North Philadelphia Civic League, an institution for improving living conditions in the black ghetto of North Philadelphia. The League fought against police brutality, slum lords and rent gougers, dishonest merchants, and a variety of other sins in our community.

One day some officials of the Presbytery of Philadelphia stood on the corner of 21st and Columbia Avenue with my father and Dr. Rice. The officials from the Presbytery asked, "Do you see that fine church building across the street? It will seat more than five hundred people, but today no more than twenty elderly white people use it for no more than an hour's worship service on Sunday mornings. The rest of the congregation has gone to the suburbs. This building has a fully equipped kitchen and dining hall, about fifteen classrooms, a bowling alley in the basement, and a full gymnasium. The Presbytery of Philadelphia will give you folks that building if you will organize a new Presbyterian church on that property."

It was exactly the kind of property the North Philadelphia Civic League was looking for to house its expanding program. I don't believe that anyone has ever seen a church organized so quickly. Almost overnight the League, to all intents and purposes, became the new McDowell Presbyterian Church. They immediately persuaded Rev. Arthur E. Rankin, the pastor of the Berean Presbyterian Church, to become their pastor. Some of the officers of the League became the officers of the church, and many of the League members left Baptist and Methodist churches to become instant Presbyterians. Fundamentally nothing about the League really changed, only the new name it took on. Its institutional commitment to and involvement in social action in North Philadelphia was deepened and broadened as the League was transformed into a church.

The McDowell Presbyterian Church soon became one of the most culturally and politically active congregations in our section of the city. My two younger brothers and I were baptized in that church, which became the center of our family life and of my father's culturally and politically dynamic world. Everything worthwhile in our community—lectures, musical concerts, a dramatic club (where, incidentally, I met my future wife), social clubs, Boy Scouts and Girl Scouts, basketball and baseball teams, even Saturday evening dances in the gym—all were sponsored by the new McDowell Church. The neighborhood in which I grew up would have been the poorer, the more oppressed, and the meaner had it not been for this church of my youth. The uplifting influence and the constant prayers of that church brought me back from the Second World War in one piece—determined to make the Christian ministry my life's vocation.

Lesson number one: The black church is still the most precious possession of the African American people. Before our slave ancestors were permitted to have legal families in this country they had black religious gatherings—a proto-church—that shaped their personalities, their family life, and their emerging culture. Never give up on the church, my brothers, for as weak and as wrong as she can sometimes be, she is still God's chosen vessel for the cultural, social, political, and economic salvation of African Americans in this land. We as a people will never rise higher than the most lofty aspirations and the most fervent prayers of our churches.

The words of William P. Merritt's great hymn, although we don't sing them anymore, still thrill our hearts and summon us men to stand up for the church. *"Rise up, O men of God! The Church for you doth wait. Her strength unequal to her task; Rise up and make her great!"*

Second, I learned early on that the major emphasis in my father's world was on young people—children and youth, both those in the congregation and those in the neighborhood. For my father and his friends, the first priority of the McDowell Church, the Crispus Attucks American Legion Post #151, the O. V. Catto Elks Lodge, the Prince Hall Masons, and the several Boy Scout Troops they organized and sponsored was to make men out of boys. Nothing was more important to them than planning and supporting activities and programs designed to help young men and women grow up.

They started, of course, with Sunday School. Then they expanded to sponsor drill teams and drum-and-bugle corps that participated in every patriotic holiday. After all, these men were veterans of the First World War. They seized every excuse to put on a uniform, to dress us boys in white ducks and white shirts so we could join them in parades down Broad Street or Ridge Avenue with flags flying and bugles echoing through the silent office buildings.

After we had outgrown the drum-and-bugle corps we were inducted into the Boy Scouts and played in the neighborhood baseball, football, and basketball teams. From there we went into adult-managed boys' clubs and recreation centers where many of us, like my first college roommate, became semiprofessional boxers, following in the footsteps of Jack Johnson and Joe Louis.

Before his death in 1973 my father was given the coveted Silver Beaver Award by the Philadelphia Council of the Boy Scouts of America. He was honored because of his many years of organizing and mentoring Scout troops and other youth activities all over the City of Philadelphia.

I hear that young people today are bored and therefore spend most of their time playing computer games and looking at TV because they can't find anything else to do. I never felt bored growing up. In my father's world the older men made it their business to see that the young boys were included in all activities where they could learn self-reliance, personal responsibility, skills in public speaking, and, above all, moral and religious values. I'm not saying that we boys made use of all these marks of authentic manhood, but they were there for us and we were encouraged to learn them.

One of the things I will always appreciate about the Men's Organization of the small Westhills Presbyterian Church where I worshiped in Atlanta is that the men tried to include the boys of the church in everything they did. I always got a kick out of seeing young fellows coming out for the monthly Saturday morning men's breakfasts and Bible study that always preceded our business meetings. Some of them came dragging their feet. They were often shy and slow to participate, but we kept them close to us in all the men's activities. Having the boys of the church present when important decisions were made helped them to realize that they were not only the church of the future but that the church of the present is their responsibility—right alongside their fathers and uncles—that they had a voice, a vote, and a role to play, now!

Lesson number two: The highest service a men's organization can render to the church is not to raise money for the congregation, offer a program for the annual Men's Day, or send delegates to some national churchmen's convention but, rather, to make a place for the boys of the congregation and the neighborhood to grow up as Christian men who will put Christ and service to the world at the center of their lives.

We must let the youth have their say. We must listen to their ideas, complaints, and suggestions, give them a voice and a job to do in every aspect of church life—even when their contributions may be flawed or even childish. Remember that Jesus taught that unless we become as little children we will never enter the kingdom of heaven. And, moreover, in Matthew 18:5 he declares forthrightly: "Whoever welcomes one such child in my name welcomes me." I believe it was the poet Wordsworth who wrote, "The child is father to the man, and I should wish my days to be, bound each to each by natural piety."

Finally, my father's world was one in which black men were supposed to be strong, courageous, and dignified, and a man's strength, courage, and dignity came from knowing, trusting, and serving God, the God and Father of Jesus of Nazareth, the God who is always on the side of those who stand up, as did Our Lord, for justice and righteousness.

I know now why dignity was so important in my father's world. It was because the white world tried to deny black men their worth. As a small boy I was always impressed that my father and his friends customarily called one another Mister. Instead of using first names they addressed each other for a long time as Mr. Allen or Mr. Cherry or Mr. Jones. Somewhere along the way I learned that this was because white men showed them little respect and, on the job, either called them by their first names or simply "boy." At work they could do little about it. But when they spoke to one another at home they repaired their wounded dignity and manhood by using the formality of Mr., a title of respect and prestige, attributes they knew they deserved and that one day the white man would be bound to give them. Dad was a little man, you might even say a shrimp of a man, but like some small poodles he thought of himself as a big dog and didn't hesitate to take on somebody twice his size when it came to defending his manhood. The white Metropolitan Insurance agents came to our house every week or so to collect the dime or quarter my mother paid for our family's "sick and death" benefits. One particular man insisted on keeping his hat on in the living room after being repeatedly asked to show my mother proper respect when he entered the house. I never saw my small father look so tall and fierce as the day he encountered that man and told him flat out, "If you don't take that hat off right now, I'm going to knock it off and throw both you and your hat into the street!"

I don't know what the man did subsequently in other houses he visited to collect insurance, but I know he snatched his hat off right off and never wore it again when he crossed our threshold.

My father was what we used to call "a race man." That meant that he was motivated by black consciousness and believed in race solidarity. For a while during the 1920s he was a Garveyite, although I don't think he strongly supported the idea of going back to Africa. During the 1930s and 1940s he challenged all forms of racial prejudice and discrimination, reminding the powers in City Hall that he had fought in France "to make the world safe for democracy." He was a leading member of the North Philadelphia Civic League, the NAACP, and the Armstrong Association, which was Philadelphia's version of the National Urban League. But the lesson he taught me about this being a world in which God is the sovereign over all men and nations had a lot to do with my decision to go to seminary and enter the ministry when I returned from Italy after the Second World War.

The God and Father of Jesus Christ made us all equal, whether black or white, rich or poor, college-educated or a high school dropout. We are all equal and commanded to deal with one another with truth, righteousness, and justice. This simple but profound truth, which I inherited from the men of my youth, is what gives me the assurance that no matter how bad things get, we will ultimately prevail if we are faithful and obedient to the One who created us. This conviction, my brothers, gives us the courage and determination to fight the good fight until, as the old folks used to say, "our change comes."

Lesson number three: It is God, not human beings, who is the ultimate ruler of this world. If we believe in the Lordship of Jesus Christ over every rule and authority, no one can permanently rob us of our manhood and our Godgiven right to life, liberty, and all the good things of this world that are in it for all of us. Thus bothers in the faith need to stand together against all who would deprive and dehumanize men, women, and children of whatever race, class, or nationality. We must constantly be organizing our communities and mobilizing our resources, and there is nothing we need fear because, as the great hymn of James Russell Lowell affirms:

> Though the cause of evil prosper, Yet 't is truth alone is strong;
> Though her portion be the scaffold, And upon the throne be wrong,
> Yet that scaffold sways the future, And behind the dim unknown,
> Standeth God within the shadow, keeping watch above His own.

Now brothers, you know as well as I that the world our fathers lived in is not the same world we live in today. But I have lived long enough to know that, although many things are radically different, many are still the same. As the French proverb tells us: "The more it changes, the more it remains the same." Race consciousness, properly understood, faith and courage, loyalty and devotion to education, self-improvement, community welfare, belief in God and commitment to the church—these are all enduring values that still remain essential for the preservation of our dignity and freedom as African American men and as human beings.

On this Father's Day we need to remind ourselves that God has not stopped calling men and boys to leadership roles in the church and the community. It may not be the same kind of leadership that my father and men like him gave in their time; but it is the same loyalty to God and country that they demonstrated seventy-five or one hundred years ago. The lessons from their world are still relevant, and we urgently need to do more to ensure that the young people of today honor the legacy those quite ordinary and uncelebrated men left us, and carry on the work they began for our liberation and redemption as individuals and as a people.

Today I salute the men and boys of this congregation, and I congratulate you for all the good things you have done and are still doing in this church and community. I charge you, on this special day, to go on to greater heights. God will go with you to uphold you, the Holy Spirit will accompany you to inspire you, and Jesus Christ Himself, our Brother, will go before you as your Leader and your Guide. Amen.

17

Struggling against Racism with Realism and Hope

We American Christians have a problem and no one knows exactly how to solve it. The problem is white racism, the frequently unconscious and unacknowledged assumption of the innate superiority of white over black, an assumption that most white Americans take in with their mother's milk and that has become institutionalized in a complex web of privileges and proscriptions that has kept us separate and unequal in this country for almost five hundred years.

If truth be told, I am weary of talking and writing about this ancient problem that ebbs and flows inexplicably year after year in American society. I have been caught up in this problem since early childhood.

I remember, as a young boy, sitting on the white marble stoop at the entrance to our house (why were the entrances to all the houses in our run-down neighborhood made of white marble steps?) I sat watching the last wave of immigrants from Eastern Europe, after the First World War, move into our block day after day. Most of the immigrant kids could not speak or read English, so we taught them, but they soon learned from the white American children they met at school that the first word they needed to learn how to pronounce, with just the right amount of derision, was *nigger.* But in spite of that, we "got along."

The immigrant children became our playmates, but they did not stay among us very long. Just as we had watched them come, we gloomily watched them go a few weeks or months later. Our neighborhood was only a temporary stopover for many of them. As soon as their fathers found good jobs they were able to hire the same moving vans that had moved them in to whisk them away—off to better residential areas where, in those days, no native-born black family had access.

I remember having to cross the invisible border, put in place by white real estate interests, and venture into those other neighborhoods to get to Fairmount Park where we liked to climb trees and play sandlot football. Crossing 26th Street frequently meant getting into a fistfight because you were in enemy territory. Then in 1943 I went off to Europe to fight another gang of racists as a private first class in the segregated U.S. army. I soldiered in the all-black Ninety-second Division—ten thousand–plus black infantrymen under the command of white field officers, because someone in Washington judged that we were incompetent and untrustworthy and could not command ourselves under fire. Once in Italy that changed slightly, and we began to see an occasional black first or second lieutenant.

When I returned home from Italy I finished college and seminary and was ordained a minister in the overwhelmingly white Presbyterian church, not because the army had made me a glutton for punishment but because—to the chagrin of some of my black Baptist and Methodist friends—I made up my mind to continue the fight against bigotry and racism at one of the sources of the sickness, in the belly of the white, upper-middle-class church into which I had been baptized.

So white racism has dogged me for as long as I can remember. And while I dislike talking or writing about it, I must. I now know that talk about prejudice and discrimination is inescapable for all of us who believe that Jesus Christ is Lord and Liberator. The action is inescapable so the talk, particularly for African Americans, is mandatory. To talk, write, and teach about racism and the struggle to abolish it is nothing less than a religious obligation that adheres to what it means to be a Christian in America. It comes with our baptism. And for those of us who have worked to develop a black theology of liberation, the ongoing struggle against racism is at the center of our talk and our action, though it does not exhaust what we are about as Christian theologians and ethicists.

Initial Presuppositions

Whenever we deal with religion and race as a topic, we ought to begin by acknowledging that in the United States the principal reason why almost all the twenty-five or so million African American church members worship in separate black congregations is because our ancestors were first introduced to Christianity in America as a racist and slaveholding religion.

There are, of course, other important reasons, but that is certainly the main one. And it is that historical mistake of Euro-American Christianity which is the most difficult to remedy. The African American historian, Vincent Harding, says it best:

> For we first met the American Christ on slave ships. We heard his name sung in hymns of praise while we died in our thousands, chained in stinking holds beneath the decks. . . . When we leaped from the decks to be seized by sharks we saw his name carved on the ship's solid sides. When our women were raped in the cabins they must have noticed the great and holy books on the shelves. Our introduction to this Christ was not propitious.[1]

In his finest book, entitled *The Seeds of Racism in the Soul of America,* the AME historian Paul R. Griffin argues that American racism did not begin among crude, booze-guzzling southern planters who gave the missionaries a hard time in colonial America but among pious Puritan divines in New England who, in order to consign black people to the lowest rank in the hierarchy of human beings, distorted biblical theology. Griffin shows how the four cardinal doctrines of scholastic Calvinism—creation, predestination, sin, and covenant—were mishandled in order to provide a theological cushion under bigotry. As a consequence, the New Canaan of the Puritans, the "City Set on a Hill," was rife with the color prejudice and discrimination against blacks who lived in its neighborhoods, no different from what I experienced as a child growing up in the "City of Brotherly Love."

> Almost from their arrival in 1630, Puritans instituted laws and practices designed to ensure that blacks would never be a part of their "holy cities." These constraints, which were forerunners of the "black codes" that would be instituted in the North in the 19th century, were a litany of human degradations shocking to find among supposedly saintly men and women. Blacks were denied unrestricted travel and had to have a pass to move from one place to another after nine o'clock in the evening. They were prevented from living next door to whites and could only own homes that were segregated in nonwhite residential areas. They were banned from owning most types of property, including . . . livestock, such as sheep, swine, and horses. Blacks were excluded from the military; prohibited from serving on juries; denied full citizenship and

> thus prevented from voting (even though they had to pay taxes); barred from jobs, because of their color or else harassed and sometimes beaten by mobs who claimed those jobs belonged to them; and segregated in schools, churches, and even cemeteries.[2]

I wrote the foreword to Griffin's book with a heavy heart. Nothing has made me feel more ashamed and disconcerted about being a black Presbyterian minister than Griffin's persistence in uncovering, with unassailable documentation, the roots of American racism in Puritanism. I will not reiterate here the many quotations he cites, to buttress his argument, from John Winthrop, Cotton Mather, Theophilus Eaton, and John Saffin, those pillars of New England Puritanism. The only point I wish to make is that, although we Reformed church leaders have skillfully sought to evade it, Griffin and others have shown that modern-day Congregationalists and Presbyterians are the unfortunate heirs of a congenital and pervasive racism, a way of thinking that cannot be attributed solely to economic factors or to the political expediencies of a brave "errand into the wilderness" or to the incivility of crass and greedy southern planters. Racism in America must ultimately be laid on the doorstep of high-flown ideas in the minds of our sanctimonious theological forbears about the God-given inferiority and degeneracy of black people.

What does that say to me as a black Presbyterian minister today, one who is committed to the clarification and propagation of a black theology of liberation within and beyond my own denomination, a theology that will get African American church members off their knees and involved in the struggle against injustice and oppression everywhere in the world? For one thing, it forces me to assume that to be "Black and Reformed," to use the title of one of Allan Boesak's hard-hitting books during the fight against apartheid in South Africa,[3] requires that I must produce the kind of theology that makes anti-racism foundational to any authentic Christian system of belief. It also reminds me that choosing to remain a member of this predominantly white church obliges me to work as hard as I can to drive the demonic power of racism out of this denomination which first taught me that the gospel was not only about repentance and personal salvation but also about transforming the world.

But how can the church itself be transformed from a racist to an antiracist community? After more than fifty years in the Christian ministry, I am embarrassed to confess that I do not have any definitive answer to that peevish, mocking question. But I am reasonably sure of two things:

first, that contextual obedience to the command to love thy neighbor as one's self is a more acceptable offering to God than any set of programmatic strategies, tactics, or techniques we might carry around in our race-relations tool kit. Most of the time we know better what needs to be done than we are able to muster the will and energy to apply it. That is partly because it is not us, but God, through God's Holy Spirit, who works within us, who must do the real work of salvation. Second, I am increasingly persuaded that we cannot expect time and history to solve the problem of racism for us. We must struggle every day with realism and hope.

The Context in Which We Struggle

In a 1997 commencement speech at the University of California, President Bill Clinton made the prediction that, "a half century from now, when your own grandchildren are in college, there will be no majority race in America." But according to demographer Nancy T. Kate, writing in *American Demographics,* in December 1997, the president was slightly off his target. Actually three out of four Americans will still belong to the white race in 2050, but many will identify themselves as white Hispanics, that is, Mexicans, Mexican Americans, Chicanos, Puerto Ricans, Cubans, Central and South Americans, and other people of Latin or Hispanic origin with the right skin color. Though some of these people will have "sepia" skin color and an attenuated cultural identity that will be quite different than the traditional Euro-American or North Atlantic orientation, most will prefer to identify themselves and their children with the older white majority in terms of social, economic, and political status, and, perhaps, religious affiliation. This is good news for the rapidly depleting mainline white churches of the nation, including, of course, the Roman Catholics.

Of particular note in the demographic picture drawn by sociologists and others is that by 2010 the Hispanic population of the United States will have overtaken African Americans as the largest minority group in the nation.[4] In fact, that may have already happened by 2004. This could have far-reaching implications. For one thing, the black-white paradigm, which has for years been the major heuristic concept for interpreting American race relations, will have to be revised to make room for a new reality. But both opportunities and dangers will result from this turn of racial/ethnic affairs in the United States. Many, perhaps most, non-Hispanic whites will be more prone to welcome "white" Hispanics into their churches, as well as to intermarry and share power with them, than blacks who were born and bred in this country. That is simply a fact of American life. And if, not surprisingly, that should be the case, how much real progress will we have made in removing the remaining obstacles to racial and ethnic justice and equality across the board?

At mid-century non-Latino whites will still be the largest ethnic group, if only in terms of a bare majority of 53 percent. The large number of new Asian and Hispanic persons making up the bulk of the remaining population will depend, of course, on a continuation of disproportionate numbers (as compared to Africans) of Latin American and Asian immigrants receiving citizenship and, as most experts predict, upon those groups continuing to have higher fertility rates than the old stock of white and black Americans.

Clearly we are in for some dramatic population shifts in terms of ethnicity. The U.S. Census Bureau's "middle series" projections report that shortly after 2050 non-Hispanic whites—the kind of people who now predominate in my own Presbyterian Church (U.S.A.)—will find themselves, for the first time in the history of the nation, a true minority. No one really knows how that will affect all aspects of American civilization, but we cannot assume that true diversity and multiculturalism will be the benevolent consequence and bring an end to the old hegemony of white over black that we have come to know so well. That uncertainty, in any case, is a part of being realistic about these changes the social scientists predict.

I predict that most of the mainline white churches, as we know them, will not fade away, as some disgusted critics have said, but will continue to exist through the twenty-first century as somewhat smaller but wealthy institutions comprising a large majority of economically secure, middle-class and middle-aged Americans, who are (1) predominantly white but not necessarily Anglo; (2) Hispanics who can and will be able to pass for white; (3) Asians and Middle Easterners who will be "colored" but will prefer to be identified with Caucasians rather than with "people of color"; native born Africans and West Indians who will try to escape identification with African Americans and make their own way toward the American "melting pot;" and the offspring of mixed marriages who will either identify themselves and their children as white or as "other."[5]

Whether there will be any African Americans and Native Americans in the predominantly white churches remains to be seen. Much depends on how we choose to deal with their dwindling presence today. If their attempts to define their own theological and cultural attributes are denied or frustrated by white theologians and Christian educators, then we may expect that the younger, most resourceful, and restive recruits for church membership among them will decline more rapidly.

In such a situation, "whiteness," as had customarily been the case in the Western hemisphere,[6] will continue to be the ostensible dividing line in both the church and the society, between the "ins" and the "outs," between the holders of effective power in the courts of the mainline churches and those who will be relatively marginalized and powerless. All reliable indexes point to the possibility that in fifty years a disproportionate number of poor Americans will still be people of color, although there will be a considerable number of impoverished people of Anglo ancestry as a result of our class-based economic system. The real difference between that time and now is that in the future more "colored people" (non-white Hispanics, Asians, and even an increasing number of African immigrants and middle-class African Americans) will find a way to escape the opprobrium of "blackness" or non-whiteness by (1) disengaging themselves from their ancestral roots; (2) abandoning the struggle for the liberation of oppressed Americans of color and lower economic status, such as the mentally ill, formerly incarcerated, and homeless; and (3) closing their eyes to the racism and white-skin privilege that will continue to plague and embarrass both the nation and the churches.

Multiculturalism and Alternative Cultural Identities

It is only realistic to assume, therefore, that although "diversity" and "multiculturalism" are gradually replacing the traditionally liberal shibboleth of "integration," we are not likely to dismantle old-fashioned white racism totally in the twenty-first century. Racial justice and anti-racism strategies will survive the effort of the courts and the intergroup relations industry to dilute the de facto separation of blacks from the mainstream and will continue to demand the attention and effort of fair-minded Christians.

The last three General Assemblies of the Presbyterian Church (U.S.A.) lifted up the themes of diversity and multiculturalism as the way forward in Christian race relations, but it seems mainly in the interest of church growth. The denomination, like their mainline Protestant sister churches, needs to replace the shrinking numbers of white or Anglo members with racial and ethnic groups that for three centuries have comprised less than 5 percent of the 1.5 million–plus membership rolls of the Presbyterians, Lutherans, Reformed Church in America, and the United Church of Christ. Certainly more diverse and multicultural churches should be welcomed and will doubtlessly help to increase the number of racial/ethnic members in what are now overwhelmingly white denominations, and should also help to blunt the Anglo-conformism of these mainline representatives of American Protestantism. But multiculturalism should not be used as an excuse to diminish efforts for justice and equality between whites and blacks both within and outside the churches. Realism about the tenacity of color prejudice and institutional racism will not permit us to substitute church growth strategies, mainly interested in counting heads, for a more aggressive program to mitigate the kind of racism that continues to manifest itself most prominently in the black-white polarity of American society.

As far as African Americans are concerned, it is clear that we are not ready to give up the African American churches, colleges and seminaries, black culture, or black militancy as we continue to seek racial, ethnic, and other forms of social justice—including justice for bisexual, lesbian, gay, and transgendered persons. Nor should we. All these ways of being human are needed on behalf of security in our own future as an African American people and the future of the nation as a whole. We know that the increase in the number of hate groups to more than 470 since 1996,[7] the brutal murder of James Byrd in Jasper, Texas, in 2000, and the murder of Amadou Diallo by New York City police all mean that violence against black people and other "strange breeds outside the covenant" is still just below the deceptively benign and benevolent surface of white America, notwithstanding the conservative evangelical and Pentecostal world revival.

The population changes that have occurred in California, Texas, Florida, and New York portend major shifts in the central cities of many other states. African Americans now find themselves in fierce competition with the newcomers for the next-to-the-last rung of the ladder of what this culture calls "success." Protestant churches seem not to have found a good way to help relieve these intergroup tensions, partly because white Protestants are not given to ecclesiastical sanctions against un-Christian behavior, and have also been too busy fleeing the areas into which the newcomers move. Not the least of their deficiencies is that the major denominations have no comprehensive or ecumenical strategy for multiculturalism. No event in the 1990s illustrates the complexity and internal contradictions of these intergroup conflicts more than the serious uprising in Los Angeles in April 1992.[8]

Maulana Karenga, chairman of the Black Studies Program at California State University (Long Beach), comments on the complexity of the Los Angeles riots in terms of alienation between competing Mexican and Central American groups and, in South Central Los Angeles, between African Americans, Latinos, and Koreans. Karenga's larger analysis of the explosive relations between the African American and the Latino populations provides some interesting and instructive insights into the nature of a valid multiculturalism and the dangers encountered on the way to achieving it. He shows how futile and immoral it is for white Christians to stand by and watch interethnic strife, hoping that it will have no deleterious impact on the majority community. He favors multiculturalism but warns against its trivialization.

> Certainly, what is proposed here is not a multiculturalism of days devoted to ethnic food and clothing, *pro forma* mention of diversity on special occasions, or recognition on calendars and workdays of holidays of various ethnicities. "Multiculturalism" here means thought and practice informed by a profound appreciation for diversity, which expresses itself in four fundamental ways. First, serious multiculturalism, of necessity, begins with mutual respect for each people and each culture. . . . Second, a substantive multiculturalism requires mutual respect for each people's right and responsibility to speak their own special cultural truth and make their own unique contribution to how this society is *reconceived* and *reconstructed*. . . . Third, a real and vital multiculturalism requires mutual commitment to the constant search for common ground in the midst of our diversity. . . . Finally, a multiculturalism which both reflects and reinforces the quest for a just and good society unavoidably requires a mutual commitment among the various peoples to a *social ethic of sharing*.[9]

All these criteria readily translate into Christian social-ethical principles familiar to most scholars, if not, unfortunately, to the people in the pews: first, the intrinsic value of each human being and every group of people in the sight of God; second, the need for humility, repentance, and (because we are all sinners who are saved by grace alone) being always ready to undergo fundamental change or conversion; third, fostering a nonhegemonic relationship among peoples, recognizing that God has given humankind a common ground for building a just and peaceful society of all the inhabitants of the earth; and, finally, affirming that such a society requires that no one person or group has the right to enjoy the good things of this earth while the rest of us are inadequately fed, clothed, housed, and cared for as free and equal children of God. That was the famous dream of Martin Luther King Jr. at the March on Washington in 1963, and it is a large part of the hope we have in Jesus Christ.

Putting the World in Order

When I was in Italy during the war I was told that every Italian is born with something called *sistemare*. I learned some Italian when the Lombardi family of Pietrasanta would come and huddle around me whenever the artillery shells came crashing in to visit us on the mountain opposite the German position on the next mountain. But I have no idea of the exact English translation for *sistemare*. I read somewhere that it has to do with an obsessive instinct to put things in order, to arrange the natural world according to some standard of elegance, to forever be tidying up one's immediate living space.

I witnessed *sistemare* in the coastal mountains of Tuscany during the Second World War. Whenever a lull came in the fighting I would watch the *paesani* start shoveling dirt and carrying rocks to shore up the terraces where they grew their olives and grapes in the shell-shocked, mine-strewn earth.

My Italian was sufficient to ask why they risked their lives rebuilding terraces when a war was raging all around them. The man I had asked looked at me, questioningly, for a moment, and then said: "Every winter the ground freezes and then thaws—rains come, and winds—maybe there's even an earthquake or a war. The soil constantly erodes. The terraces crumble and slide down the mountainside. So every year we have to build them up all over again. For hundreds of years we have done this. It is our life."

Without wanting to seem pessimistic—it is un-Christian—I believe that the struggle against racism resembled the Italians' continual rebuilding of their ever crumbling terraces. Racism is America's original sin; the struggle against it is perennial. The struggle is boring, tiring, frustrating, but that is its nature and it will not change. Every year we have to repeat all over again what we did to combat racism last year and the year before and the year before that. Racism is indigenous to the fallen world, the sinful environment in which we all must live. It is one of the most stubborn and messiest parts of our living space. That should not so much discourage us as it ought to clarify what our moral responsibility is in the best and worst of times. We need to know assuredly that it falls to every generation to continue to work while the bombs are falling, to rebuild the terraces of realism and hope against racism's perennial and inevitable destructiveness, to tidy up the world of interracial and interethnic relations in faithfulness and obedience to Christ.

Each of us must do his or her part wherever we are. That is what the Lord demands of us. That is our Christian *sistemare,* our contextual obedience: to keep on struggling all our lives, with realism and with hope, against the demonic power of racism.

Notes

INTRODUCTION

1. Molefi Kete Asante, who, with other Africanists, invented the term *Afrocentrism,* prefers the prefix *Afro.* Although I, too, have used that prefix commonly known to African Americans for years, I now choose to use *Afri* because it derives more directly from the word *Africa.*

2. Line from the third stanza of Matthew Bridges's great hymn, "Crown Him with Many Crowns, The Lamb Upon The Throne" (1851).

3. James H. Evans Jr., *We Have Been Believers: An African American Systematic Theology* (Minneapolis: Fortress, 1992), vii.

4. Margaret Walker, "We Have Been Believers," in *This Is My Country: New and Collected Poems* (Athens: University of Georgia Press, 1989).

5. Jacquelyn Grant, *White Woman's Christ and Black Woman's Jesus: Feminist Christology and Womanist Response* (Atlanta: Scholars, 1989), 217.

6. John S. Mbiti, *African Religions and Philosophy* (New York: Praeger, 1969), 5–6.

7. John Lovell Jr., *Black Song: The Forge and the Flame, the Story of How the Afro-American Spiritual Was Hammered Out* (New York: Macmillan, 1972).

8. John S. Mbiti, *African Religions and Philosophy,* 67–68.

9. Molefi Kete Asante, *The Afrocentric Idea* (Philadelphia: Temple University Press, 1987), 3. See also idem, *Afrocentricity: The Theory of Social Change* (Philadelphia: Temple University Press, 1980); and *Kemet, Afro-centricity and Knowledge* (Trenton, N.J.: Africa World Press, 1990). A number of other black scholars have contributed to this concept, including C. A. Diop, *The Cultural Unity of Black Africa* (Chicago: Third World, 1978); Maulana Karenga and Jacob H. Carruthers, eds., *Kemet and the African World View: Selected Papers* (Los Angeles: University of Sankore Press, 1986); *The African American Holiday of Kwanzaa, A Celebration of Family, Community and Culture* (Los Angeles: University of Sankore Press, 1988); John G. Jackson, *An Introduction to African Civilization* (New York: Negro Universities Press, 1969); Yousef ben Jochannan, *African Origins of the Major "Western Religions"* (New York: Alkebu-Lan

Books, 1970); J. Deotis Roberts, *Africentric Christianity: A Theological Appraisal for Ministry* (Valley Forge, Pa.: Judson Press, 2000); Peter J. Paris, *The Spirituality of African Peoples* (Minneapolis: Fortress, 1995). Cain Hope Felder has made a notable contribution to these perspectives linking African and African American histories and cultures. See his "Cultural Ideology, Afrocentrism, and Biblical Interpretation," in James H. Cone and Gayraud S. Wilmore, eds., *Black Theology: A Documentary History* (Maryknoll, N.Y.: Orbis Books, 1993), 2:188. Perhaps the most popular and influential work among the many in this genre is Maulana Karenga's *Kwanzaa: Origin, Concepts, Practice* (San Diego, Calif.: New African American, 1988), which is responsible for the increasing observance of Kwanzaa in African American communities across the nation. See also Ndugu T'Ofori-Atta, *Christkwanza* (Atlanta: Strugglers Community Press, 1991).

10. Cain Hope Felder, "Cultural Ideology, Afrocentrism, and Biblical Interpretation," in James H. Cone and Gayraud S. Wilmore, eds., *Black Theology: A Documentary History, 1980–1992* (Maryknoll, N.Y.: Orbis, 1993), 2:188.

11. J. Deotis Roberts, *Africentric Christianity* (Valley Forge: Judson Press, 2000), 14.

1. WHAT IS AFRICAN AMERICAN RELIGIOUS STUDIES?

1. Despite the warning of St. Clair Drake that the North American diaspora never developed an African American culture (*The Redemption of Africa and Black Religion* [Chicago: Third World Press, 1970], 19), I am using the term *African American* in most contexts interchangeably with *Afro-American,* because it has gained vogue in most black communities today and bespeaks a certain ideological (Africentric) orientation toward African identity that has almost always been a disideratum of the black church.

2. The two are not, of course, strictly synonymous. Black church studies has an institutional bias for African American Christianity. Black religious studies is concerned with the full spectrum and phenomenology of all black religions, particularly in the New World. The terms, however, are often used interchangeably, and I will do so here.

3. Gunnar Myrdal, *An American Dilemma,* 2 vols. (New York: Harper, 1944). See vol. 2, chap. 40, "The Negro Church."

4. This should not be taken as an uncritical endorsement of the present fourfold division of the curriculum of most white seminaries. Rather, it is a recognition of the status quo and a conscious decision not to make a frontal attack on the traditional disciplines, which would be a premature confrontation with the theological education elite. Unfortunately this elite already considers black religious studies to be dangerously eccentric—unlike what some intended to inculcate into their African American doctoral students.

5. Clifford Geertz, *The Interpretation of Culture* (New York: Basic Books, 1973), 89. See also John H. Morgan, ed., *Understanding Religion and Culture: Anthropological and Theological Perspectives* (Washington, D.C.: University Press of America, 1979).

6. Geertz, *The Interpretation of Culture*, 90.

7. Following Geertz's paradigm I have formulated the following operational definition of black religion: By *black religion* reference is made to a system of symbols deeply embedded in the culture of people of African descent. This symbol system, formed in slavery from Christian instruction and remnants of African religions has been preserved in the historic black Christian churches. The system acts to establish powerful psychosomatic moods and motivations in believers by evoking conceptions of a normally hostile world that blacks generally relate to white oppression, and in which both provisional accommodation and protest are found to be so necessary for survival and liberation, with the help of mystical or divine powers, that the psychosomatic moods and motivations seem uniquely appropriate for overcoming present distress and for guaranteeing a future and happy existence in a world to come.

8. Gayraud S. Wilmore, "Tension Points in Black Church Studies," *The Christian Century*, April 11, 1979; slightly revised.

9. James H. Evans, "Black Church Studies and the Theological Curriculum," in Gayraud S. Wilmore, ed., *African American Religious Studies: An Interdisciplinary Anthology* (Durham: Duke University Press, 1989), 24.

10. Manning Marable, "Black Studies: Marxism and the Black Intellectual Tradition," in Bertell Ollman and E. Vernoff, eds., *The Left Academy* (New York: Praeger, 1986), 3:57.

2. REINTERPRETATION IN BLACK CHURCH HISTORY

1. University of Chicago Press, 1968); see Robert T. Handy, "Negro Christianity and American Historiography," 91–112. See also Thomas R. Frazier, "Changing Perspectives in the Study of Afro-American Religion," *Journal of the Interdenominational Theological Center* 6, no. 1 (fall 1978): 51–68.

2. Joseph R. Washington, *Black Religion: The Negro and Christianity in the United States* (Boston: Beacon, 1964).

3. William J. Walls, *The African Methodist Episcopal Zion Church: Reality of the Black Church* (Charlotte: AME Zion, 1974).

4. Charles H. Long, "Perspectives for a Study of Afro-American Religion in the United States," *History of Religions* 2 (August 1971): 58.

5. A sampling of some of the most important publications in English by some of these writers would include Cheikh Anta Diop, *The African Origin of Civilization: Myth or Reality* (New York: Lawrence Hill, 1974); Yosef ben Jochannan, *African Origins of the Major "Western" Religions* (New York: Alkebu-Lan,

1970); Willis N. Huggins and John G. Jackson, *Introduction to African Civilizations* (Secaucus, N.J.: Citadel, 1970); J. C. De Graft-Johnson, *African Glory: The Story of Vanished Negro Civilizations* (Baltimore, Md.: Black Classic, 1954); Chancellor Williams, *The Destruction of Black Civilization* (Chicago: Third World, 1976); Ulysses D. Jenkins, *Ancient African Religion and the African American Church* (Jacksonville, Fl.: Flame International, 1978); and Molefi Kete Asante, *The Afrocentric Idea* (Philadelphia: Temple University Press, 1987). No list like this would be complete without mentioning the several works of English author Basil Davidson, who has been a popular writer of great proficiency on African history since 1960. See *Black Mother: The Years of the African Slave Trade* (Boston: Little, Brown, 1961); *The Lost Cities of Africa* (Boston: Little, Brown, 1970); *The African Past: Chronicles from Antiquity to Modern Times* (Boston: Little, Brown, 1994); and *The African Genius: An Introduction to African Cultural and Social History* (Boston: Little, Brown, 1969).

6. As early as 1948 J. Olumide Lucas traced Egyptian elements in Yoruba religion. See J. O. Lucas, *The Religion of the Yorubas* (Lagos: C.M.S. Bookshop, 1948); and idem, *Religions in West Africa and Ancient Egypt* (Apapa, Nigeria: Nigerian National Press, 1970). That Lucas's theories have been disputed by some West African historians cannot detract from the possibility of the influence of a resurgent nationalism that is protective of indigenous origins, but other scholars, like the Ghanaian Kofi Asare Opoku (*West African Traditional Religion,* FEP International Private, 1978), have great respect for the Archdeacon's scholarship, although they have reservations about some of his conclusions.

7. See Randall K. Burkett, *Black Redemption: Churchmen Speak for the Garvey Movement* (Philadelphia: Temple University Press, 1978).

8. Research on black sects and cults has been helpful in this regard since the 1930s. See, for example, the work of Arthur H. Fauset, Howard M. Brotz, Joseph R. Washington, and the studies on black Pentecostalism by the late Professor James S. Tinney of Howard University.

9. E. Franklin Frazier, *The Negro Church in America* (New York: Schocken, 1964), 85–86.

10. Some of the works I refer to here are John W. Blassingame, *The Slave Community,* rev. enl. ed. (New York: Oxford University Press, 1979); Vincent Harding, "Religion and Resistance among Antebellum Negroes, 1800–1860," in August Meier and Elliott Rudwick, eds., *The Making of Black America* (New York: Atheneum, 1969); Vincent Harding, "The Religion of Black Power," in Donald R. Cutler, ed., *The Religious Situation: 1968* (Boston: Beacon, 1969); Eugene G. Genovese, *Roll, Jordan, Roll: The World the Slaves Made* (New York: Pantheon, 1974); Mechal Sobel, *Trabelin' On: The Slave Journey to an Afro-Baptist Faith* (Westport, Conn.: Greenwood, 1979); Albert J. Raboteau, *Slave Religion: The "Invisible Institution" in the Ante-Bellum South* (New York: Ox-

ford University Press, 1978); Lawrence E. Levine, *Black Culture and Black Consciousness* (New York: Oxford University Press, 1977); Leonard Barrett, *Soul-Force: African Heritage in Afro-American Religion* (Garden City, N.Y.: Anchor, 1974); Henry H. Mitchell, *Black Belief: Folk Beliefs of Blacks in America and West Africa* (New York: Harper and Row, 1975); and James H. Cone, *The Spirituals and the Blues* (New York: Seabury, 1972).

11. Benjamin E. Mays, *The Negro's Church* (New York: Institute of Social and Religious Research, 1933); Mark Miles Fisher, *Negro Slave Songs in the United States* (Ithaca, N.Y.: Cornell University Press, 1953); Howard Thurman, *Jesus and the Disinherited* (New York: Abingdon-Cokesbury Press, 1946); Charles H. Long, *Significations: Signs, Symbols, and Images in the Interpretation of Religion* (Philadelphia: Fortress Press, 1986); J. Deotis Roberts, *Roots of a Black Future: Family and Church* (Philadelphia: Westminster Press, 1980); George D. Kelsey, *Racism and the Christian Understanding of Man* (New York: Scribner, 1965).

12. Gayraud S. Wilmore, *Black Religion and Black Radicalism* (New York: Doubleday, 1972).

13. Peter G. Hodgson, *Children of Freedom* (Philadelphia: Fortress Press, 1974); Leonard E. Barrett, *Soul Force* (Garden City, N.Y.: Doubleday, 1974); Randall K. Burkett, *Garveyism as a Religious Movement* (Metuchen, N.J.: Scarecrow Press, 1978); Randall K. Burnett and Richard Newman, eds., *Black Apostles: Afro-American Clergy Confront the Twentieth Century* (Boston: G. K. Hall, 1978); C. Eric Lincoln, *The Black Church since Frazier* (New York: Schocken, 1974); J. Deotis Roberts, *Africentric Christianity: A Theological Appraisal for Ministry* (Valley Forge, Pa.: Judson Press, 2000). For a good discussion of the Herskovitz-Frazier debate see Norman E. Whitten, Jr., and John F. Szwed, eds., *Afro-American Anthropology: Contemporary Perspectives* (New York: Free Press, 1970), 23–60.

14. John Blassingame, *The Slave Community* (New York: Oxford University Press, 1972); Sterling Stuckey, *Slave Culture: Nationalist Theory and the Foundations of Black America* (New York: Oxford University Press, 1987); Eugene G. Genovese, *Roll, Jordan, Roll: The World the Slaves Made* (New York: Pantheon, 1974); Lawrence W. Levine, *Black Culture and Black Consciousness* (New York: Oxford University Press, 1977); Lawrence N. Jones, "They Sought a City: The Black Church and Churchmen in the Nineteenth Century," *Union Seminary Quarterly Review* (Spring 1971, 253–272); Mechal Sobel, *Trabelin' On* (Westport, Conn.: Greenwood, 1979); Albert J. Raboteau, *Slave Religion: The "Invisible Institution" in the Antebellum South* (New York: Oxford University Press, 1978).

15. Carter G. Woodson, *History of the Negro Church,* 3rd ed. (Washington, D.C.: Associated Publishers, 1972), 196–208.

16. Blassingame, *The Slave Community,* 133.

17. Benjamin Quarles, *Black Abolitionists* (New York: Oxford University Press, 1969), 81–82.

18. Wilmore, *Black Religion and Black Radicalism,* 168–186, 213–219. See also "The Role of Afro-America in the Rise of Third World Theology: A Historical Reappraisal," in Kofi Appiah-Kubi and Sergio Torres, eds., *African Theology En Route* (Maryknoll: Orbis, 1979).

19. See the seminal article by James S. Tinney, "Black Origins of the Pentecostal Movement," *Christianity Today,* October 10, 1971; and Leonard Lovett, "Black Holiness and Pentecostalism: Implications for Ethics and Social Transformation" (Ph.D. dissertation, Emory University Candler School of Theology, 1977). Tinney's writings on the subject are voluminous. Bibliographical references for his published and unpublished work are available in the library of Howard University Divinity School in Washington, D.C.

20. Joseph H. Jackson, *A Story of Christian Activism: The History of the National Baptist Convention, U.S.A., Inc.* (Nashville: Townsend, 1980), 325–326, 279.

21. Howard D. Gregg, *History of the African Methodist Episcopal Church: The Black Church in Action* (Nashville: AME Sunday School Union, 1980), 392–421.

22. Robert S. Lecky and H. Elliot Wright, *Black Manifesto: Religion, Racism, and Reparations* (New York: Sheed and Ward, 1969), 176.

3. BLACK RELIGION

1. W. E. Burghardt Du Bois, *The Souls of Black Folk* (New York: Fawcett, 1961), 141.

2. Ibid., 143.

3. For example, one could say that a radical religious liberation orientation inspired the Denmark Vesey and Nat Turner rebellions of 1822 and 1831, respectively, and that the newly independent African Methodist Episcopal churches of the North were cooperating with groups like the American Moral Reform and Phoenix Societies of Philadelphia and New York that were seeking to elevate the life of urban blacks through education, moral reform, and cultural refinement. Similarly, in the storefront Pentecostal churches of the inner city, between the two world wars, there was a reversion to some of the same patterns of emotionalism, dissociation, and other forms of religiosity known on the African continent that helped the first slaves brought to America survive the brutality of plantation life in the early nineteenth century.

4. Richard F. Burton, *The Proverbs: Wit and Wisdom from Africa* (New York: Negro University Press, 1969), 25.

5. Chinua Achebe, *Things Fall Apart* (Greenwich, Conn.: Fawcett, 1959), 164.

6. John W. Blassingame, *The Slave Community: Plantation Life in the Ante-Bellum South* (New York: Oxford University Press, 1972), 33.

7. Charles Colcock Jones, *The Religious Instruction of Negroes in the United States* (Savannah: T. Purse, 1842), 125.

8. Mechal Sobel, *Trabelin' On: The Slave Journey to an Afro-Baptist Faith* (Westport, Conn.: Greenwood, 1979), 296.

9. Blassingame, *Slave Community,* 206.

10. Lewis V. Baldwin, *The Mark of a Man: Peter Spencer and the African Union Methodist Tradition* (Lanham, Md.: University Press of America, 1987), 15.

11. Martin R. Delany, *The Condition, Elevation, Emigration, and Destiny of the Colored People of the United States* (Baltimore, Md.: Black Classic Press, 1993 [1852]), 44–45.

12. Professor Delores Williams, of Union Theological Seminary in New York City, combines the elevation and survival motifs into a dyadic emphasis which she terms "the survival/quality-of-life tradition" of the African American church and community. This, she concludes, is a female-centered tradition originally appropriated from the Bible, emphasizing God's positive response to the black family rather than capitulation to the degrading, hopeless conditions of black existence during and after slavery. See Delores S. Williams, *Sisters in the Wilderness: The Challenge of Womanist God-Talk* (Maryknoll, N.Y.: Orbis, 1993), 6.

13. See Henry Highland Garnet, *Walker's Appeal, with a Brief Sketch of His Life* (New York: J. H. Tobitt, 1848); and Herbert Aptheker, *"One Continual Cry," David Walker's Appeal* (New York: Humanities, 1965).

14. James H. Cone, *Black Theology and Black Power* (New York: Seabury, 1959. Cone, who teaches at Union Theological Seminary in New York, is to the field of systematic theology what King was to the field of social ethics. The substance and significance of his brilliant and courageous reinterpretation of Christian theology for African Americans and people of the Two-Thirds world are unparalleled.

15. See Stokely Carmichael and Charles V. Hamilton, *Black Power: The Politics of Liberation in America* (New York: Random House, 1967).

16. See Jawanza Kunjufu, *Hip Hop vs. Maat: A Psycho/Social Analysis of Values* (Chicago: African American Images, 1993). I do not mean to debase all of Hip Hop culture. Some of these young people have used their talents and the aesthetics of the ghetto streets to revitalize an attenuated African American urban culture with demands for honesty, compassion, solidarity, and the critical deconstruction of bourgeois values that have robbed our communities of their Africentric heritage and political salience. For this perspective on Hip Hop culture, see Manning Marable, *The Great Wells of Democracy: The Meaning of Race in American Life* (New York: BasicCivitas Books, 2002), 255–269. Nevertheless, the examples of this lifestyle that most of us see on nighttime television are rarely

conducive to the kind of common civility, Africentric spirituality, principled nonviolence, and progressive democracy that has been in the best tradition of the African American community in the United States.

17. Martin Luther King Jr., *Where Do We Go from Here? Chaos or Community* (New York: Harper and Row, 1967), 134.

4. WOMANIST THOUGHT AS A RECOVERY OF LIBERATION THEOLOGY

1. James H. Cone, *A Black Theology of Liberation* (Philadelphia: Lippincott, 1970), and idem, *God of the Oppressed* (New York: Seabury, 1975); J. Deotis Roberts, *Liberation and Reconciliation: A Black Theology* (Philadelphia: Westminster, 1971), and idem, *Black Political Theology* (Philadelphia: Westminster, 1974).

2. The absence of a strong emphasis on race in white Christian feminist writings was one important impetus for the initial development of womanist thought, although credit must be given to the white feminist movement for raising the consciousness of black Christian women. In some respects black womanists have been more conservative or moderate than white feminists on the left of the theological spectrum. Black Christian womanists, nevertheless, have majored in areas of black subordination, marginalization, and neglect in white and black mainstream male/female theology and church affairs that no one else has been greatly moved to talk about or rectify.

3. James H. Cone and Gayraud S. Wilmore, *Black Theology: A Documentary History, 1966–1979* (Maryknoll, N.Y.: Orbis, 1980).

4. Not all the women whose names appear in this list can be classified as womanist thinkers and activists, but all are working in some respect on African American religious studies and are part of the cadre of black women scholars who are leaders and role models for both feminist and womanist seminary students working under them as well as for female clergy already in the churches.

5. Here I refer to black women whose writings are grounded in secular feminist theory, such as Toni Cade Bambara, Alice Walker, Patricia Hill Collins, Audre Lourde, Gloria Wade-Gayles, Angela Davis, Michelle Briggs, Barbara Smith, Paula Giddings, Ntozake Shange, Toni Morrison, Michelle Wallace, and bell hooks.

6. C. Eric Lincoln and Lawrence H. Mamiya, *The Black Church in the African American Experience* (Durham, N.C.: Duke University Press, 1990), 303–304.

7. Diana L. Hayes, *And Still We Rise: An Introduction to Black Liberation Theology* (New York: Paulist, 1996), 178–179.

8. Karen Baker-Fletcher, *A Singing Something: Womanist Reflections on Anna Julia Cooper* (New York: Crossroads, 1994); Kelly Brown Douglas, *The*

Black Christ (Maryknoll, N.Y.: Orbis, 1994; Mercy Amba Oduyoye, "Reflection from a Third World Woman's Perspective: Women's Experience and Liberation Theologies," in Virginia Fabella and Sergio Torres, eds., *Irruption of the Third World: Challenge to Theology* (Maryknoll, N.Y.: Orbis, 1983); and A. Elaine B. Crawford, *Hope in the Holler: A Womanist Theology* (Louisville: Westminster John Knox, 2002).

9. A. Elaine Brown Crawford, *Hope in the Holler: A Womanist Theology* (Louisville: Westminster John Knox, 2002), 116–117.

10. Alice Walker, *In Search of Our Mothers' Gardens* (New York: Harcourt Brace Jovanovich, 1983), xi.

11. Kelly Brown Douglas, *The Black Christ,* 109.

12. James H. Cone and Gayraud S. Wilmore, *Black Theology: A Documentary History, 1980–1992, vol.* 2 (Maryknoll, N.Y.: Orbis, 1993), 83.

13. Jacquelyn Grant, *White Women's Christ and Black Women's Jesus: Feminist Christology and Womanist Response* (Atlanta, Ga.: Scholars, 1989), 221.

14. During the 1990s a serious effort for reconciliation was quietly attempted by the Kelly Miller Smith Institute, a think tank for black religious professors and pastors at the Divinity School of Vanderbilt University under the direction of Forrest E. Harris Sr., but after publishing two volumes entitled *What Does It Mean to Be Black and Christian?* the experiment failed for lack of adequate financial support from both the churches and the university.

15. Katie G. Cannon, *Black Womanist Ethics* (Atlanta, Ga.: Scholars, 1988), 164.

16. Ibid., 174.

5. "DOING THE TRUTH"

1. *The Secular Relevance of the Church* (Philadelphia: Westminster, 1962) was the first book in the Christian Perspectives on Social Problems series, which I edited for Westminster Press during the period from 1959 to 1963, when I was teaching and doing graduate studies in Madison, New Jersey, and in Philadelphia.

2. The source of this point of view is I Corinthians 1:27–28a, which seems to have been written with people like black African and African American Christians in mind: "But God chose what is foolish in the world, to shame the wise; God chose what is weak in the world to shame the strong; God chose what is low and despised in the world, things that are not to reduce to nothing things that are" (RSV).

3. Roger Bastide, *African Civilizations in the New World* (New York: Harper and Row, 1971); and George Easton Simpson, *Black Religions in the New World* (New York: Columbia University Press, 1978). The writings of W. E. B. Du Bois early on expressed his lifelong interest in the African origins of black

religion and may have inspired Benjamin E. Mays's classic work, *The Negro's God: As Reflected in His Literature* (New York: Atheneum, 1969), with a preface by Vincent Harding. That work was first published in 1938 and represents one of the early writings by an African American author to offer a broad-gauged assessment of the nature and history of black religion. Today, partly as a result of the black studies movement of the 1960s, several works of this genre by African American writers are available, but much more needs to be done to render a thoroughly researched and comprehensive view. I mention some of the best-known authors and titles elsewhere in this volume.

4. Carter G. Woodson, *The History of the Negro Church* (Washington, D.C.: The Associated Publishers, 1921).

5. C. Eric Lincoln and Lawrence H. Mamiya, *The Black Church in the African American Experience* (Durham, N.C.: Duke University Press, 1990).

6. St. Clair Drake, *The Redemption of Africa and Black Religion* (Chicago: Third World, 1970); and James W. St. G. Walker, *The Black Loyalists: The Search for a Promised Land in Nova Scotia and Sierra Leone, 1783–1870* (New York: Africana, 1976).

7. Paul Lawrence Dunbar, "We Wear the Mask," *The Complete Poems of Paul Lawrence Dunbar* (New York: Dodd, Mead), 1913.

8. Joan M. Martin, *More Than Chains and Toil: A Christian Work Ethic of Enslaved Women* (Louisville: Westminister John Knox Press, 2000), 140.

6. WHAT IS AFRICAN AMERICAN CHRISTIANITY?

1. The author and publisher have made every attempt to document and research the quoted material included in this revised edition of this chapter. Since the publication of the first version, most of the author's research, which was conducted at the Presbyterian Historical Society in Philadelphia and the Schomburg Center in New York City, is now inaccessible. "When I wrote the book in 1980," says G. Wilmore, "I was probably influenced by the success of Nathan T. Huggins's *Black Odyssey: The African American Ordeal in Slavery* (New York: Random House, 1978), which has no notes. . . . The style is conversational and storytelling rather than a work of 'scientific historiography.'"

7. AFRICAN BEGINNINGS

1. The Confession of Alexandria of the AACC can be found in Gerald H. Anderson and Thomas F. Stransky, C.S.P., eds., *Mission Trends, No. 3* (New York: Paulist Press and Eerdmans, 1976), 132–34.

2. The ignominy of the defeat at Adowa was never forgotten by the Italians. "Writing to a young man bound for 'the African war' in 1935, the veteran Gabriele d'Annunzio urged him to wipe out its memory, for he could still feel on

his shoulder 'the scar, yes the shameful scar, of Adowa.'" Cited in A.H.M. Jones and Elizabeth Monroe, *A History of Abyssinia* (New York: Negro Universities Press, 1969), 145.

3. In 1895 a historic conference on the relationship of African American churches to the churches of Africa was held at Gammon Theological Seminary in Atlanta, under the leadership of Professor John Wesley Edward Bowen Sr. of the Gammon faculty. Significantly the First Pan-African Christian Church Conference, which brought together African and African American Christian scholars and church leaders, was held at the Interdenominational Theological Center (ITC) in Atlanta, which includes Gammon as one of its six constituent seminaries, from July 17 to July 23, 1988. The theme of African and African American church solidarity was renewed at this important conference organized and chaired by Professor Ndugu T'Ofori-Atta of the ITC faculty. The papers and addresses of the 1988 conference are contained in a double issue of the *Journal of the Interdenominational Theological Center* 16 (fall 1988; spring 1989).

4. See Cheikh Anta Diop, *The Cultural Unity of Black Africa* (Chicago: Third World, 1978); and Charles S. Finch, "The Kamitic Genesis of Christianity," in Ivan Van Sertima, ed., *Nile Valley Civilizations: Proceedings of the Nile Valley Conference, Atlanta, September 26–30, 1984* (Journal of African Civilizations, November 1984).

5. Among works by Africans and African Americans, dating from the Second World War to the present, are Cheikh Anta Diop, *The African Origin of Civilization: Myth or Reality* (New York: Lawrence Hill, 1974); J. C. deGraft Johnson, *African Glory: The Story of Vanished Negro Civilizations* (Baltimore, Md.: Black Classic, 1986); Ivan van Sertima and Larry Williams, eds., *Great African Thinkers: Cheikh Anta Diop* (New Brunswick, N.J.: Transaction, 1986); John G. Jackson, *Introduction to African Civilizations* (Secaucus, N.J.: Citadel, 1980); Willis N. Huggins and John G. Jackson, *An Introduction to African Civilization: With Main Currents in Ethiopian History* (New York: Negro Universities Press, 1969); Yosef ben Jochannan, *African Origins of the Major "Western Religions"* (New York: Alkebu-Lan, 1970); Molefi Kete Asante, *Kemet: Afrocentricity and Knowledge* (Trenton, N.J.: Africa World Press, 1990); Maulana Karenga, *Selections from the Husia: Sacred Wisdom of Ancient Egypt* (Los Angeles: University of Sankore Press, 1984); and Chancellor Williams, *The Destruction of Black Civilization: Great Issues of Race from 4500 B.C. to 2000 A.D.* (Chicago: Third World, 1974).

6. There are several well-known works in print at this time that deal with this field of Africentric studies but begin with material in the Hebrew Bible. We cannot go into this special area in this chapter, but among helpful books I would recommend the following by African American scholars of Old Testament literature: Alfred G. Dunston Jr., *The Black Man in the Old Testament and Its World* (Philadelphia: Dorrance, 1974); Charles B. Copher, *Black Biblical Studies*

(Chicago: Black Light Fellowship, 1993); Cain H. Felder, *Troubling Biblical Waters* (Maryknoll, N.Y.: Orbis, 1989); Cain H. Felder, ed., *Stony the Road We Trod: African American Biblical Interpretation* (Minneapolis: Fortress, 1991); and Walter A. McCray, *The Black Presence in the Bible* (Chicago: Black Light Fellowship, 1990).

7. John S. Mbiti, *African Religions & Philosophy* (New York: Praeger, 1969), 48.

8. Noel Q. King, *Christian and Muslim in Africa* (New York: Harper and Row, 1971), 3.

9. John G. Jackson, *Introduction to African Civilizations* (Secaucus, N.J.: Citadel, 1970), 134; citing E. A. Wallis Budge, *Osiris: The Egyptian Religion of the Resurrection,* 2 vols. (New Hyde Park, N.Y.: University Books, 1961), 1:174.

10. The Solomon-Sheba story is preserved in the treasured Ethiopian work called the *Kebra-Nagast* (Glory of kings), said to be a translation of a Coptic original found in Constantinople before A.D. 325. See Jean Doresse, *Ethiopia* (New York: Frederick Ungar, 1959), 13–14.

11. The proximity to Palestine made possible a strong Jewish presence in both Egypt and Ethiopia during the centuries following the Exodus. Philo reported that the Jewish population of Egypt reached one million, with two hundred thousand Jews dwelling in Alexandria alone. See C. P. Groves, *The Planting of Christianity in Africa,* 2 vols. (London: Lutterworth, 1948), 1:36.

12. We learn that the eunuch's name was Judich from the historian Eusebius of Caesarea (*Ecclesiastical History,* 2.1.13).

13. Bishop Athanasius of Beni-Suef and Bahnasa, *The Copts through the Ages* (Arab Republic of Egypt Ministry of Information, n.d.), 5. One of the greatest public celebrations in modern Egypt was held in the new Cairo Cathedral on June 25, 1968, in recognition of the nineteen hundredth anniversary of the martydom of St. Mark, the founder of the Egyptian church.

14. For a brief but excellent treatment of the invention of monasticism in the Egyptian desert and the exploits of black Christians in the earliest days of the African church, see Martin de Porres Walsh, O.P., *The Ancient Black Christians* (San Francisco: Julian Richardson, 1969); see also a neglected but highly authoritative study by Cyprian Davis, *The History of Black Catholics in the United States* (New York: Crossroad, 1990), 1–27.

15. Walsh, *Ancient Black Christians,* 5–6. The story is also found in the *Acta Sanctorum* of the Roman Catholic Church.

16. *The Church of Ethiopia: A Panorama of History and Spiritual Life* (Addis Ababa: A Publication of the Ethiopian Orthodox Church, 1970), 3–6.

17. Doresse, *Ethiopia,* 64.

18. Groves, *Planting of Christianity in Africa,* 139.

19. Cited in ibid., 141–42.

20. Giovanni Fantini, *Christianity in the Sudan* (Bologna: EMI, 1981), 25.

21. Groves, *Planting of Christianity in Africa,* 49–50.

22. Fantini, *Christianity in the Sudan,* 199–202. Rumors persisted through the Middle Ages that small communities of Christians were scattered west and north of Dongola as far as Bornu and the Lake Chad area. That would have placed Nubian Christianity not too far from what is now Nigeria. Several hopeful Catholic missions were dispatched from Rome to contact these black Christians in the Lake Chad area but apparently without success. Nevertheless, Nubian Christianity seems to have existed in an attenuated form as late as the eighteenth century. See William Y. Adams, *Nubia: Corridor to Africa* (Princeton, N.J.: Princeton University Press, 1984), 542–43.

23. Ibrahim Abu-Lughod, "Islam in Africa," in the *World Encyclopedia of Black Peoples;* Vol. 1: *Conspectus* (St. Clair Shores, Mich.: Scholarly Press, 1975), 284.

24. These are the Oneness of God, prayer five times a day, the giving of alms to the poor, the annual pilgrimage to Mecca, and fasting from dawn to sunset during the sacred month of Ramadan. Some Muslims add the *Jihad,* or Holy War, against the enemies of Allah.

25. King, *Christian and Muslim in Africa,* 23–24.

26. Sir Harry H. Johnston, *The Colonization of Africa* (Cambridge: Cambridge University Press, 1930), 85.

27. Groves, *The Planting of Christianity in Africa,* 129. For important details on developments in the western Sudan during the period of the great empires of Ghana, Mali, and Songhai to the nineteenth century, with suggestions for teaching this history to African Americans, see Willis N. Huggins and John G. Jackson, *An Introduction to African Civilizations* (New York: Negro Universities Press, 1969), 122–39.

28. Elizabeth Isichei, *A History of Christianity in Africa: From Antiquity to the Present* (Grand Rapids, Mich.: Eerdmans, 1995), 54.

29. Groves, *Planting of Christianity in Africa,* 131.

30. Lamin Sanneh, *West African Christianity: The Religious Impact* (Maryknoll, N.Y.: Orbis, 1983), 53.

31. Ellen Gibson Wilson, *The Loyal Blacks* (New York: G. P. Putnam's, 1976), 151.

32. Ibid., 222.

33. For detailed discussions of the evangelization of West Africa by Africans and African Americans, and continued missionary collaboration, see Lamin Sanneh, *West African Christianity* (Maryknoll, N.Y.: Orbis, 1983); David B. Barrett, *Schism and Renewal in Africa: An Analysis of Six Thousand Contemporary Religious Movements* (Nairobi: Oxford University Press, 1968); Sandy D. Martin, *Black Baptists and African Missions: The Origins of a Movement, 1880–1915* (Macon, Ga.: Mercer University Press, 1989); Leroy Fitts, *Lott Carey: First Black Missionary to Africa* (Valley Forge: Judson, 1978); Walter L. Williams,

Black Americans and the Evangelization of Africa, 1877–1900 (Madison: University of Wisconsin Press, 1982); E. A. Ayandele, *Holy Johnson: Pioneer of African Nationalism* (London: Frank Cass, 1970); St. Clair Drake, *The Redemption of Africa and Black Religion* (Chicago: Third World, 1970); and "The First Pan-African Christian Church Conference," July 17–23, 1988: Papers and Addresses, *The Journal of the Interdenominational Theological Center* 16 (fall 1988–spring 1989).

34. A classic source of information about early independency in Africa is Barrett's *Schism and Renewal.* See also Nathaniel I. Ndiokwere, *Prophecy and Revelation: The Role of Prophets in the Independent African Churches and in Biblical Tradition* (London: SPCK, 1981); and Adrian Hastings, *African Christianity* (New York: Seabury, 1976).

35. Johnston, *Colonization of Africa,* 48, 51.

36. Cited by Albert J. Raboteau, *Slave Religion: The "Invisible Institution" in the Antebellum South* (New York: Oxford University Press, 1978), 47.

37. Kofi A. Opoku, "The West through African Eyes," *International Journal of African Studies* 4 (December 1996): 87.

38. King, *Christian and Muslim in Africa,* 113.

39. Cited by the African American bishops in a pastoral letter, September 9, 1984, "What We Have Seen and Heard," David T. Shannon and Gayraud S. Wilmore, eds., *Black Witness to the Apostolic Faith* (Grand Rapids, Mich.: Eerdmans, 1985), 72.

8. THE BLACK MESSIAH

1. Willis N. Huggins and John G. Jackson, *An Introduction to African Civilizations* (New York: Negro Universities Press, 1969), 55.

2. Thomas F. Gossett, *Race: The History of An Idea in America* (Dallas: Southern Methodist University Press, 1963), 3.

3. Winthrop D. Jordan, *White Over Black* (Baltimore: Penguin Books, 1969), 18.

4. Frank M. Snowden Jr., *Blacks in Antiquity* (Cambridge, Mass.: Harvard University Press, 1970), 179.

5. Snowden, *Blacks in Antiquity;* cited in William R. Jones, *Is God a White Racist? A Preamble to Black Theology* (Garden City, N.Y.: Doubleday, 1973), 5.

6. Roger Bastide, "Color, Racism, and Christianity," in John Hope Franklin, ed., *Color and Race* (Boston: Houghton Mifflin, 1968), 37.

7. Eulalio R. Baltazar, *The Dark Center: A Process Theology of Blackness* (New York: Paulist, 1973), 46.

8. Gay L. Byron, *Symbolic Blackness and Ethnic Differences in Early Christian Literature* (New York: Routledge, 2002), 124. See also Robert E. Hood, *Begrimed and Black: Christian Traditions on Blacks and Blackness* (Minneapolis:

Fortress, 1994); Charles B. Copher, *Black Biblical Studies: An Anthology of Charles B. Copher* (Chicago: Black Light Fellowship, 1993); Randall C. Bailey and Jacquelyn Grant, eds., *The Recovery of Black Presence: An Interdisciplinary Exploration* (Nashville: Abingdon, 1995); Cain Hope Felder, *Troubling Biblical Waters: Race, Class, and Family* (Maryknoll, N.Y.: Orbis, 1989); and Vincent L. Wimbush, "Introduction: Reading Darkness, Reading Scriptures," in Vincent L. Wimbush, ed., *African Americans and the Bible: Sacred Texts and Social Textures* (New York: Continuum, 2000).

9. Newbell N. Puckett, *Folk Beliefs of the Southern Negro* (Chapel Hill: University of North Carolina Press, 1926), 545.

10. William R. Jones, *Is God a White Racist? A Preamble to Black Theology* (Garden City, N.J.: Doubleday, 1973), 9.

11. Joseph R. Washington, *The Politics of God* (Boston: Beacon, 1967).

12. For the theologian who best represents the position presented in this chapter and whose work has been a continuous inspiration to me, see James H. Cone, *God of the Oppressed* (New York: Seabury, 1975).

9. BLACK CONSCIOUSNESS

1. A small group of white theologians welcomed the advent of black theology in the late 1960s and were not afraid to acknowledge that blackness, as a symbol of oppression and ultimate liberation *from* oppression, was a much needed corrective to the theology and praxis of the mainstream white churches. Frederick Herzog, the original inspiration for this chapter, was possibly the first in the United States to let his interests be known. His tour de force was a provocative exposition of the Gospel of John entitled *Liberation Theology: Liberation in Light of the Fourth Gospel* (New York: Seabury, 1972), a book that was both a welcome surprise for those who were trying to create a black liberation theology and an embarrassing shock to many of his white colleagues.

2. Unfortunately most of us were too involved in the movement trying to empower the African American community to worry too much about Herzog's support or the support of our work by other white theologians. Under other circumstances we might have formed a tight interracial coalition, although the effort of Father Sergio Torres ("Theology in the Americas") to do just that failed. I recall, however, that some of us were grateful for this rather aberrant white professor, Fred Herzog, in—of all places—North Carolina, where court-ordered desegregation was being bitterly fought in Charlotte and Wilmington. Here was a white seminary professor who could bring the two words *black* and *theology* together without choking in the process. James Cone once observed that Herzog was the only white theologian he knew who was prepared to reorder the priorities of the new political theology in the light of black oppression. "Whatever else may be said about Herzog's *Liberation Theology*," Cone wrote, "it is concrete evidence

that white theologians do not have to remain enclosed in their little white boxes" (*God of the Oppressed* [New York: Seabury, 1975], 50).

3. C. Eric Lincoln, *The Black Church since Frazier* (New York: Schocken, 1974), 106.

4. Victor Anderson, *Beyond Ontological Blackness: An Essay on African American Religious and Cultural Criticism* (New York: Continuum, 1995).

5. Gabriel M. Setiloane, "I am an African," in *Mission Trends No. 3, Third World Theologies,* ed. Gerald H. Anderson and Thomas F. Stransky, C.S.P. (New York: Paulist, 1976), 130–131.

6. Frederick Herzog, *Justice Church: The New Function of the Church in North American Christianity* (Maryknoll, N.Y.: Orbis, 1980), 146.

10. WHAT IS BLACK THEOLOGY?

1. I use North America rather than the United States in order to include our Canadian brothers and sisters who are also wrestling with the issue of black religion and theology in their nation. See, for example, the story of black religion and theology in Vincent D'Oyley, ed., *Black Presence in Multi-Ethnic Canada* (Vancouver: University of British Columbia and the Ontario Institute for Studies in Education, 1978).

2. Charles S. Brown, "Present Trends in Black Theology," *Journal of Religious Thought* (fall–winter 1975): 61.

3. Ibid., 62.

4. Hugh Ross Mackintosh, *Types of Modern Theology: Schleiermacher to Barth* (London: Nisbet, 1937), 3.

5. William R. Jones, "Toward an Interim Assessment of Black Theology," *The Christian Century* 89 (May 3, 1972): 513–17.

6. For the entire statement on black theology by the National Conference of Black Christians (formerly the National Committee of Black Churchmen), see Warner N. Traynham, *Christian Faith in Black and White* (Wakefield, Mass.: Parameter, 1973), 109–11.

7. Anonymous, "The Sons of Africa: An Essay on Freedom," in Dorothy Porter, *Early Negro Writing, 1760–1837* (Boston: Beacon, 1971), 17.

8. Nathaniel Paul, "An Address on the Celebration of the Abolition of Slavery in New York," July 5, 1827, a Library of Congress pamphlet, 15–16.

9. James H. Cone, "The Content and Method of Black Theology," *Journal of Religious Thought* (fall–winter 1975): 96.

10. See the essay by James H. Cone, "From Geneva to Sao Paulo: A Dialogue between Black Theology and Latin American Liberation Theology," in James H. Cone and Gayraud S. Wilmore, *Black Theology: A Documentary History,* 2 vols. (Maryknoll, N.Y.: Orbis, 1993), 377.

11. The fact that this statement, adopted by the BTP in August 1977, was not published in the revised Cone-Wilmore documentary history for the period from 1966 to 1992, and that it represented the highest point of the radicalization of black theology and the coming together for the first time of strategic elements in the African American religious and political communities, deserves to be investigated. It is not too outlandish to speculate the possibility of sabotage by the same undercover agencies of the federal government that infiltrated and broke up the Black Panther Party and other radical alliances in the black community during the Nixon administration in the early 1970s.

12. BLACK POWER, BLACK PEOPLE, AND THEOLOGICAL RENEWAL

1. From "A Message to the Churches from Oakland, California," cited in Gayraud S. Wilmore and James H. Cone, *Black Theology: A Documentary History, 1966–1979* (Maryknoll, N.Y.: Orbis, 1979), 105.

2. *New York Times,* July 31, 1966; for the full statement, see Wilmore and Cone, *Black Theology,* 23–30.

3. Vincent Harding, "No Turning Back," in *Renewal* (October–November, 1970): 8.

4. For example, the 179th General Assembly of the United Presbyterian Church (1967) encouraged Presbyterians "to view the phenomenon of Black power within the context of the White power we exercise, seeing in it both the legacy of frustrated aspirations and the promise of a newly assertive self-identity." The Assembly also commended the NCNC statement to the churches and recommended the study of its "action implementations" by predominantly white congregations.

5. For the statements from the black and white caucuses, see Wilmore and Cone, *Black Theology,* 43–47.

6. The denominational black caucuses included the United Methodists, three Lutheran bodies, the United Church of Christ, the Episcopal Church, two Presbyterian churches, the American Baptist Convention, the Disciples of Christ, and the Unitarian-Universalists. Several of these caucuses were still meeting in the 1990s. Added to their number are at least two Roman Catholic caucuses and one among black evangelicals. During the 1960s the AME Zion Church had a group of radical young churchmen who called themselves the Sons of Varick. Other African American churches did not have formally organized black power caucuses, but many NCBC members met informally within several black denominations. See Leon W. Watts, "The National Committee of Black Churchmen," *Christianity and Crisis* (November 2 and 16, 1970): 237–243.

7. Harding, "No Turning Back," 13.

8. The statement, drafted by John Hurst Adams, who would later become presiding bishop of the AME Church, held it to be a "tragic mistake for well-meaning whites to attempt to bypass the black church in an effort to relate directly to the ghetto." It was adopted on April 4, 1968, the very day King was assassinated, and was mailed to more than eight hundred denominational executives, inviting them to negotiate with grass-roots church and community leaders in order to "surrender power." Many of them replied that they resented the language of confrontation and polarization.

9. It is true, nevertheless, that the majority of the more than one thousand NCBC members belonged to all-black denominations. They were generally younger seminary graduates who were disillusioned with the conservatism of both the churches they pastored and their denominations.

10. IFCO was formed by ten national white churches, under pressure from the caucuses, as a coalition for the development and funding of community organizing in African American and Hispanic American communities—usually along the lines of the Alinsky model of "rubbing raw the sores of discontent." In 1969 its board of directors consisted of twenty-three blacks and Hispanic, and seventeen white representatives of national religious and social service agencies. The first IFCO executive staff persons, Lucius Walker Jr., a Baptist minister, and Louis Gothard, a Unitarian layman, were also founding members of NCBC.

11. IFCO News Release, May 5, 1969.

12. James Forman was born in Chicago in 1928. He was baptized and confirmed in the AME Church. After serving in the military for four years and earning a B.A. in political science and public administration at Roosevelt College, he did graduate work in government and African studies at Boston University. Between 1963 and 1965 Forman took over the SNCC program in Hattiesburg, Mississippi, from Bob Moses, and met with many black and white clergy who came down from the North to work mainly in voter registration under the auspices of the NCC and the United Presbyterian Church. See Michael Hamlin and the staff of Black Star Publishing, *The Political Thought of James Forman* (Detroit: Black Star, 1970); and James Forman, *The Making of a Black Revolutionary* (New York: Macmillan, 1971).

13. Stephen C. Rose, "Putting It to the Churches," in Robert S. Lecky and H. Elliott Wright, *The Black Manifesto* (New York: Sheed and Ward, 1969), 102.

14. *Tempo* (June 1, 1969): 7.

15. "Rationale for Restitution," a pamphlet published by St. George's Episcopal Church, Stuyvesant Square, New York City, n.d.

16. A "Declaration of Revolution" presented on May 23, 1969, to the WCC meeting at Notting Hill, England, demanded 500,000 pounds sterling to be used to set up a defense fund for political prisoners in South Africa and for the "Panther 21" in the United States, various sums for African liberation movements, funds to develop an international publishing house, and the public disclosure of

WCC assets and financial investments. A direct outgrowth of the Notting Hill action was the creation of the WCC Programme to Combat Racism, which allocated more than 1 million dollars to liberation movements and racial justice programs worldwide. See John Vincent, *The Race Race* (New York: Friendship, 1970), 42–48.

17. *The Christian Century* (January 4, 1967): 10.

18. Vincent Harding, "The Religion of Black Power," in Donald R. Cutler, ed., *The Religious Situation: 1968* (Boston: Beacon, 1968), 31.

19. Albert B. Cleage Jr., *The Black Messiah* (New York: Sheed and Ward, 1968), 277. See also idem, *Black Christian Nationalism: New Directions for the Black Church* (New York: William Morrow, 1972).

20. Ibid., *The Black Messiah,* 111. On the concept of the Black Messiah, see James H. Cone, *A Black Theology of Liberation, Twentieth Anniversary Edition* (Maryknoll, N.Y.: Orbis, 1990), 119–124; and William L. Eichelberger: "Reflections on the Person and Personality of the Black Messiah," *The Black Church Magazine* 1, no. 2 (1972): 51–63.

21. George D. Kelsey was one of the first black ethicists to teach in a major white seminary. He was a professor at Drew University during the 1950s. His principal work was *Racism and the Christian Understanding of Man* (New York: Scribner's, 1965).

22. James H. Cone, *Black Theology and Black Power, Twentieth Anniversary Edition* (Maryknoll, N.Y.: Orbis, 1989), 39.

23. "Black Theology—A Statement of the National Committee of Black Churchmen," in James H. Cone and Gayraud S. Wilmore, *Black Theology: A Documentary History, 1966–1979* (Maryknoll, N.Y.: Orbis, 1993), 37. A bibliography of black theological writings between 1979 and 1993, compiled by Mark L. Chapman, is appended to volumes 1 and 2. See also an excellent bibliographical essay by J. Deotis Roberts, "Black Theological Ethics," in *Journal of Religious Ethics* 3 (spring 1975): 69–109; see also Diana L. Hayes, *And Still We Rise: An Introduction to Black Liberation Theology* (New York: Paulist, 1996), 198–214.

24. Cone and Wilmore, *Black Theology,* 38.

25. Ibid., 39.

13. THE ROLE OF AFRICAN AMERICA IN THE RISE OF THIRD-WORLD THEOLOGY

1. The highly regarded E. Franklin Frazier, in his *Negro Church in America* (New York: Schocken, 1964), misdirected scholarly attention to symbiotic and socialization features of institutional Christianity in the African American community to the neglect of resistance and protest elements that were more fundamental to slave religion. Joseph R. Washington's influential *Black Religion: The*

Negro and Christianity in the United States (Boston: Beacon, 1964), similarly misconstrued the theological content of black faith. Washington tried to correct his earlier impressions but seemed to remain ambivalent. See the introduction to his *Black Sects and Cults* (Garden City, N.Y.: Doubleday, 1972).

2. See Franz Fanon, *The Wretched of the Earth* (New York: Grove, 1968); and C.L.R. James, *A History of Pan-African Revolt* (Washington, D.C.: Drum and Spear, 1969).

3. Those theologians whose work best reflects the influence of black American theology are Allan Boesak and Bongani Mazibuko (South Africa), Idris Hamid and Joyce Bailey (the Caribbean), Sergio Torres and Gustavo Gutierrez (Latin America), C. S. Song (Taiwan), Burgess Carr, Kofi Opuku, and Kofi Appiah-Kubi (West Africa), and Eulalio P. Baltalzar (the Philippines).

4. Cited in Daniel A. Payne, *History of the African Methodist Episcopal Church* (New York: Arno, 1969), 91.

5. Ibid., 293.

6. For a classic study of this development, see George Shepperson, "Notes on Negro American Influences on the Emergence of African Nationalism," reprinted in Melvin Drimmer, ed., *Black History: A Reappraisal* (Garden City, N.Y.: Doubleday, 1969), 491–511.

7. For a comprehensive historical account, including the early history of Liberia, see Rodney Carlisle, *The Roots of Black Nationalism* (Port Washington, N.Y.: Kennikat, 1975).

8. The late Horace Mann Bond wrote an extended analysis of the impact of Lincoln University, and the African students in attendance there from 1857 to 1954, in his posthumous work, *Education for Freedom: A History of Lincoln University, Pennsylvania* (Princeton, N.J.: Princeton University Press, 1976), 487–550.

9. Drake, *Redemption of Africa* (Chicago: Third World, 1970), 11.

10. Rotberg and Mazrui, *Protest and Power,* 488, 573, 808, and passim.

11. The pioneering work of Randall K. Burkett made a good beginning, but, unfortunately, it was not followed up by African American church historians and theologians. See Randall K. Burkett, *Garveyism as a Religious Movement* (Metuchen, N.J.: Scarecrow, 1978); and his co-authored book with Richard Newman, *Afro American Clergy Confront the Twentieth Century* (Boston: Hall, 1978).

12. Even before Abidjan, Clinton Marsh, a prominent African American Presbyterian pastor, later to become moderator of the General Assembly of the denomination, was influential in promoting the social justice agenda of liberal Protestantism as executive director of the fledgling AACC. Earlier Dr. Marsh had served as a staff person in Religion and Race for the United Presbyterians in Nebraska.

13. The author and the Rev. J. Metz Rollins, then the executive director of NCBC, were the visiting delegates.

14. *Profile of the All-Africa Conference of Churches, Programme* 1972/73, 8.

15. Ofori-Atta is African American and has played an unsung role in fraternal relations between African and African American scholars and churches. See his *Christkwanza: An African American Church Liturgy* (Atlanta: Strugglers' Community, 1991); and his introduction to "The First Pan-African Christian Church Conference, July 17–23, 1988, Atlanta, Georgia: Papers and Addresses," in the *Journal of the Interdenominational Theological Center* 16 (fall 1988/spring 1989).

16. The papers of the Ghana Consultation appear in *Journal of Religious Thought* 32 (fall–winter 1975).

17. John Mbiti, "An African Views American Black Theology," *Worldview* (August 1974).

18. Ibid., 43.

19. James H. Cone, "A Black American Perspective on the Future of African Theology," in idem and Gayraud S. Wilmore, *Black Theology: A Documentary History, 1966–1979, vol. 1* (Maryknoll, N.Y.: Orbis, 1993), 393–394. Mbiti's original article is also in this volume, 379ff.

20. Desmond M. Tutu, "Black Theology/African Theology: Soul Mates or Antagonists?" in *Journal of Religious Thought* 32 (fall–winter 1975): 25–33; reprinted in Cone and Wilmore, *Black Theology,* 379–392.

21. Tutu, "Black Theology/African Theology," 20.

22. Cone and Wilmore, *Black Theology,* 398–399.

23. Manas Buthelezi, "Toward Indigenous Theology in South Africa," in Sergio Torres and Virginia Fabella, eds., *The Emergent Gospel: Theology from the Underside of History* (Maryknoll, N.Y.: Orbis, 1978), 56.

24. See the reports of the Third-World delegates to the First Pan-African Christian Church Conference at the Interdenominational Theological Center in Atlanta, July 1988 (*Journal of the Interdenominational Theological Center,* 16 [fall 1988/spring 1989]).

14. WHAT IS THE RELEVANCE OF BLACK THEOLOGY FOR PASTORAL MINISTRY?

1. See for example, James H. Harris, *Pastoral Theology: A Black Church-Perspective* (Minneapolis: Fortress, 1991), 63.

2. W. E. B. Du Bois, *The Souls of Black Folk* (Greenwich, Conn.: Fawcett, 1961), 23.

3. Martin Luther King Jr., *Where Do We Go from Here? Chaos or Community* (New York: Harper and Row, 1967), 134.

4. Gayraud S. Wilmore, "Cultural Renewal: The Vocational Responsibility of the Black Church," unpublished paper read at the annual meeting of the Society for the Study of Black Religion (SSBR), October 1985.

5. In July 1964 a rally was called in New York by the Congress of Racial Equality (CORE) that developed into a clash with the police in which twelve officers and nineteen marchers were injured. For several days the police fought blacks in the Bedford-Stuyvesant section of Brooklyn and in Harlem. Blacks fought back with Molotov cocktails, bricks, and bottles, and the police with gunfire. Many people were injured. See *Report of the National Advisory Commission on Civil Disorders* (New York: Dutton, 1968), 36.

6. *Presbyterian Outlook,* May 25, 1981, 9.

7. James M. Washington, ed., *A Testament of Hope: The Essential Writings of Martin Luther King, Jr.* (San Francisco: Harper & Row, 1986), 279.

8. On the pneumatological basis of black theology, see Theo Witvliet, *The Way of the Black Messiah: The Hermeneutical Challenge of Black Theology as a Theology of Liberation* (Oak Park, Ill.: Meyer-Stone, 1987.

9. James H. Cone, *Black Theology and Black Power* (New York: Seabury, 1969).

10. Joseph A. Johnson Jr., *Proclamation Theology* (Shreveport, La.: Fourth District Press, 1978).

11. Cecil W. Cone, *The Identity Crisis in Black Theology* (Nashville: African Methodist Episcopal Church Press, 1975); and Henry H. Mitchell, *Black Belief: Folk Beliefs of Blacks in American and West Africa* (New York: Harper & Row, 1975).

12. Henry H. Mitchell and Nicholas C. Lewter, *Soul Theology: The Heart of American Black Culture* (San Francisco: Harper and Row, 1986). See dust jacket and page 11.

13. William H. Grier and Price M. Cobbs, *Black Rage* (New York: Basic Books, 1968), 22.

14. Ibid., 196–97.

15. Thomas C. Oden, *Pastoral Theology: Essentials of Ministry* (San Francisco: Harper & Row, 1983), x.

16. James H. Cone, *Speaking the Truth: Ecumenism, Liberation, and Black Theology* (Grand Rapids, Mich.: Eerdmans, 1986), 31–32.

17. *The Atlanta Constitution,* March 3, 1987, A4.

18. Witvliet, *The Way of the Black Messiah,* 88.

19. Ibid., 170.

20. Cone, *Black Theology and Black Power,* 151.

15. BLACK CHRISTIANS, CHURCH UNITY, AND ONE COMMON EXPRESSION OF APOSTOLIC FAITH

1. Accurate church membership figures are hard to come by. Perhaps the most recent and reliable data on the membership statistics and other characteristics of American Protestant and Roman Catholic churches can be found in C.

Eric Lincoln and Lawrence H. Mamiya, *The Black Church in the African American Experience* (Durham, N.C.: Duke University Press, 1990). For a full picture one would have to add increasing numbers of African Americans who in the last thirty or forty years have converted to Islam and other "non-Western" religions.

2. George D. Kelsey, *Racism and the Christian Understanding of Man* (New York: Scribner's, 1965).

3. Cited in Dorothy Porter, *Early Negro Writing, 1700–1837* (Boston: Beacon, 1971), 630.

4. Liele and George were the earliest slave preachers to demonstrate that liberation was at the heart of their Christian confessions by leaving the United States in the 1780s and founding the first independent churches for free blacks in Jamaica and Sierra Leone, respectively. Cone and Roberts are the two leading systematic theologians of contemporary black liberation theology in the United States.

5. David T. Shannon and Gayraud S. Wilmore, eds., *Black Witness to the Apostolic Faith* (Grand Rapids, Mich.: Eerdmans, 1988). This chapter is a revised version of my article in the volume published by Eerdmans for the Commission on Faith and Order of the National Council of Churches.

6. From *A Report of the Fifth Assembly of the World Council of Churches, Section II* (Geneva: World Council of Churches, 1976), 19.

7. The phrase used by Pope VI at Kampala inviting African Christians to bring "gifts of blackness" to the whole church. Cited in Shannon and Wilmore, eds., *Black Witness*, 72.

17. STRUGGLING AGAINST RACISM WITH REALISM AND HOPE

1. Vincent Harding, "Black Power and the American Christ," in Floyd B. Barbour, ed., *The Black Power Revolt* (Boston: Porter E. Sargent, 1968), 86.

2. Paul R. Griffin, *Seeds of Racism in the Soul of America* (Cleveland: Pilgrim, 1999), 22.

3. Allan Boesak, *Black and Reformed: Apartheid, Liberation, and the Calvinist Tradition* (Maryknoll, N.Y.: Orbis, 1984).

4. Middle estimates of population characteristics by race as early as 2010 project whites at 247 million; blacks at 42 million; Hispanic origin at 41 million; American Indian, Eskimo, and Aleut at 2 million; Asian and Pacific Islanders at 15 million; the result is a total population of 101,744,000 non-whites compared to 247,193,000 non-Hispanic whites (rounded figures from the *Statistical Abstract of the United States, 1997* [Department of Commerce, Bureau of Census, 1997], 7).

5. The concept of race used by the Bureau of the Census reflects self-identification by respondents, that is, the individual's self-perception of his or her racial identity. It does not presume any biological or anthropological definition.

In 1990 the "other" category provided for persons who did not want to identify with any specific group. "Hispanic origin," incidentally, is defined correctly as an ethnicity (Mexican-American, Chicano, Mexican, Puerto Rican, Cuban, Central or South American, or other Hispanic origin) (ibid., 9).

6. In Theodore Allen's important work, *The Invention of the White Race,* 2 vols. (New York: Verso, 1994), Vol. 1, *Racial Oppression and Social Control;* Vol. 2, *The Origins of Racial Oppression in Anglo-America,* the author shows how Scottish, Irish, and German immigrants were molded into a single inclusive category of "white people" in order that the white elites could discourage rebelliousness and threatening solidarity among working class people of all colors, and thereby ensure the elites social and economic hegemony over the new nation. "This 'key paradox of American history' as Allen calls it,'" writes Bob Hulteen of *Sojourners* Magazine, "the metamorphosis of servants, tenants, farmers, and merchants into a cohesive group—creates a democracy built on certain race assumptions."

7. The figures are from the Southern Poverty Law Center in 2000.

8. For the demographic setting of the 1992 riots and how the ethnic profile of the rioters and those attacked differ from the civil rights riots of the 1960s, see Mark Baldassare, ed., *The Los Angeles Riots: Lessons for the Urban Future* (Boulder, Colo.: Westview, 1994).

9. Maulana Karenga, "Black and Latino Relations: Context, Challenge, and Possibilities," in Ishmael Reed, ed., *Multi-America: Essays on Cultural Wars and Cultural Peace* (New York: Viking Penguin, 1997), 196–97.

Index